W9-BXY-303

CONTENTS

PREFACE

In March of 2003, the United States invaded Iraq, intending to replace a bellicose and undemocratic regime with, at least, one friendlier to the United States. The day after the bombing started a dozen senior citizens led a march of several hundred people protesting the war down the main street in Nevada City, California, a town of just over three thousand people. Upon reaching the major crossroads in this small tourist town, they sat on plastic buckets, linked arms, and refused to move—even after police ordered them to disperse to allow traffic to pass. The members of this core *Crossroads* group had planned their actions in advance, but a few dozen others spontaneously joined them. Determinedly nonviolent, they submitted to arrest and spent most of the day being arraigned.

All of those arrested were offered the opportunity to settle their criminal cases by pleading guilty to some kind of public disruption and accepting either fifty-three hours of community service or three days in jail as punishment. Most did so. Fifteen of the protesters, however, were determined to present their claims in court; essentially, they argued that they were acting to protest the war and be part of a process to reduce harm. Sympathetic lawyers from as far away as San Francisco took on their criminal defenses *pro bono,* that is, for free.

Nevada City is a small town in the middle of a beautiful part of California. Its main street is dotted with independent shops selling coffee, books, and souvenirs to tourists. Virtually everyone involved in the case knew all of the others, running into each other while shopping, watching a school play, or attending a meeting. Through negotiations with the trial judge, the antiwar activists agreed to forego a jury trial if they would be allowed to present an expert witness on the politics of protest.

Searching on the Internet, the lawyers found me, an academic who has been studying and writing about the politics of protest, social movements, and antiwar movements for more than ten years. I agreed to testify at the trial of the first five protesters and spent several hours on the phone talking with their attorneys about what I could truthfully say under oath, based on reading, research, and writing in this area. I came into court after local police had established that the demonstrators had blocked traffic and had refused to disperse when police had asked them to do so.

Having sworn to tell the truth, I testified that dramatic protests, like the one in Nevada City, could be part of a larger process that might change the conduct of the war. Citing examples from other social movements in the United States, I explained that the arrests in Nevada City, far from the place where decisions about U.S. military policy are made, could inspire others to take action, could give journalists additional opportunity to examine the premises and conduct of the war, and could encourage opponents of the war in government to continue their own efforts. Further, as part of a larger social movement, the Nevada

THE
POLITICS OF
PROTEST

Social Movements in America

David S. Meyer
University of California, Irvine

New York   Oxford
OXFORD UNIVERSITY PRESS
2007

Oxford University Press, Inc., publishes works that further Oxford University's
objective of excellence in research, scholarship, and education.

Oxford   New York
Auckland   Cape Town   Dar es Salaam   Hong Kong   Karachi
Kuala Lumpur   Madrid   Melbourne   Mexico City   Nairobi
New Delhi   Shanghai   Taipei   Toronto

With offices in
Argentina   Austria   Brazil   Chile   Czech Republic   France   Greece
Guatemala   Hungary   Italy   Japan   Poland   Portugal   Singapore
South Korea   Switzerland   Thailand   Turkey   Ukraine   Vietnam

Published by Oxford University Press, Inc.
198 Madison Avenue, New York, New York 10016
http://www.oup.com

Oxford is a registered trademark of Oxford University Press

Library of Congress Cataloging-in-Publication Data

Meyer, David S.
   The politics of protest: social movements in America / David S. Meyer.
      p. cm.
   Includes bibliographical references and index.
   ISBN-13: 978-0-19-517354-3 (alk. paper)
   ISBN-10: 0-19-517354-6 (alk. paper)
   ISBN-13: 978-0-19-517353-6 (pbk. : alk. paper)
   ISBN-10: 0-19-517353-8 (pbk. : alk. paper)
   1. Protest movements—United States. 2. Political activists—United States. 3. United
States—Social conditions—1980- I. Title.

HN59.2.M49 2006
327.1'72'0973090511—dc22   2005051837

Printing number: 9 8 7 6 5 4 3 2 1

Printed in the United States of America
on acid-free paper

*To Zena, Jean, and
the world they will help make*

City activists could force proponents of the war to answer questions about their goals and strategies and might even change the way the war was conducted as policymakers anticipated answering such questions. I answered questions from the defense attorneys and the judge for about ninety minutes. The prosecutor, who wanted to keep the focus on the nature of the traffic infraction, didn't ask me anything.

I left the stand, and the court took a recess for lunch. I enjoyed a spectacular vegetarian lunch prepared by another protester whose trial would follow. We ate, sitting around a crowded table with the defendants, their attorneys, and other protesters who had accepted community service or jail time or were still awaiting trial. It became clear that the one protest against the war covered by the trial was a small part of the politics of a committed community. And it was but one activist event in so many lives that had rich and diverse trajectories of activism. Most of the activists had been active for many years and would continue to work against war and for their visions of social justice. Over lunch, I learned of the Peace Center of Nevada County, which they had begun to organize in response to the war.[1]

After lunch, each of the defendants was allowed to make a statement to the court. The judge listened respectfully to their views about the war, justice, and the politics of their lives. He then announced that he would not have to retire to chambers but instead was prepared to render his verdict right away. Finding all of the defendants guilty, he gave each the choice of community service, a fine, or three days in jail. Essentially, he offered each of the activists the same choices as those who had pled guilty and avoided trial; perhaps he showed a little more flexibility. He allowed one of the defendants to give the money for his fine to a charitable group rather than to the city and also announced that he would count a wide variety of activities as community service. Although these people defined their lives through service to the community, most refused this offer on the principle that they had nothing to compensate for: they took the jail time.

Explaining that the jail food wasn't very good and not always suitable for vegetarians, the judge ordered the defendants to report for their sentences after dinner. Further, he gave them credit on their sentences for the time they had spent being arraigned. Given the way the local jail worked, this meant they would be released roughly twelve hours after they entered, spending one night in jail.

Although the judge listened to my testimony respectfully and asked a few questions, I don't think what I said affected the outcome of the trial in any way. I think that he allowed me to testify out of respect to his neighbors, knowing that he—but perhaps not a jury—would be able to keep a perspective on balancing his view of the law with political and moral commitments. He seemed to be trying to be as sympathetic as he thought he could be to the activists; he just didn't see any latitude within the law to declare their blocking of the street was not a crime.

---

[1] The Peace Center is now well established as a site for organizing peace activism in northern California. In addition to continuing to oppose U.S. participation in the war in Iraq, the center has taken on a wide range of related issues, including a campaign for peaceful, rather than violent, toys. The center supports local and national efforts to turn out for demonstrations and letter-writing campaigns, as well as an essay contest for high school students. It manages an online discussion list that is wide ranging in its political concerns. The center's other ongoing activities include a gardening club, a film series, and a "Women in Black" series of vigils to commemorate the suffering in Iraq. See http://www.ncpeace.org

Talking to the protesters and their supporters, I felt grateful to be with them and to be able to offer something in respect for their ongoing efforts to make the world better. Several asked if anything I'd written resembled the testimony I'd given. Most academic writing, however, is directed to smaller questions about social movements in the context of larger theories about how they work and to a specialized audience of scholars that shares the same concerns and vocabulary. I'd hoped I could do a little better.

I had been approached by Jennifer Knerr about writing a more general book on protest in American politics, and in the wake of the Nevada City trial, I began to think that such a book, putting together a lot of ideas and findings in a comprehensive frame and accessible language, might be useful to activists who want to change the world, as well as to students and more advanced scholars. This describes the genesis and goals of *The Politics of Protest*.

Jennifer, John Green, Peter Labella, and the anonymous reviewers for Oxford University Press also helped me conceptualize this book. Kelsy Kretschmer was invaluable in helping me track down the details of historical events; she was also an insightful first reader of everything in the book, providing a helpful critical eye. Additionally, many of the ideas in this book have been worked out in other research, particularly in collaborative efforts with Steve Boutcher, Lynn Chancer, Catherine Corrigall-Brown, Bill Gamson, Josh Gamson, Will Hathaway, Doug Imig, Helen Ingram, Val Jenness, Sharon Kurtz, Rob Kleidman, Sam Marullo, Debra Minkoff, Ellen Reese, Tom Rochon, Belinda Robnett, Deana Rohlinger, Charlotte Ryan, Traci Sawyers, Suzanne Staggenborg, Sid Tarrow, and Nancy Whittier. I'm particularly grateful to Deana Rohlinger, Sarah Soule, and Sid Tarrow for helpful comments on the manuscript. To these friends, and to the inspirational activist community of Nevada City, California, I offer my heartfelt thanks—and this book.

INTRODUCTION

Protest is everywhere in American politics. We romanticize protest as a political tactic in our history, teaching schoolchildren about the Boston Tea Party, John Brown's raid on Harpers Ferry, and at least a little bit about the famous civil disobedients Rosa Parks and Martin Luther King Jr. But protest movements are hardly confined to the distant past. In the past few years, activists have staged dramatic demonstrations, including civil disobedience, against the war in Iraq, radical environmentalists have firebombed car dealers marketing "Hummers," and students in Massachusetts have refused to take standardized tests. This is an idiosyncratic selection, not the most dramatic or most important events. The more important point is that protest and social movements have become essential features of contemporary American life.

On a somewhat larger stage, dramatic demonstrations against globalization follow the international meetings of the World Bank and the International Monetary Fund around the globe. The issues range from abortion rights to civil liberties to health care policy to global inequality. People take to the streets when they don't think they can get what they want any other way, and the number of people who might take to the streets in the service of a cause has increased tremendously. As the range of people and issues involved in social movements in America continues to diversify and grow, so do the tactics of social movement activists. Increasingly, protest is an addition, rather than an alternative, to politics as usual, as elected officials address demonstrations and sometimes even get arrested.

It's not that there aren't other means of politics available. The United States continues to hold elections routinely for local, state, and national office. The number of established interest groups in Washington, D.C., has expanded over the past three decades to such an extent that anyone with any cause can find an organization trying to press the cause through institutional channels. And throughout much of the United States, emergency measures allow disgruntled citizens to undo the actions of their governments. Lawsuits in which the government is a defendant are continual. And, in California, where I write, a new governor took office through a recall procedure in which hundreds of thousands of citizens signed petitions to revisit an election only months old. One group, ferret owners, eagerly anticipated his election, thinking he would be more responsive to their interests than was his predecessor.

In short, there is no shortage of institutional means to employ for influence. At the same time, protest and social movements continue. This presents us with something of a paradox: in a country that prizes democracy and offers numerous institutional means of political participation, social movements and protest represent a challenge. In order to understand American politics, we need to understand protest movements. It is not so much that movements represent politics by other means today, but rather that the means of politics now includes social movements.

This book is about understanding social movements in America, where they come from, how and why they develop, and how they sometimes matter. Social movements sometimes influence, the broader cultural climate, public policy, organizations and established political institutions, and, most obviously, the people who participate in them. The American political context is one that allows, indeed, invites, a broad range of political participation and manages tremendous conflict.

The first chapter describes the design of the American constitutional system. The founders, particularly James Madison, had a paradoxical insight: that stability requires flexibility. They designed a system of multiple access points to bring dissent out into the open, where it could be more easily managed. The American polity retained the capacity to crush dissent but more commonly could embrace and diffuse it. Of course, social movements have flourished in this American context, starting before the American Revolution, through the Civil War, two world wars, the Cold War, and into the present day. We review what people who study social movements think these movements are. The definitions all contain some amount of sloppiness, because movements themselves are rarely tidy affairs, with loose and elastic boundaries and varieties of demands and tactics, ranging from approaches that seem just like conventional politics to those that don't even make explicitly political claims. Nonetheless, social movements develop in response to the rules and practices of mainstream political conflict, although not always in accord with those rules and practices. We will consider how the American constitutional design shapes the landscape on which social movements emerge, develop, and sometimes affect influence.

In Chapter 2, we look at why people choose protest instead of—or in addition to—more conventional means of pursuing their interests. Psychological factors, although certainly important, explain less about why movements sometimes emerge strongly than do political factors. Although some people are so firmly committed to a particular cause that they will always act on its behalf, and others will never engage in politics, the vast majority of people fall somewhere in between, engaging in movement politics when they think it's necessary and potentially effective. We can best understand the ebbs and flows in social protest on particular issues by focusing on more conventional politics and public policy. To a large degree, the government plays a large role in shaping the sort of opponents it will face, the tactics they will employ, and, most significantly, the issues they will press. Social movement activists sell ideas, to be sure, but how attractive those ideas are is more likely to be influenced by the context than by how well the ideas themselves are packaged. In this regard, it's much like the umbrella salesman on the streets of a major city. Pricing, placement, and marketing matter, but not so much as whether or not it's raining. The circumstances that favor or impede the development of a movement are political opportunities for mobilization. Strategies matter, but not abstractly; instead, effective organizers pick their tactics, allies, and issues with careful consideration of the larger environment. We then look at the formal organizations that provide the infrastructure for social movements during times of mobilization and that hold their identity in less volatile periods. Finally, we look at, and dismiss, the notion that ideas automatically translate into social movement action by looking at the "big books myth."

In Chapter 3, we return to the social-psychological factors that make activists. Older accounts of protest movements, and contemporary politicians challenged by movements, often point to psychological factors in seeking to explain—and especially to discredit—social movements. In fact, when we look carefully at most social movement activists, disparaging explanations that emphasize pathology don't stand up well. Most of the active people are socially well connected, slightly better educated, and better adjusted than their inactive colleagues. Becoming an activist is rarely the result of a dramatic moment of conversion; rather, it is an ongoing process in which an individual comes to see himself or herself as a member of a larger group, one whose efforts might make a difference politically and give meaning to a life. Activists come from, and join into, strong social networks that organize much of what they do.

This all said, unlike tighter leadership cliques, broad social movements rarely have someone working the door as a bouncer. The site of a demonstration, for example, is like a bright light attracting all kinds of people, including entrepreneurs who want to sell sodas at a profit, organizers who want to promote different ideas, and cranks and crazies whose personal dramas play out in the developing history and drama of a social movement. Political opponents and targets are often quick to promote the activities of these crazies as emblematic of a movement, and all movements have to struggle to define and control those energetic allies they would not choose or recruit.

In Chapter 4, we examine the diversity within social movements. It is a grammatical convenience to talk about social movements as unitary actors: the peace movement, the antitax movement, the environmental movement, and so forth. In fact, however, movements are looser formations, pulling together formal organizations, grassroots groups, and unaffiliated individuals. The boundaries between movement sectors are also fuzzy, such that women's organizations sometimes ally with traditional peace groups, antiabortion activists sometimes work with partisans of educational reform, and environmental groups work on issues only tangentially related to the environment. At the same time, organizations that share political goals often compete for the same supporters even as they cooperate in terms of influence. Movement leaders need to manage their relationships with other movements, forging coalitions that are sometimes long-lived, and also need to manage diversity within their ranks, affording participants enough autonomy to maintain their energy and participation but coordinating enough unity that a movement's efforts aren't diluted and its message remains clear. Political opponents also respond to this diversity, offering a mix of concessions and sanctions that generally works to divide social movements, moderating their impact. This is, we will see, the way Madison designed the American political system to work.

In Chapter 5, we examine what social movements do, considering the strategy and tactics of social protest. Movements are based around belief and shared interests, but more than this, they are defined by social action. When social movement activists engage a political issue, they choose from a large menu of tactics of influence, ranging from political violence to mainstream political participation. Every tactical choice carries different risks and potential benefits. A group's choice of a tactic has consequences for participants, often defining who they are to themselves, their potential allies, bystanders, targets, and opponents. An effective tactic demonstrates the extent and intensity of commitment to targets, energizes supporters, and piques the interest and sympathies of bystanders. In picking tactics, organizers must be mindful of the experiences of those they intend to mobilize or influence, because everyone involved evaluates a new action in terms of what he or she thinks has happened in the past. Because opponents, supporters, and bystanders can all respond to political action, the circumstances in which tactics are chosen are volatile. A good choice on one day may be a weak one soon afterward. Strategy means employing a series of tactics and demands over a period of time in ways that benefit both political and organizational goals. Importantly, because of the diversity within movements, any significant challenge will include a variety of groups employing a broad range of tactics, ranging from, at least, demonstrations to conventional politics.

Activists make choices about tactics mindful of the likely reactions of authorities, supporters, opponents, and bystanders. But most of those audiences do not interact directly with the activists or even observe their work close-up. Rather, information about activist events is communicated through mass media. In Chapter 5, we examine the changing nature of mass media in the United States and how this changing nature affects not only what activists do, but also how we see it.

In Chapter 6, we consider one common, and often dramatic, tactic: civil disobedience. This tactic, willful and open defiance of the law, is one that has grown increasingly common in the United States. Civil disobedience, like protest in general, has a long tradition in American politics, but one that leads to frequent misunderstandings about what it means. Activists and analysts frequently discuss civil disobedience in terms of moral witness and moral absolutes. Although this may be part of what happens, here we are particularly concerned with the role of civil disobedience in protest movements, so we examine how this tactic affects the development of social movement coalitions and their relations with authorities, supporters, opponents, and bystanders.

In Chapter 7, we focus on the development of social movements into some kind of stable entities, because the peak of a movement is always inherently unstable. The height of a movement's activity is defined by larger numbers of people doing something that is, for them, unusual. This means that even at the peak of mobilization, when all kinds of things seem possible, activists and politicians are thinking about the next day. Entrepreneurial politicians seeking influence or higher office try to find ways to capture some portion of a movement's energy, visibility, and resources, adopting new rhetoric, embracing new policy prescriptions, and recruiting activists and leaders. At the same time, organizers seek to carve out a stable basis of support to allow them to continue to make some claim on political institutions and the public imagination. The process of turning the exceptional into something more routine, something repeatable, predictable, and sustainable, is institutionalization. One part of this process is building an infrastructure of new institutions outside of government; another part is making inroads into government, planting ideas and actors into stable positions inside the state. Something is always lost, of course, in making the move toward politics indoors, but it's not clear that movements that take the institutional road become less effective in promoting policy reform or social change. This is, by the way, a function of the system that Madison designed at work.

Protest, always a fixture in American politics, has become increasingly common. Once the province of those poorly positioned to be effective in more conventional politics, it is now employed as part of a strategy for all sorts of causes. With increasing frequency, even elected officials, who presumably have more direct means of access and influence, not only explicitly align themselves with movements, but also engage in civil disobedience, expressing frustration at their potential influence through more conventional means of affecting influence. And although the popular image of protest politics is anchored in the civil rights movement of the 1960s and expressed most frequently in the antiglobalization and antiwar protests of the contemporary era, protest has never been the exclusive province of the political left. Indeed, in contemporary politics, with increasing frequency more than one side of a political struggle employs protest politics as part of its strategy.

In Chapter 8, we examine the diffusion of protest tactics and styles across the political spectrum. The growing attractiveness of protest tactics reflects both the perceived efficacy of the protests of the past and the perceived inaccessibility of mainstream politics to citizen concerns. The growth of social movements on both sides, proclaiming a recurrent politics of polemic and crisis, undermines both the capacity of government to make policy coherently and the faith of citizens in government—thus propelling social protest. In effect, we have a social movement society (Meyer and Tarrow 1998). When, however, protest is not the exclusive province of the disadvantaged, but a standard part of the contemporary political rhetoric, the disadvantaged and their concerns become crowded out of all kinds of politics.

In Chapter 9, we consider the political payoff of social protest by looking at the connection of social protest to policy reform. Because the conditions that promote social change are also those that promote social protest, disentangling the independent influence of movements on policy is no easy matter. Further, because movements are based on a politics of stark and extreme demands, and our institutional politics prize seeking compromise and negotiation and promoting incremental reforms, social movements virtually never get all they ask for—or at least what their strongest supporters ask for. This doesn't mean, however, that such movements don't matter. In fact, government action—and proposed government action—is both a provocation and a response to social movements. Sometimes, in fact, moderating or stalling a proposed reform is a social movement success, albeit one reflected by stability rather than policy change. By laying out the dynamics of the policy process in America, we can see distinct places in the process where social movements might make a difference, and we'll see specific examples in which they have affected the outcome of policy. At the same time, in a complicated and often convoluted process of policy reform, it's not always those who promote change who take credit for it. We will analytically separate the process of influencing policy from the process of claiming credit for influence. The stakes of successfully claiming credit, of course, are extremely high, for the sake not only of historical accuracy, but also for mobilizing effective citizen action in the future.

The terrain we've covered in this book demonstrates quite clearly that social movements sometimes matter. Historically, the partisans and activists who've helped promote massive changes in policy and culture have often been people with extremely limited conventional political resources, poor people, ethnic and political minorities, and even students. Recognizing that this is the case imposes a large burden on all of us. In Chapter 10, we're reminded that citizen action propelled by average people, people like us, means that we have a responsibility for improving the communities we live in. All kinds of things are possible.

AMERICA AND POLITICAL PROTEST

Political Institutions and Dissent

Although the notable colonists were dressed as Indians, no one familiar with the political scene in Boston in 1773 would have been unable to identify them on the night of December 16 as they clambered aboard a ship and started throwing crates of tea into Boston Harbor. Sam Adams, speaking to a crowd at a mass meeting on the tea tax, announced that the meeting could do no more to "save the country." In response to this signal, men in the back of the crowd began "warwhoops" as groups of lightly camouflaged colonists rushed through the streets to the harbor. Smearing a bit of cork across their faces, they made little attempt to conceal their identities or their purposes. They were joined by spontaneous—and undisguised—volunteers, swelling the numbers of protesters from more than 110 men to perhaps more than 200; more than 1,000 watched. They quickly emptied the hull of its contents and hurled the crates of tea into the sea, while being careful to do no additional damage. The only injury was to one man, accidentally hit by a falling crate of tea, and he quickly recovered.

In order to finance foreign wars, King George III had imposed several new taxes on the colonies, including one on tea, this time wrapped in a subsidy to the East India Company. Rather than quietly refusing to pay the tax, much less to acquiesce to it, colonists across America rejected new tea shipments. In Boston, in opposition to the governor, firebrand patriots staged the dramatic raid to announce not only their opposition, but also their identity, determination, and future plans. This tale of protest against one of many new taxes imposed by King George III is frequently told and often cited as the start of the American revolutionary campaign that resulted in the birth of a new nation.

If the disguises weren't enough to prevent the British from prosecuting the men who led the charge against tea, the strong solidarity of the revolutionaries in Boston was. One man who turned in a neighbor to the British was tarred and feathered, then forced to parade through the streets wearing a sign identifying him as an informer. No one else talked, and Britain announced it would punish the entire city instead by closing the port of Boston to all trade (Griswold 1972). More significantly, word of the "tea party" spread across the colonies, alerting, encouraging, and terrifying those who heard of it. This party demonstrated the willingness of some Americans to resist new taxes (without representation) to finance British wars abroad. This demonstration was important in sending a message to both British authorities and to other colonists. In effect, the emergence of visible and dramatic resistance set the political agenda for all concerned: American independence. Most Americans, then as now, preferred to think about things other than politics, and most hoped for more moderate solutions than a revolutionary war. Sam Adams's cousin, John Adams, writing decades afterward, estimated that, at best, one-third of the colonists supported the revolution, with another one-third largely uninterested in politics altogether (Marina 2004). The Boston Tea Party was designed to polarize the population, to force the colonists to choose sides. For this purpose, Sam Adams said, majorities aren't important. "It does not require a majority to prevail," he proclaimed, "but rather an irate, tireless minority keen to set brush fires in people's minds."[1]

Histories of the American Revolution frequently start with a recounting of the Boston Tea Party. Dramatic resistance, effected in costume, makes for a nice story, and the incident symbolizes a broad range of resistance, most of it less dramatic. Colonists resisted other taxes and British authority more generally, more frequently with bold talk than theatrical action. The rebels wrote letters and made promises, all with the dual intent of sparking the imaginations of their supporters and stoking the fears of their opponents. They wanted to inspire and mobilize the colonists while threatening the British with hints of unspecified aggression in the future. (If they would throw tea into the ocean, what else might they do?) The tea party was only a small part of a much larger revolutionary movement, which included passionate rhetoric and guerrilla war.

The tea party provides a convenient place to start the story of the birth of the United States as well as an opportunity to begin our inquiry of social movements in America. We'll start by thinking about social movements as distinct political phenomena, something clearly related to more familiar kinds of political efforts, but apart from them at the same time. From the Boston Tea Party, we'll consider the larger kind of dramatic and unconventional politics it represented. We'll then return to the flow of events from the Boston Tea Party, focusing particularly on how the colonists' experience of government and rebellion led them to set up a government that presented a peculiar mix of obstacles and opportunities for future social movements.

TEA PARTY OR SOCIAL MOVEMENT?

The Boston Tea Party was a dramatic and important event; in itself, however, it wasn't a social movement, but rather part of a larger campaign. In looking at social movements in the United States, we must first confront the extraordinarily broad range of definitions that follows the phenomenon. The notion and language of social movements run through popular culture and the academy, and there is absolutely no consensus about what they mean. In "Alice's Restaurant," a comic song depicting his modest acts of draft resistance, Arlo Guthrie starts to approach a definition we can work with. Asking members of his audience to walk into the draft board and sing a chorus of the song, Guthrie emphasizes the importance of numbers. "If one person does it, they'll think he's crazy and won't take him . . . but if 50 people, can you imagine 50 people a day walking into the draft board and singing a chorus of Alice's Restaurant, well, they'll think it's a social movement, and that's what it would be folks . . ." In some ways the song, which provided the core of a popular movie, is an artifact

---

[1] http://www.brainyquote.com/quotes/quotes/s/samueladam134183.html

of the sixties. Still, Guthrie has performed the 18-minute tale for nearly 40 years. Moreover, without any academic purpose, Arlo Guthrie identifies a movement as something with a political purpose in which sufficient numbers of people undertake unusual action that is designed to disrupt the regular functioning of an institution and to threaten to do more.

When we turn to more academic definitions, the same elements that Guthrie identifies remain, but there is much else. McCarthy and Zald (1977: 1217–18) define social movements as "A set of opinions and beliefs in a population which represents preferences for changing some elements of the social structure and/or reward distribution of a society." In their view, there needn't be action to be a movement. In stark contrast, Tarrow (1998: 4) defines a social movement as "collective challenges based on common purposes and social solidarities, in sustained interaction with elites, opponents, and authorities." For him, social movements are essentially defined by the action, not the ideas. For Tarrow, and for others, the state is the critical actor that makes the development of social movements possible. But we can observe that the language of movements is used to refer to all kinds of efforts in which the state is hardly an important target or interlocutor, such as hip-hop, vegetarianism, or punk. As David Snow (2005) points out, numerous authorities can be challenged by social movements: religious, artistic, and familial authorities. And Melissa Wilde (forthcoming), in a pathbreaking book, argues that the best way to understand Vatican II was as the result of a social movement.

We can argue about definitions, but invariably people with competing ideas talk past each other, trying to make room for the kinds of movements that interest them. Definitions always exclude in order to provide clarity, and the term *social movement* belongs to both popular and scholarly language. We need to think about definitions that help us understand something important, and by excluding some things to focus on others, we hope to make sense of what we do look at and to figure out general patterns. The way an artistic and literary movement, such as the Harlem Renaissance, works figures to be quite different from the way the women's movement of the 1960s swept across the United States and through government. The important thing is to specify a field of concern, develop concepts of use in understanding it, then assess what other sorts of phenomena might profitably be understood by employing the same concept.

The social movements that people study affect how they think about movements—as forces for democracy and justice or as harbingers of intolerance and hatred—and affect what scholars look at when they try to explain social movements. Although the history of social movements in America is quite long, dating back well before the Constitution, most scholarship in the United States is of a more recent vintage.

The first wave of scholarship on social movements, mostly in departments of sociology and political science, commenced in the 1950s as a reaction to the horrors of a social movement elsewhere: fascism in general and Nazism in particular. Scholars were not disinterested but rather were passionately aware of the dangers of a society that seemed to have gone mad and at tremendous costs to the world. Most scholarship focused on the dangers of movements of the right and traced social protest to psychological disabilities. William Kornhauser (1959), for example, proposed that people join social movements because they are insufficiently connected to state and society through intermediary social and political groups. They turn to social movements because they seek connection and because they lack other options. Lipset and Raab's (1973) study of right-wing movements also emphasized the importance of intermediary associations, linking people to the broader society. Oddly, these scholars were writing when the civil rights movement was erupting into larger public visibility without visible signs of aggregate psychological dysfunction and when well-integrated, often well-heeled and committed religious people were protesting against nuclear weapons and nuclear fallout—again, without visible psychological disabilities. Scholars offered generalizations on movements based on their readings of particular cases.

When the social movements of the 1960s erupted, the template of Nazism was sometimes applied to understand why students, in particular, were challenging authority and sometimes breaking the law. But empirical studies of social movement activists found that the student activists were more socially engaged and better psychologically adapted than their less active counterparts (e.g., Keniston 1968). Scholarship turned to consider protest as a choice that people with claims sometimes make, a "resource" (e.g., Lipsky 1970; McCarthy and Zald 1977) to be employed to enhance political influence.

Here we will pay close attention to the political context in which social protest takes place, the grievances that activists have, the strategies and tactics they employ to try to get what they want, the life they create within a social movement to keep people engaged, and the responses from government and authorities.

For this book on the *politics of protest,* we will think about social movements as *collective and sustained efforts that challenge existing or potential laws, policies, norms, or authorities, making use of extrainstitutional as well as institutional political tactics.* This definition leaves much out, but by limiting what we consider here, we can establish some basic concepts to develop a foundation for understanding a critical and recurrent expression of politics in the United States.

Let's take apart some of that definition. To begin, social movements are the products of collective efforts rather than individual and disconnected actions; some activists organize in groups, whereas others orchestrate their own actions in harmony or counterpoint with broader political trends. They join together for some common purpose. Importantly, they do not need to agree on everything. In the Boston Tea Party, for example, some of the tea-tossers wanted to spark a revolution and national independence, whereas others wanted Britain to be more respectful of the colonists and to offer some gesture of political inclusion. No doubt others were caught up in the passion of the moment and were less clear about their ultimate political objectives. Although it's a linguistic convenience to think about *the* social movement (the antiwar movement, the women's movement, the civil rights movement, the labor movement, and so on), real political movements are comprised of diverse coalitions of actors, generally with a range of ideas, resources, and institutional identities.

By "sustained" I mean something that continues over a period of time. The Boston Tea Party was an *event* that was part of a larger *campaign* against the new taxes and part of a larger social movement that ended, finally, with a successful war of independence—if not a real social revolution. Social movements string together events and campaigns as part of an extended effort to achieve real gains politically. Over the course of a social movement effort, different groups will be more prominent, offering distinct emphases and demands and employing a wide variety of tactics. The dramatic events that garner public attention comprise a tiny portion of what individuals and organizations do to advance their ideas.[2]

---

[2] Tilly and Tarrow (2006) distinguish between the "base" of a movement or its infrastructure, and its "campaigns," that is, a series of events directed toward a specific goal.

Over time, some groups will be better positioned in relation to authorities than others will be, and differences within a movement will become critical to affecting its development and ultimate impact. Sometimes, as in winning a revolutionary war or losing a decisive political or military battle, movements have distinct endings. Much more commonly, however, the lifespan of a social movement has ambiguous beginnings and endings (Whittier 1995). Social movements draw their inspiration, ideas, organizations, and personnel from people involved in other campaigns and movements (Meyer and Whittier 1994), and some elements and organizations almost always continue on after the peak of a social movement, albeit with fewer members, less visible activity, and far less interaction with mainstream politics (Taylor 1989).

On the matter of challenge, we must start with the premise that people don't take on the costs and risks of participating in a social movement unless they have some kind of a serious grievance with some powerful authority. The vast majority of people would surely prefer to manage the issues in their lives without politics of any kind and surely to avoid the hassles and dangers of mobilization most of the time. When they do get involved to some degree, they prefer to undertake the most routine, easiest, least disruptive, and most predictable sorts of political participation: voting, calling an elected official, participating in a political party. Social movement politics, in contrast, are mostly unpredictable, and their influence is uncertain and always difficult to trace. Of course, people have a variety of motivations for doing anything, but large-scale participation in any social movement is conditioned on substantial dissatisfaction with some element of government policy and a level of cynicism, frustration, or pessimism about getting a response without social protest.

This doesn't mean, however, that all such people abandon more conventional means of politics; rather, something is added to normal politics. At the time of the Boston Tea Party, other colonists were writing letters and seeking meetings. Movements are defined by common purposes uniting people doing very different things: working in political campaigns, going to meetings, signing petitions, organizing demonstrations, maybe throwing rocks, breaking windows, getting arrested, and *always* making opponents worry about what's coming next. Some portion of a social movement's activity takes place outside mainstream political institutions, and the connection of these efforts to what goes on inside mainstream institutions, more than anything else, defines the trajectory and impact of a social movement.

Authorities are those people in position to respond not only to the efforts of social movements, but also to their claims. For the most part, we'll be focusing on social movements that are directed toward some level of government, but movements also challenge authorities in other settings, including religious orders, corporations, and universities (Snow 2005). In the course of a movement campaign, authorities must make decisions about both categories of response: how to manage the conduct of dissidents and how to handle the issues that are animating the social movement. These decisions are, of course, related, and frequently sharp strategic divisions among people in power provide opportunities that activists can exploit by making the right tactical choice.

While social movement activists and their allies work inside and outside of political institutions to advance their claims, most people do little more than watch. Social movements rarely take up more than a small portion of the population in favor of their efforts— or in opposition. Joining a social movement means leaving the role of spectator and entering the political field of play. Between one hundred and two hundred colonists crowded onto the small tea party ship, emptying its contents within an hour, and a sizeable crowd grew as the party rolled on (Labaree 1964; Griswold 1972). Because movement strategies are generally the province of those ill positioned to win through conventional tactics alone, they have an interest in how those watching respond to what they do. In this regard, a tactic is a kind of performance, and savvy activists are attentive to their audiences (Tilly 1994). Indeed, paradoxically, the response of the bystanders is often the most important factor in determining what happens next. Social movements can provoke a range of responses, including, at least, fear, disgust, and sympathy. They can call forth coordinated action for or against their efforts. As E. E. Schattschneider (1960) pointed out nearly fifty years ago, the people to watch in any fight are in the crowd. Schattschneider notes that it is the losers in any conflict who have an interest in expanding its scope and bringing in new actors to the conflict. This is what social movements do. When social movements are successful, authorities and bystanders think not only about the political efforts of activists, but also about their demands and gripes.

Sometimes, as in the case of the Boston Tea Party, bystanders are actually standing close by and can see activists and authorities. But the messages of movements are also conveyed by those who tell their stories. The tale of the Boston Tea Party was repeated across the colonies and written in the newspapers of the day. Over time, the variety of conduits of information, and the speed with which a story is conveyed and repeated, has increased dramatically. As more distant audiences can be reached, even around the globe, the potential scope of a conflict has increased tremendously. We'll see that activists are attentive to how mass media perceive and portray them and their efforts and to how those portrayals can influence how activists think of themselves.

The basis of a challenge is some kind of grievance, and people have grievances about all kinds of things, which we can think of as their *interests,* which may be nearby and material or relatively distant and abstract. Direct interests are generally based on material goods, that is, the distribution of stuff that influences how people live their lives. People are concerned about who has how much property and how they can improve their own material situations. They are concerned about their wages, the taxes they pay, and the services they get for those taxes. When people protest against taxes, we understand that they are trying to protect their perception of their interests. When workers strike for higher wages, we see the same thing at work. Similarly, citizens protest to keep libraries open in their communities, to get their trash picked up more routinely, to ensure the presence of police, to oppose a military draft that might put them in harm's way.

In a way that is sometimes related, citizens also engage in social movements about values and about what Dieter Rucht (2000) describes as "distant issues," that is, issues that are likely to be global or transnational in effect and in resolution (also see Tarrow 2005). We can extend Rucht's concept to include issues distant from the way in which people live their lives. People who will never visit a national park, for example, still engage in protest about keeping lands pristine and protected in distant parts of the country and often engage in politics about rain forests in other parts of the world. They join social movements about U.S. policy toward other countries and about military posture more generally. And people protest about providing or preventing abortion or scientific research using stem cells or teaching a foreign language or "creation science" in public schools, even when these policies might be far from the more concrete issues in their lives. Our concept of *interests* must be expanded to include values and concerns. Individuals who would never choose—or have the chance to choose—an abortion are no less passionate about their beliefs about the practice than are those who do make such a choice. People who are unlikely to spend time in prison, much less face execution themselves, are passionately engaged in an ongoing debate on the death penalty. In many ways, the conflicts about values are more disruptive and difficult because they are less amenable to compromise. Of course, within a social movement, people have distinct and individual reasons for committing to political action.

Because the goals and actions of people within a social movement vary, and because they all may change over time, and because the responses of authorities are critical factors that influence how important an issue seems and how necessary a particular tactic seems and how risky participation in a movement is, we need to look at those challenged in order to understand social movements. This means we need to look at the challenges and opportunities provided by mainstream politics. In the United States, this means we need to look at the laws, rules, and policies of the American government. People protest when they believe that they won't get what they want otherwise and that they *might* get it if they do take action. In other words, *potential activists must see participation in a social movement as both necessary and potentially effective in order to stage a large event.* These conditions are set by the rules, practices, and institutions of the existing government.

Social movements trace dynamic trajectories, with activists moving in and out of collective action and with authorities responding in different ways. As with other kinds of politics, the process is always in flux, so that the people who write letters on one day may choose to take to the streets the next or simply to return to their individual concerns. How authorities respond to both the claims and the efforts of social movements is obviously critical to understanding the broader pattern of development and potential influence of social movements. In order to begin to understand these processes, we need to pay close attention to the context in which social movements emerge. Here, focusing on social movements in the United States, we will start with the development of the Constitution, and this will take us back to the aftermath of the Boston Tea Party.

THE FOUNDING

On the day after the Boston Tea Party, there was a lot of cleaning up to do. The tea-tossers escaped individual punishment, but the warning shots in the revolution were now heard by all, and people took sides. The spiral of activities culminated in the revolutionary war, in which the British lost possession of the colonies. Having ousted the British, the colonies faced newly mobilized democratic sentiment, fed on the polemical rhetoric needed to get men to leave their families and fight through long, cold winters with little pay. Revolutions promise massive change, and those who fight them can imagine even what no one says explicitly. Those who read Thomas Paine's inflammatory *Common Sense* imagined democracy, people making decisions about the things that affect their lives—regardless of how much property they own or the extent of their education. Abolitionists heard the end of slavery. Those who heard the Declaration of Independence that Jefferson assembled imagined a new political and economic equality, hinted at by the phrase "pursuit of happiness." They engaged in local politics with a vigor, passion, and effect that threatened the very same interests that spurred the revolution. It made sense, as Jefferson outlined it, for decisions to be made by rational citizens who understood and had to live with the consequences of those decisions. People believed that power corrupts and feared the concentration of power in an executive or in a distant legislature. It made sense for the locus of power to be near the sites at which it would be administered.

Citizens, newly titled and fully engaged from the revolution, didn't go home and wait to be governed. They took up the challenges of politics in their communities, forging rules that would make the concentration of power represented by King George III impossible and trying to set up governments that would be more responsive to their perceptions of their interests. With power decentralized across thirteen colonies, the coalitions that governed varied tremendously, as did the rules. Pennsylvania was probably the most radical of the states; its Constitution, written in the revolutionary fervor of 1776, called for, instead of a single governor, a council of twelve that would annually choose a president. It imposed strict term limits on all elected positions, and the most important positions were contested annually. And, like many other states, Pennsylvania did away with property requirements for voting altogether (Rakove 1979; Wood 1993).

In Massachusetts, a coalition of merchants and bankers gained control of the state legislature and assembled a state constitution largely drafted by John Adams. Property qualifications for voting and holding office remained, albeit at much lower levels than prior to the revolution. Adams designed for the state a political system that would limit not only the power of an executive, but also the potential influence of the masses. Dubious about direct democracy from the outset, Adams was candid about his concerns. In a country where most people didn't own property, political equality would allow the propertyless to unite and vote to redistribute wealth. Indeed, he believed it was inevitable. For Adams, such a possibility was clearly antithetical to the national interest and the survival of the colony. His constitution divided power between three branches of state government: two houses of the legislature, a senate and a general assembly; an executive branch led by a governor; and a court whose members the governor would appoint.

The Massachusetts government served some interests better than others. In western Massachusetts, as today, farmers were dependent upon debt to manage their businesses. They borrowed money, mostly from creditors in the eastern part of the state, to put their crops in, planning to repay their debts with money earned from their harvests. Obviously, this enterprise was loaded with risk. Key to the farmers was the cost of credit. The farmers supported a flexible fiscal policy, which meant they wanted government to put more money into circulation. Providing more money, and injecting some amount of inflation, allowed farmers to repay loans more easily than did the tight fiscal policy favored by creditors. In Massachusetts, the farmers lost on this issue again and again. In the summer of 1786, facing foreclosures because they were unable to pay their loans and reacting to the state legislature's rejection of their petitions for paper money, farmers began staging rebellions. Daniel Shays, formerly a captain in the revolutionary army, led the most active opposition. In August of 1786, rebels mobbed the courthouse in Northampton to prevent legal foreclosure of farms. Shays and up to six hundred lightly armed farmers staged similar actions against courts in towns across western Massachusetts, leading the governor to meet their force with more than four thousand militia in Springfield. On January 25, 1787, Shays's supporters surrounded the arsenal in Springfield, capturing some merchants and looting some stores along the way. Exchanging fire inside the arsenal, the two sides fought sporadically over the next week until the Shaysists were ambushed and scattered. Whereas some of the rebels gave up, others, including Shays, sought to organize in other states.

Although the state was ultimately able to put down the rebellion and jail Shays and the other rebels, ultimately executing two, it was a difficult and scary time. The possibility of insurrection, represented by Shays's campaign, sent a shudder through politicians and governments across the United States. The threat of less violent, but no less disruptive, popular democratic politics around issues of currency was perhaps even scarier. Legislators sent out a call for a national convention to reform the Articles of Confederation and improve the national government (Brown 1987; Szatmary 1980; Wood 1993).

Meeting in secret in Philadelphia in the summer of 1787, representatives of most of the colonies argued about the structure of the new government. All agreed that the Articles of Confederation was unwieldy and unworkable and that direct democracy was no answer. They disagreed, however, on much else, including the process of representation, the powers of an executive, slavery, and foreign policy. Throughout the vigorous debates among the founders, the most influential person in the room was the recording secretary, James Madison. Barely five feet tall and slight, in the shadow of war heroes and charismatic speakers, Madison was quiet in public but actively negotiated with all of the factions at the convention, seeking compromises that could hold together the convention and ultimately the colonies as well. The Constitution that emerged was remarkably similar to the one adopted in Massachusetts less than ten years earlier.

In seeking ratification of the Constitution, Madison and his allies, Alexander Hamilton and John Jay, wrote polemical essays extolling its virtues. Published in New York newspapers, these *Federalist Papers,* replete with the prejudices, misjudgments, and disagreements among the authors, serve as a kind of Rosetta Stone for interpreting and understanding American political theory and American politics. To be sure, these essays were written as practical arguments to engage supporters, not as coherent pieces of an abstract theoretical treatise. Nonetheless, in these essays we can see how the founders thought about the purposes and strengths of the government they had helped design. In these essays, the founders explained their efforts to try to steer a course between avoiding the tyranny of a monarch, such as they'd experienced under British rule, and avoiding the imagined tyranny of the mob, represented by Shays's Rebellion. Importantly, although this balance was on the minds of many of the drafters, the Constitution that emerged was less an explicit and coherent strategy than a negotiated political document, with room for all the contradictions and inefficiencies of compromise.

The calculations, negotiations, and consequences of the American Constitution are the subject of tremendous elaboration and debate, which I will not repeat here (but see Dahl 1956). In summarizing the structure of American government, I mean to focus on those elements that affect the way in which citizens who want something organize, where they might target their efforts, and how the government can respond. We can think about the federal design in terms of five Fs: **factions** (groups of interested citizens), **fragmentation** (of power), **filtering** (of passions), **fighting** (on policy), and **frustration**—of all those concerned.

"If men were angels," Madison writes in *Federalist* 51, they would not need government. In fact, he contends, everyone is looking out for his or her own interests. Assume that people will always think of themselves first, Madison argued, and take appropriate precautions. (In some ways, this is an odd revelation coming from a man—and a group—who had dedicated a large amount of uncompensated time to the constitutional project.) Madison saw conflict about interests as unavoidable and imagined that the most salient issues would always be about property rather than about abstract values. When he writes that it is impractical to give all persons the same interests, he is referring directly to the distribution of goods. Citizens would unite in groups based on interest, which he described as **factions,** and attempt to make the government work for them. Because all persons would be looking out for his or her interests, which would always be in conflict, a stable government must be able to manage conflict and maintain itself (Matthews 1995).

The Constitution laid out a blueprint for a government that was premised on distrust. Its basic design divided power to make it hard for any interested group, or "faction," in Madison's terms, to use the power of the government without broad and sustained support from a range of other actors. On one level, this was an explicit attempt to avoid the tyrannies of monarchs and mobs. On another level, however, it was a recipe for a government that would be able to do less. This itself was a fine outcome for those who were doing fairly well as things were, but it was surely less responsive to those who might need help or protection from government. By dividing power, the Constitution guarded against the abuse of power; even if one part of government fell into enemy hands, that faction would be unable to do much with it; it would be difficult for *anyone* to make much use of this government. This tension and this reality, a slow and unresponsive government wrapped in rhetoric about democracy and participation, confront all Americans to this day.

We see more when we look more directly at the constitutional design. First, those at the Philadelphia convention agreed that the United States needed to be more united, at least in terms of dealing with foreign and domestic threats. They wanted a national government that could, at least, borrow and repay currency, raise and fund an army, and conduct foreign policy. At the same time, all of the rhetoric of having government located at a level near the citizens who might influence it was a constant pressure to maintain the state and local governments. The federal compromise divided power between the states and the federal government, affording citizens governance from at least two distinct, although completely entangled, units. Although the Constitution set aside some roles exclusively for the federal government (e.g., raising an army, conducting foreign policy, printing money), in many policy areas both the states and the federal government could make claims to have primacy in making decisions. Immediately, the constitutional design presents incipient activists with multiple targets. Further, because of the Supremacy Clause (Article VI), the Constitution assures that state governments will be constrained in responding to the demands of their own citizens. Even with the federal divide, the Constitution ensures that the national government will win any battle it wants to contest. In this way, federalism allows the separation of access to government from influence on matters of policy. But this is just the beginning.

Power was further divided within the federal government between the legislative branch and the executive branch, with the potential influence of a third branch of government, the judiciary. The legislature, clearly meant to be the most powerful branch of government, was itself further divided into two houses, the Senate and the House of Representatives, with members serving different constituencies and elected on somewhat different timetables. In order for any government action to occur, majorities in both houses had to agree to every detail of a bill. Bicameralism ensured some institutional brakes on action of any kind and created a system that prizes compromise and incrementalism, that is, slow change that occurs in small bits at a time. The ship of state would be like an aircraft carrier or ocean liner, which would turn slowly if at all. The agendas of the House and the Senate diverged somewhat, with the Senate given additional responsibilities for policing foreign policy and high-level appointments—responsibilities denied the House of Representatives, which the founders assumed would be more volatile and responsive to mass publics. Implementation of policies, however, was separated from the legislature altogether, given to an executive who controlled a bureaucracy, leaving lots of room for stalling, slowing, and modifying.

Popular influence on who actually held all these positions was meant to be severely limited and filtered. In a classic democracy, citizens would choose decision makers, who would have to face an electorate relatively frequently in order to ensure that they responded to popular will. The founders, however, were not interested in this kind of democracy. In the original design, Supreme Court justices were to be appointed to life terms by the executive; the executive himself would be chosen by electors chosen by the state legislatures, and the Senate would be chosen by the state legislatures as well. The president and senators would also enjoy relatively long terms (four and six years, respectively). One-half of one branch of government, the House of Representatives, would be filled by popular elections that were conducted more frequently—every two years. The passions of the public as represented in these elections, however, would be restrained by the other elected officials in the federal government, chosen by more informed, more advantaged, and more limited electorates. The design was intended to include popular participation, but not to be bound by it.

Allocation of senators, two per state, gave smaller states, and particularly states in the South, an undemocratic electoral and political advantage that has continued to this day. At the time, this advantage was particularly important in making it essentially impossible for Congress to act on slavery, thus frustrating the abolitionist movement and keeping the southern states engaged in the Union (Wills 2003). More broadly, the founders assumed that the Senate would represent something of a national aristocracy, the best and the brightest the states had to offer. Enjoying long terms, senators would be free to think about the national interest more than popular demands. Because the terms were staggered, with only one-third of the Senate up for election at any time, quick response to popular moods would be unlikely. The Senate then would serve to consider, cool out, and moderate the initiatives from others.

The founders assumed, mostly incorrectly, as it turned out, that the membership in the House would fluctuate tremendously in response to passing moods and conditions in the country. Even here, however, they installed institutional structures to promote moderation. Most significantly, they created an electoral system based on single-member districts. Representative seats, apportioned to the states based on populations, would be contested in distinct geographic areas. The candidate for office who won a plurality of votes would gain the seat, with supporters of other candidates left to wait for the next election. By design, this meant that smart aspirants for office would position themselves in the imagined political and ideological center of their districts. To be sure, some districts would be far more liberal and others more conservative, but the successful candidates would largely win office by marginalizing the more extreme—and minority—positions in their districts, a kind of **filtering** built into the system. Savvy candidates who lost elections would themselves have to build coalitions toward the center in order to compete in the future. Of course, the same filtering would take place in the House itself, where majority votes were needed to pass legislation.

This was the only place in the national government where citizens would enjoy the potential of direct influence through voting. The structure of government effectively encouraged activists of all stripes to concentrate their efforts on electing sympathetic candidates to the House but made sure that those efforts would be based in coalition-building and compromise. Once in office, no matter how committed and partisan, representatives would have to compromise and coalition-build further. (Importantly, the founders didn't envision the development of a party system that would facilitate the building of more stable coalitions of diverse interests. Indeed, they were all active opponents of the development of political parties. Even Jefferson, who formed the first national party in pursuit of office, criticized the very notion of political parties.)

Madison's vision of a large and growing republic would have the effect of complicating the process of coalition-building by multiplying the number of interests. He realized that in order to ensure a large buy-in to the system among the range of factions in the United States, it was critical to prevent the emergence of permanent cleavages in which one group not only lost all the time, but also saw no prospect of ever winning. By continually bringing in new interests through expansion, the system made it possible for coalitions to form and break relatively easily, so that any group could always find potential partners in politics and could envision progress, if not complete victory, on the issues of its concern.

State and local governments would be more accessible to dedicated activists. At the same time, even with the freedom to set up their own republican governments, all of the states have developed remarkably similar forms of governance, embracing the separation of powers, the divisions of power and responsibilities among local and larger governments, and the principle of checks and balances. The same jigsaw puzzle of governance at the federal level was replicated at local levels and with the same effects.

Madison and his colleagues were concerned about limiting both dedicated minorities and majorities, and most, being well off and well educated, recognized themselves as a potentially threatened minority. As Madison described it, although a democratic system would control minorities, it might do so too well, and it could fall prey to the passions of temporary—or misguided—majorities, particularly the propertyless masses. The republican system promised by the Constitution was sure to frustrate everyone's political aspirations at least part of the time. The founders imagined a polity with broader participation, but surely not mass democracy. Most states retained some kind of property qualification and age restrictions for voting—for white men. Slaves, obviously, could not vote. It would take more than seventy years and a bloody war to change the Constitution to end slavery and provide the vote to former slaves and nearly another century before the federal government worked seriously to protect their descendants' voting rights. Women began to win suffrage later, state by state, culminating in a constitutional amendment in 1920 (Banaszak 1996; McCammon 2001). Another constitutional amendment, ratified in 1971, lowered the voting age to eighteen—partly a political response to an antiwar movement featuring young men who stubbornly pointed out that they could not vote to replace the men who were sending them to risk their lives in a war abroad.

Even without anticipating these extensions of the franchise, the constitutional system protected the country from transparent democratic rule. The founders designed the system with numerous "veto points," that is, places where an interested and active minority could stop something from happening. Initiative, particularly for broad reforms or new policies, would be very difficult to effect. Nonetheless, the system had to offer sufficient access in order to keep a range of constituencies more invested in the system than in any particular policy outcome. Importantly, even within this system, because power was fragmented throughout various branches of government, it was hard to trace the actual initiative for any action, and social movement leaders and institutional political actors competed to "claim credit" for their influence. Was the Voting Rights Act of 1964 a triumph of the civil rights movement, or was it the victory of a president, Lyndon Johnson, who was committed to doing something bold and great for the country, and was a master of manipulating the legislative process and legislators? Obviously, both factors were critical, but to emphasize one or the other teaches very different lessons to Americans about politics and collective action.

Moreover, the consequences of social movements often extend far beyond the apparent boundaries of a challenge. Once in mainstream politics and culture, social movement ideas become redefined and can animate opponents as well as supporters. Ideas rattle around political institutions and get picked up, reframed, and redeployed in ways that would appall their initiators. Thus, opponents of affirmative action are now fond of quoting Martin Luther King's speech to a crowd of 250,000 protesters on the steps of the Lincoln Memorial. Surely King's dream that his children would "one day live in a nation where they will not be judged by the color of their skin but by the content of their character," articulated in a time when gross economic and social inequality was supported by explicitly discriminatory laws and contracts, was directed to a politics that those critics would find abhorrent. In a different kind of example, the movement against the war in Vietnam led political leaders to reformulate American politics and policy to make future antiwar movements, if not wars, less likely and less dangerous. The government ended the draft and, until the end of the twentieth century, embraced a doctrine that called for engagement in wars only with overwhelming force.

In essence, the Madisonian design was all about *institutionalizing dissent,* bringing political conflict into the government in order to confine the boundaries of claims that activists might make and to invite partisans to struggle using conventional political means rather than taking up arms or opting out of the system. The theory was that conflict inside government is preferable to conflict between the government as a whole and dissenters. This choice came at a price, however, that of a responsive and active federal government. Veterans of the colonial experience and the Articles of Confederation, a majority of the founders were prepared to pay this price—and to impose their choices on others.

When the Constitution was ratified and came into effect in 1789, in conjunction with the new Bill of Rights, a dimension was added to the constellation of political prospects for activists. The large purpose of the Bill of Rights was to limit further the capacity of the federal government to act in accord with majorities of the moment. By limiting government restrictions on basic civil liberties, specifically speech, assembly, press, and religion, the Constitution allowed a broad range of interests to try to mobilize visibly, rather than taking their concerns underground. Again, this had the paradoxical effect of stabilizing the political system and preventing the development of large revolutionary movements.

Of course, the American government hasn't always lived up to the ideals expressed in the Constitution, particularly on issues of civil liberties. Further, many of the details of governance and the structure of American political institutions have changed in ways the founders could not have anticipated. At the same time, the basic effect of key principles of the Constitution—separation of powers, single-member electoral districts, checks and balances, and especially federalism—works pretty much as the founders intended. As Dahl (1956) has noted, although the founders were wrong about all of the details, their notions of how the final product would work turned out to be prescient.

First and foremost, the founders imagined that factions would virtually automatically form around interests and that organized groups would be able to pursue their interests persistently and effectively. Nearly fifty years later, however, based on his visit to America, Alexis de Tocqueville (2000) wrote that even the process of forming organized groups led to compromise and filtering of interests. Presuming, like Madison, that everyone is simply looking out for his or her own narrow interests, Tocqueville noted that the system required citizens, if they wanted to be effective at all, to develop a sense of "self-interest, rightly understood," that is, the need to compromise and bargain with potentially interested supporters. Interests, at least as perceived, turned out to be less uniform than Madison anticipated, and the process of mobilizing interests turned out to be more difficult, rent with compromises all by itself.

The founders imagined that the presidential elections would usually be deadlocked and thus decided in the House of Representatives. This has happened twice. Almost always, the Electoral College exaggerates and emphasizes a popular election, although three times it undermined it.[3] A Supreme Court decision in 1962 (*Baker v. Carr*) placed serious restrictions on the size and boundaries of electoral districts within states, but this did not change the fundamental effect of the single-member district system, which channeled conflict into elections and led representatives to find the political center of their districts. To be sure, in the last fifteen years, state legislatures, aided by sophisticated computer programs, have developed aggressive redistricting strategies to favor incumbents and minimize uncertainty in elections. This has led to a far larger number of seats that are effectively "safe" for one party or the other, representatives who serve narrower constituencies within the major parties, and a more polarized House of Representatives. At the same time, there is still a diversity of opinion within the House, and the legislature itself is still constrained by the other branches of government.

In 1913, the Seventeenth Amendment to the Constitution provided for the direct election of senators, but the staggered six-year terms and the selection of what might be called an "aristocracy," natural or not, have occurred pretty much as the founders anticipated. The founders might have been surprised to see the development of a reasonably stable two-party system, although the electoral rules they developed basically ensured this outcome (Downs 1957), yet both parties work to channel conflict and build coalitions toward the political center. In short, reforms and miscalculations on so many of the particulars haven't affected the way the governmental structure affects the development of social movements and citizen politics more generally.

On civil liberties, although the Bill of Rights is remarkably clear on basic premises, presidents since John Adams and up to George W. Bush have tried, with some success, to limit the access of their political opponents to meaningful audiences through the press. The American government has sometimes prosecuted people for their political beliefs, most notably during the 1950s, when Senator Joseph McCarthy fronted a campaign against Communists (and people who might look like or know Communists) in America. More recently, the Patriot Act has given the federal government broad powers to fight terrorism that make

---

[3] The loser in the popular vote triumphed in the Electoral College three times: Rutherford B. Hayes defeated Samuel Tilden in 1876; Benjamin Harrison defeated Grover Cleveland in 1888; and George W. Bush defeated Al Gore in 2000, aided by explicit intervention from the Supreme Court.

citizen oversight very difficult. It's important not to ignore such drastic departures from the principles of civil liberties. At the same time, throughout American history, citizens have been generally afforded some amount of political freedom to try to recruit others to their causes. The principle of free speech is the belief that even the most heinous ideas are less threatening and more manageable when out in the open. In the United States, the largest share of social movement politics has taken place in public, with all of the constraints and opportunities that offers. Similarly, although there have been serious limitations on the freedom of the press historically, the principle of a free press means that activists can try to use mainstream media to glean information about issues of their concern and use mainstream media to convey their concerns and efforts to others. Again, the idea is to bring dissent into the open, without letting it build into a potentially revolutionary movement.

Finally, in a paradox of democracy, the Constitution is ambiguous about the role of the Supreme Court and the legal system in the process of making policy. The establishment of judicial review, however, early in the nation's history provided claimants with the promise of influence without majorities, as well as another potential veto point. The fact that the Supreme Court can invalidate any state law or act of Congress or the president, in theory, means that activists can imagine hot-wiring the political process, skipping the difficulties of building broad public support in favor of crafting a fine argument and enlisting the support of the federal government. That judicial decisions on racial segregation and abortion rights provided not only policy change, but also inspiration and support to social movements encouraged movement activists to consider the courts in a way the founders could not have envisioned.

WHAT THE MADISONIAN DESIGN
MEANS FOR SOCIAL MOVEMENTS

The structure of government established by Madison and the other founders affects the prospects and tactics of challenging social movements in several distinct ways:

1. The guarantee of civil liberties encourages those dissatisfied with any government policy to take their claims public and to attempt to convince others to join them. Clandestine organizing flourishes when the United States retreats from constitutionally protected liberties.

2. Activists who wish to influence policy will need to build broad coalitions to establish enough strength to gain notice of the general public and elected officials.

3. This means that organizers will, ultimately, simplify and soften their messages in order to reach a larger number of people.

4. Elected officials will always have an interest in responding to insurgent movements. Those in the most secure positions will be slowest to respond. Ambitious or threatened politicians will be quick to jump on the momentum of a social movement, articulating positions designed to steal its fire or to capitalize on its opponents.

5. As a result, movements will generally be able to find more or less committed allies in government who will want to speak for them.

6. Politicians who claim allegiance to movements will enjoy considerable autonomy in defining what activists really want and what they will settle for.

7. Elections will provide routine opportunities and constraints for social movements. Organizers will generally have to decide whether to participate in electoral politics and, if so, how, these decisions are of great consequence.

8. Federalism and an often ambiguous separation of powers and responsibilities will offer activists a kind of shell game, as they must search for open institutions with the capacity to respond to their concerns.

9. The existence of judicial review will provide a constant temptation to activists, who will imagine the possibility of coopting a branch of government to struggle against majorities. Of course, the Supreme Court has historically been reluctant to rule against majorities and has had severe limitations on actually enforcing its decisions in any case.

10. The history of social movements and social change will be contested, and institutional actors will always be better positioned to claim credit for a movement's influence than with any social movement. When movements are given credit for their influence, their goals and terms will be defined by institutional actors who may have very different purposes.

Here I've outlined some basic approaches to understanding social movements in the United States. I've emphasized that social movements live in a state of dynamic interaction with the political mainstream, at least when they are potentially significant. Because they are related to mainstream politics, they are deeply influenced by the structures and rules in mainstream politics—even if they challenge those structures and rules. Essentially, by setting up the rules as they did, the founders established the playing field for both institutional politics and the social movements that challenge them. But setting up the struggle doesn't determine outcomes, even though it does advantage some actors, interests, and approaches. The structures we've described bound the battles, but the birth, development, and influence of social movements reflect the active leadership and strategic choices that activists make, as well as the responses of their opponents and allies in mainstream politics. Knowing the basic rules, the lay of the land, however, allows us to go further to figure out what's next.

CHAPTER 2

WHY PROTEST?

The Origins of Movements, Opportunities, and Organizations

Twenty-nine people sat on park benches in front of New York's City Hall on a summer day in 1955, holding signs calling for an end to the nuclear arms race, to nuclear testing, and to nuclear weapons altogether. On any normal day, thousands of New Yorkers would pass by those benches and see the demonstrators, but this wasn't any normal day. June 15 was the day of a citywide air raid drill, and the peace demonstrators were immediately noticed mostly by police, who arrested them. They were charged with disobeying police orders during a required drill and sent that same night before a judge, who likened them to murderers for attempting to undermine the U.S. war against Communism, and the Soviet Union in particular. He found them guilty but suspended any jail sentence (Miller 1982).

But the air raid demonstration was projected around the world, along with speeches from foreign leaders, including Pope John XXIII, condemning nuclear weapons. The most famous of the activists was Dorothy Day, who had spent the previous thirty years primarily fighting poverty. After a mystical vision, Day had founded the Catholic Workers, a group of religiously inspired activists who took their own vows of poverty and spent their lives trying to live their interpretation of the Gospel, working for peace and justice.

The air raid demonstration is a viable entry into several larger points, but we can start with a relatively small one: context gives an action meaning. The demonstration in front of City Hall would have been a legal and negligible action on any other day, but on the day of a civil defense drill unprecedented in size and scope, it was not only illegal, but also extremely visible and meaningful. And even on that day there were many other places in New York City where the Catholic Workers could have gone to avoid arrest rather than to find it. Like those activists, we want to understand those contingencies of time and place, about when an issue becomes actionable and about where it can be challenged.

In this chapter, we are going to examine the opportunities and constraints that activists face in launching social movements. Social movements are episodic, even though the issues on which they mobilize are far more persistent. We will try to understand why movements on issues come and go and how their trajectories reflect something important and lasting about American politics. We will start with the premise that for large social movements to emerge, people need to believe that participation in a protest movement is needed to get some part of what they want and that the movement might be effective, in other words, that protest is both necessary and potentially effective.

EPISODES OF PROTEST AGAINST NUCLEAR WEAPONS

The campaign against nuclear weapons is a good place to start our investigation. Nuclear weapons have been a critical component, and a contested issue, in American foreign policy since at least August 6 and 9, 1945, when the United States dropped nuclear bombs over Hiroshima and Nagasaki in the closing days of the war against Japan. The critical question for us is why, in the face of an apparently constant grievance, the nuclear arms race, protest has been so episodic, confined to four important eruptions or campaigns, two of which were international.

Almost immediately after the end of the war, public concern about nuclear weapons spread across the country. Nuclear weapons were something new and something very scary. Regardless of one's belief about the necessity of bombing Japan to end a terrible world war, the early reports of the horrors of Hiroshima and Nagasaki were disturbing. John Hersey's (1989) report from Hiroshima, published first in the *New Yorker* and then as a slim book, detailed human carnage from one weapon that was previously unthinkable. The immediate response, from clergy and political leaders, was a call for careful consideration of how these weapons had changed the world. Scientists spearheaded a public education effort, founding organizations to promote discussion about nuclear weapons, most notably the Federation of American Scientists, which publishes the *Bulletin of the Atomic Scientists*. Activists called for the international control of nuclear weapons. This possibility faded in 1947 with the onset of the Cold War, and American nuclear anxiety took a backseat to other issues for nearly eight years.[1]

A broader and more volatile peace movement emerged in 1954, prodded by the issues of radioactive fallout from nuclear tests. Dorothy Day's civil disobedience was an early event in this long campaign, which flourished worldwide until 1963. It included nonviolent civil disobedience, sometimes by groups, but often by brave individuals, designed to disrupt testing, undermine the arms race, and project the issue of nuclear weapons to a larger audience. Albert Bigelow (1959), for example, sailed a small boat, *The Golden Rule,* into a nuclear test site in the Pacific, hoping that he could delay a nuclear test. The movement also included publication of books and magazines, production of movies, lobbying in Congress, art exhibits, international meetings of scientists and activists, local organizing, and questions in presidential debates. The movement receded in 1963 after the United States, the Soviet Union, and Britain signed the Limited Test Ban Treaty, which prohibited atmospheric testing.

A somewhat smaller antinuclear weapons campaign emerged in response to the development of antiballistic missiles (ABM) at the end of the 1960s. Such missiles—their effectiveness still only a theoretical possibility—are supposed to destroy incoming nuclear weapons before they can damage American missiles or cities. Protests against ABMs were large in American cities that were scheduled to host them from 1968 until 1972, when the Soviet Union and the United States signed a treaty limiting ABMs in number and deployment. The ABM treaty remained in effect until 2000, when President George W. Bush announced the U.S. intention to abandon it.

---

[1] For accounts of the cycles of antinuclear weapons protest in America, see Wittner 1984, as well as Wittner's comprehensive global histories 1993, 1997, 2003. See also Meyer 1990, 1993a, b.

Finally (at least at this writing), the early 1980s brought the emergence of a nuclear freeze movement in the United States, which called for a "bilateral freeze" on the production, testing, and deployment of nuclear weapons. The freeze movement worked in some coordination with European movements against the deployment of new nuclear weapons in western Europe. These movements faded when the United States and the Soviet Union reinvigorated the arms control process in 1985. Indeed, in an episode emblematic of the nature of American political institutions, when Ronald Reagan, the prime target of the freeze movement, won reelection in 1984, he declared his victory as a "mandate" for arms control, a process he had not only neglected in his first term, but also excoriated.

How can we understand the episodic nature of protest on the issue of nuclear weapons? If the problem is that of the existence of nuclear weapons and the continued technological arms race, why isn't protest against nuclear weapons continuous? Obviously, sustaining a social movement is extremely difficult, but why do large movements emerge at the times they do? Is the answer the efforts of organizers? Although this seems to make sense, a little search reveals the persistence of some individuals and organizations throughout the entire period. In other words, there are always activists trying to call attention to the dangers of nuclear weaponry, but only sometimes are they able to win broader public attention and engage many other people. Why?

If we answer the questions about nuclear weapons protests, we can begin to understand the episodic nature of other kinds of social movements. Looking at the history of movements against nuclear weapons, it makes sense to recall our dictum about people needing to believe that protest is both necessary and potentially effective in order to engage in sustained collective action. Nuclear weapons should be a hard sell to most activists. It's not that the dangers of nuclear war can't be made apparent, it's more that the dangers of nuclear war are distant from most lives. Most Americans have never seen a nuclear missile, and believing that people have the prospect of engaging with and understanding policy on the issue is usually a long stretch.

By looking at the context surrounding the dramatic episodes of protest about nuclear weapons, however, we can begin to understand how changes in circumstance make some claims more credible and allow long-time activists access to a broader audience. Like the umbrella salesman on the street, technique may matter, but more significant is the visible threat of rain. The first campaign against nuclear weapons, commonly referred to as the "scientists' campaign" or the "campaign for international control," faded with the prospects for international control. It's not that nuclear weaponry or the threat of nuclear war seemed less important; rather, it was the space for protest and the prospects for influence that disappeared. Immediately after the end of the Second World War, there seemed to be both an urgency and a possibility for a new collective approach to international security, which entailed some supranational organization. This possibility collapsed, however, even as the United Nations appeared with the onset of the Cold War. As an example, look at the trajectory of Cord Meyer Jr., founder of the World Federalists Organization and one of the proponents of international control of nuclear weapons. Along with many others, he came to see the Soviet Union, rather than the weapons themselves, as the primary threat to peace and shifted his efforts from peace activism to working in the newly created Central Intelligence Agency (Wittner 1993; Divine 1978). Meanwhile, the federal government offered promises of developing nuclear energy that would provide cheap, clean, and reliable power, channeling discussion of the nuclear issues to power, rather than war. In short, government policy, framing and responding to world events, made it harder for activists to portray a present danger or to project seemingly viable alternatives. Not only was government less open to such alternatives, but also it was less tolerant of those who might challenge the dominant approach to national security.

Protest against nuclear weaponry reemerged strongly just a few years later, but it did so less because activists had found new tactics than because new issues had emerged and new opportunities seemed to open. In 1954, a Japanese tuna trawler, the *Lucky Dragon,* was covered with radioactive fallout from a nuclear test in the Pacific, ultimately killing all on board (Divine 1978). The tragedy publicized by atomic scientists and others, connected the hazards of nuclear tests to the larger conduct of the arms race. The threat of nuclear war, a potential danger, was connected to the actual hazards of the arms race, even absent a war. Political space for mobilization was also enhanced by factors well outside the control of antinuclear activists. The war in Korea over and Joseph Stalin dead, in 1953 the possibilities of alternatives to the Cold War seemed to emerge.

At the same time, U.S. policy became notably more aggressive. The movement grew as government spending on the military in general, and nuclear weapons in particular, was increasing dramatically and as the United States was seeking to deploy a broader range of nuclear weapons in a broader range of strategic and tactical roles. Mobilization ebbed and flowed from 1954 to 1963, diminishing during presidential election years and when the arms race seemed more manageable or the Soviet Union more threatening. The ratification of the Limited Test Ban Treaty, which banned atmospheric tests, took some of the proximate threats of the arms race off the agenda. Although military support for American ratification of the treaty was bought by the promise of more tests, albeit underground, managing the dangers of radioactive fallout by moving the tests underground made it more difficult to mobilize public concern and made it easier for many Americans to trust institutional politics and the Kennedy and Johnson administrations to manage the dangers of the arms race.

The campaigns against ABM development and deployment were facilitated by dissident scientists who had lobbied against ABM development inside government and lost, working in coalition with local activists who didn't want ABMs to be sited near their homes. By reconfiguring and limiting the program in response to costs, perceived efficacy, and political vulnerability, President Nixon defused the movement. Signing an arms control accord with the Soviet Union limited the potential number of ABM missiles and sites. He then opted to set up only one ABM site, located in North Dakota, far from any urban centers, with the mission of defending a missile field. This system was ultimately deployed for only a few months in 1974.

The nuclear freeze movement took off also in response to a new and expensive escalation in the arms race and a more generally aggressive turn in American foreign policy. The nuclear freeze idea had circulated in both arms control and activist circles since the early 1960s, but it had failed to generate much intellectual traction or popular support. In 1979, in response to an initiative from the pacifist American Friends Services Committee (AFSC), arms control analyst Randall Forsberg grafted this arms control policy into a broader agenda for remaking American foreign policy. Forsberg framed her nuclear freeze proposal as both a policy alternative and a strategy for political action. It is unlikely, however, that her freeze proposal would have been more successful than its predecessors had not circumstances changed to make activists and the broader public more receptive.

In 1978, in response to both world events and domestic political troubles, President Jimmy Carter increased spending on the military in general and nuclear weapons in particular. Republican candidate Ronald Reagan ran against Carter from the right, charging Carter with valuing arms control more than American security and blaming Carter for leaving America undefended. Carter tried, unsuccessfully, to use fear of nuclear weapons and nuclear proliferation to salvage his electoral fortunes; in 1980, Reagan defeated Carter in a landslide of historic proportions, bringing Republicans control of the Senate at the same time.

Immediately advocates of arms control and foreign policy restraint were shunted into the political wilderness. The Reagan administration implemented large military budget increases on top of the increases Carter had already built into the budget, raising spending on the military to a level unknown in peacetime. At the same time, Reagan purged from his council advocates of arms control and detente with the Soviet Union. He replaced them with conservative activists and experts openly disdainful of the entire arms control process, breaking off negotiations with the Soviet Union and renouncing—though not violating—the unratified SALT II agreement. And he continued preparations for deploying, for the first time in nearly twenty years, intermediate-range nuclear weapons in western Europe.

All told, Reagan's strategic posture, aggressively criticized by mainstream—but out-of-government—experts, made it easy for citizens to get concerned about the arms race, nuclear weapons, and the new administration's capacity to handle the tasks of national security. Deploying cavalier rhetoric in confirmation hearings, considering the possibility of millions of casualties in a nuclear war, for example, the administration's security team and the policies they advanced proved attractive targets for activists with a range of grievances with the president.

Aided by more focused antinuclear activism in western Europe that was directed against hosting new missiles, the freeze movement grew quickly, taking up a variety of critics of the administration in its wake. When the freeze movement demonstrated its strength through large victories in referenda, through nonbinding resolutions in hundreds of town meetings and city council endorsements, and through the assembly of one million people in New York City's Central Park, ambitious politicians saw mileage in joining the freeze movement or at least some of its elements. The freeze became a popular stick to use in beating the president.

But when new actors picked up that stick, they used it for their own purposes, redefining the freeze as something compatible with their own previous positions on national security. Democratic candidates for office variously linked the freeze with increased spending on conventional weapons or support for newer, single-warhead strategic nuclear weapons. As the freeze movement became more visible and more popular it also became more diffuse and accessible, and as it became more diffuse and accessible, it became even more popular. Broad and shallow support isn't exactly what most of the organizers wanted, but support of any kind is very hard to turn away or to qualify. The criticisms and the proposals of the nuclear freeze were redefined with astonishing rapidity. In 1982, for example, while watching French television, I was shocked to see President Ronald Reagan claim to be a leader of the movement that had identified him as its prime target.

Nonetheless, by 1984, after the House of Representatives had passed a vacuous and nonbinding nuclear freeze resolution and after six of seven Democrat presidential hopefuls (including eventual nominee Walter Mondale) had endorsed a nuclear freeze resolution, Ronald Reagan's victory was, in fact, a kind of mandate for arms control. As the organizations that animated the freeze movement began to falter and the freeze started to fade on the public scene, Reagan sent Vice President George Bush to the funeral of

Soviet leader Konstantin Chernenko, carrying a personal note for the new Soviet leader, Mikhail Gorbachev. The handwritten note emphasized Reagan's newly visible interest in working on arms control. "You can be assured of my personal commitment to working with you and the Soviet leadership," it read, "In that spirit I would like you to visit me in Washington at your earliest convenient opportunity" (quoted in Cannon 1991: 746). In the next few years, the arms control process spun out of Reagan's control as Gorbachev accepted proposals the Reagan administration had designed to be rejected. In the Eastern bloc, reform also spun out of control, leading to democratization in some contexts. By the end of 1989, state Communist governments had fallen in Czechoslovakia, Hungary, Poland, and East Germany, followed shortly by Bulgaria and Romania. East and West Germans danced on top of the Berlin Wall. Two years later, the Soviet Union itself broke up. Superpower arms control was a less salient issue for many activists in a world with only one superpower.

EXPLAINING CYCLES OF PROTEST

From these brief narratives, we can see the relationship of antinuclear mobilization to the broader political context, tracking cycles of protest in relation to changes in policy and politics.[2] Without taking anything away from the activists who actually comprised the social movement, we have to understand that circumstances during the 1980s made it first more, then less, possible to stage a broad antinuclear movement. Activists' efforts were critical, to be sure, but would not have been enough without favorable opportunities.

From these cases, we can identify the basic clusters of variables that constitute what we can call the "structure of political opportunities" (Meyer 2004; Tarrow 1998; Tilly 1978; Eisinger 1973; Kitschelt 1986). Scholars offer very different definitions of political opportunities (Meyer 2004), but Tarrow's (1998: 19–20) treatment offers an economical place to start: "consistent—but not necessarily formal, permanent, or national—dimensions of the political struggle that encourage people to engage in contentious politics." Opportunities don't automatically translate into protest but rather set the conditions in which activists work.

Now we can return to the antinuclear weapons movement and its ebbs and flows over nearly fifty years and read back through that history to identify factors that made mobilization more or less likely and that could be translated to other social movements. We start with our premise that substantial numbers of people need to believe that participation in a social movement is necessary and at least potentially effective.

First, in the case of all four episodes of antinuclear protest, the broad movement was preceded by the development of a *grievance,* resulting from a new policy problem: the introduction of nuclear weapons into world politics; the fallout from nuclear testing; the introduction of antiballistic missile systems; and a new escalation of the arms race, unfettered by arms control. These grievances all reflected real or potential changes in politics to which citizens could respond. To be sure, once established as a fixture in international politics, the

---

[2] On protest cycles, see Tarrow 1998.

potential grievance of nuclear weapons has been a persistent possible target for challenge. Most of the time, however, that is not sufficient to mobilize activism or even much public attention. This is true for many other social movement causes as well, ranging from opposing discrimination against any group to seeking tax fairness. Sometimes, however, a small change in a large problem, or a critical incident, allows activists to raise—or reraise—the broad political issue.

Second, activists responded to the rules and norms of American politics. The constitutional framework we reviewed in the first chapter set the basic parameters of the political game in the United States, and those parameters exercise great sway over just what's possible and what seems possible. Beyond that, however, every issue brings with it a particular obstacle course of institutions and procedures. Effecting change in nuclear policy means influencing different people than does effecting change in educational policy, for example. What's more, those rules, norms, and broad cultural values change over time—to be sure, partly in response to social movements. Thus, we'd expect activists on behalf of gay and lesbian rights to have different options for making their claims in 2000 than they had twenty-five years earlier.

Third, activists needed sufficient *political space* or openness to organize. With the start of the Cold War in 1947, questioning national security policy was tantamount to enlisting in the Communist Party and being prosecuted for it. The end of the Korean War, followed shortly by Stalin's death, afforded new openings in politics, making it safe to come out against the bomb.

Fourth, institutional politics had to appear unresponsive to activists' concerns. In all of these cases, activist mobilization was inversely related to the apparent prospects of working through more conventional politics. Presidents, by responding to the movement rhetorically, balancing bellicose statements toward the Soviet Union with appropriate concern and sobriety about the dangers of nuclear war and offering arms control initiatives, can undermine the grounds for going to extrainstitutional politics (Meyer 1995).

Fifth, in truth, most activists are generally not terribly well attuned to the intricacies of security doctrine. They are, however, responsive to signals from people who are attuned to these intricacies. When experts can press their cases directly to the president, they generally do so, leaving the public mostly disengaged. When, however, they are unable to do so, they may go public. Experts comprise one sort of political or cultural elite that can be an asset to social movements. The term *elite* is hard to define, but we can think about people who enjoy disproportionate status or influence in politics or society. The prospects for successful and broad mobilization are substantially enhanced either when some faction of those elite is available for movement leaders to use or when those elite try to stoke mobilization themselves.

In the case of the antinuclear movement, both of these things happened. Every broad public mobilization had been promoted by dissident scientists or strategists who no longer enjoyed sufficient influence within the higher levels of government to believe that they could affect influence without outside help. The popular movements were also aided by the presence of well-known actors and artists or other celebrities who proved to be valuable assets for activists. Celebrities bring media attention to social movements and their issues and for obvious reasons aid in raising funds and crowds as well (Meyer and Gamson 1995).

PROTEST AND POLITICAL OPPORTUNITIES: CIVIL RIGHTS

We can state these elements of political opportunity somewhat more generally and then see how they hold up for other movements and other issues. The key elements of political opportunity include salient public grievances; a political context that includes both institutional rules and public values; political space for activist mobilization; political alignments, particularly on the issue of concern; and availability of elite support, usually a function of elite schisms.

We can take this broad roadmap and look at another social movement that has ebbed and flowed throughout American history—the American civil rights movement. We can have some general sense of how the movement, subject to a great deal of attention and analysis, emerged, how it reached a peak of sorts in the early 1960s, and how it transformed into something else over the course of the next decades.

The existence of a grievance for African Americans dates back well before the founding to slavery; only rarely, however, were most Americans positioned to see discrimination by law and culture as something sufficiently salient—or sufficiently tractable—to mobilize broad support. Committed activists tried to raise the issue and tried to coopt allies in institutional politics, establishing the NAACP in 1909—along with other organizations and campaigns—as a vehicle for doing so. Demographic factors aided in spreading public concern with racism, and not only in the South. The collapse of the cotton economy in the South led to the Great Migration of African Americans from the South to northern cities, breaking down well-established routines of social control in both contexts. Still, in the 1930s, President Roosevelt saw more to lose than to gain by embracing the cause of civil rights at that point in the form of an antilynching law (McAdam 1982).

World War II entailed a massive mobilization and relocation of both black and white Americans and, although men fought in segregated units, created a climate for reexamining the structure of race relations in the United States. In addition to internal pressures, the United States, trying to craft an international alliance against the Soviet Union, was constantly reminded of its own deficiencies in freedom and democracy at home (Dudziak 2000; Layton 2000). Responding to these pressures, President Truman announced, via executive order, that racial segregation in the armed forces would end. This built on narrow, but favorable, Supreme Court decisions that invalidated the policy of racial exclusion at some white-only educational institutions (Kluger 1975). At the same time, these political changes reflected and encouraged similar changes in popular beliefs such that the president of the Brooklyn Dodgers baseball team felt safe enough to hire Jackie Robinson as the first black player in major league baseball in the twentieth century. All of these events put race relations and civil rights policy on the political and social agenda.

Politicians responded to these issues in a wide range of ways. Hubert Humphrey, a young senator from Minnesota, a state with a small black population, made a passionate speech at the Democratic national convention in 1948, identifying civil rights as the most significant issue and challenge of his time. Strom Thurmond of South Carolina, also a young senator, responded to that speech and to Truman's policies by walking out on the convention and running against Truman in the general election with a new party, the Dixiecrats, built fundamentally on resisting any change in civil rights policy. Labor leaders argued about how to mobilize black workers and overcome racial prejudice to build the labor movement (Goldfield 1997).

Civil rights activists mobilized in a range of ways, including filing the critical lawsuit *Brown v. Board of Education.* Importantly, the pressures of the Cold War and the political responses to the earlier claims of civil rights afforded activists some political space in which to mobilize, that is, the federal government afforded a level of protection to African Americans, no matter how modest, that they could not count on previously—in an era of lynch mobs. In the 1950s, Congress considered several civil rights bills and passed a weak one in 1957. Meanwhile, activists executed both community campaigns and political organizing, creating a kind of synergism in which reforms inspired activism that provided additional reforms.

In the early 1960s, aided by media attention and the influx of activists from the North, civil rights came to be an issue that captured national attention. Boycotts, sit-ins, marches, and freedom rides all drew support and opposition, making civil rights the essential issue on the American political agenda and generating a national march on Washington, where organizers argued behind the scenes about which issues and rhetoric they might use to take advantage of this special moment. In 1964, President Johnson pushed the Voting Rights Act through Congress and the Civil Rights Act the following year. The legislation gave federal endorsement to a few critical demands of civil rights activists and left many others untouched. This exacerbated growing rifts within the movement among those who wanted to focus on a broader definition of civil rights and stress economic issues, those who wanted to take the opportunities of enhanced voting rights to work through the system, and others who were dubious about white participation in some of the movement's key organizations.

As the Vietnam War grew in political visibility, and as riots spread across American cities, splits within the civil rights movement grew more difficult to manage. Over the following decades, many of the civil rights organizations that animated the movement at its height continued efforts, but a rift grew between more moderate groups and their radical flank (Robnett 2002). At the same time, the status of African Americans in America changed significantly, if not to the extent that civil rights activists demanded. John Lewis, heroic director of the Student Non-Violent Coordinating Committee (SNCC), forced out of the leadership, eventually turned to more conventional politics and in 1986, roughly two decades after SNCC imploded, won election to the U.S. House of Representatives.

Synthesizing Political Opportunities and Activism

In both cases, the civil rights movement and the antinuclear weapons movement, we see a strong relationship between activists and institutional authorities and an ongoing interaction between the movement and the structure of political opportunities it faced. However, important differences between these relationships underscore the complexity of opportunities and activism.

In both cases, the grievances around which activists organized were long-standing, but new changes in policy—or proposed changes in policy—afforded an opportunity to raise broader issues. For the antinuclear weapons movement, however, activism increased in response to policies that activists found more threatening. In contrast, civil rights activism increased, at least initially, when government seemed more responsive. In this way, civil rights activism was part of a synergistic spiral of reform, working off and encouraging policy reforms. In contrast, antinuclear weapons activism served as a brake on government initiative, inhibiting unwelcome policies.

The two movements faced radically different institutional contexts in that antinuclear weapons activists challenged a policy made exclusively at one level of government, generally well insulated from citizen pressures. Even members of Congress would express frustration at being unable to influence the conduct of government. In contrast, the challenges that civil rights activists faced involved the federal government, but more commonly proximate grievances against local governments. Indeed, in the 1950s and 1960s, the civil rights movement depended upon the intervention of the federal government *against* state governments, and many of the tactics employed were designed specifically to engage the federal government and outside allies. The antinuclear movement has sometimes tried to use the Supreme Court but found minimal success. And its efforts to exert pressure on the president by appealing to international law or outside allies have been largely unsuccessful.

In discussing political space, it's important to acknowledge that the United States is normally treated as a very open polity, in comparison with other countries, even other wealthy liberal democracies. This said, political openness varies by constituency and over time. Throughout the first half of the twentieth century, it was difficult for African Americans to find safe spaces in which to organize, and even in the 1950s, the safe space of the churches proved critical (Morris 1984). Without doubt, the movement grew in response to greater political openings—at least until formal openings for voting, when things became more complicated.

In contrast, the antinuclear weapons movement was usually afforded a great deal of openness in society. Animated largely by white, well-educated, and relatively advantaged people, activists did not fear repression, except for a brief and critical period early in the Cold War, when any claims critical of U.S. nuclear weapons policy raised the specter of the Soviet threat and Communism. In both cases, political circumstances had to be sufficiently open to allow safe organizing and mobilizing, but not so open and inclusive as to undermine the perceived necessity of protest. Routine access to institutional politics that seems meaningful reduces urgency for a political movement and undermines the prospects of mobilization.

The concept of political opportunity structure was first advanced by a political scientist studying the urban riots of the 1960s. Peter Eisinger (1973) was concerned about why *some* large cities experienced riots while others didn't. Seeing poverty and discrimination everywhere, Eisinger looked at the means for redress that were readily available to dissatisfied people. He assessed urban governments in terms of the open or closed nature of their political structures and found that cities in the middle of the spectrum were most likely to be visited by riots. In effect, cities that allowed no prospect for influence could effectively discourage or repress dissent, whereas cities that were open to the claims of the poor could institutionalize conflict before it erupted in riot. We can trace the relationship between openness and opportunity for protest on a curve, finding protest most likely at its center.

We can trace the curve in explaining the development of both of the movements we've looked at over the past sixty years. In the case of the antinuclear weapons movement, government closing of claims of activists at the start of the Cold War put a lid on dissent, driving activists underground or, more frequently, to other issues and approaches. The end of McCarthyism opened a chance for antinuclear weapons activists to organize, and they did so until government built institutional spaces for their concerns. For example, President Kennedy established the Arms Control and Disarmament Agency in 1963, explicitly chartered to maintain a voice for negotiations and limitations to the arms race. When government appears to be addressing activist concerns, large social movements are unlikely to emerge. Certainly radical pacifists and others will not be satisfied by the moderate responses of management and negotiation, but they are unable to mobilize a broader audience on behalf of their ideas. Since that time, antinuclear weapons mobilization has taken off in response to government exclusion of the views of moderation, in other words, when these views are pushed out and up the curve.

The story of African American civil rights mobilization runs along broadly similar lines, albeit over a much longer period of time. After World War II, increased concern with civil rights, driven by a number of factors, afforded partisans increased safety to mobilize and increased the prospects of some responses from government. Both deliberate government action and unpredictable circumstances pulled a constituency usually excluded from meaningful access to political institutions into the realm of possibility. As real, albeit limited, reforms were effected, the civil rights movement coalition began to fragment as some large portions of the movement's potential leadership were pulled off the high point of the curve into government. Protest mobilization is now more likely to take place when those in government are crowded out or when policies further restrict access of African Americans to the full benefits of American life, again pushed back up the curve of openness.

The nature of available political space is a function of what issues are monopolized by well-established political institutions. This results from the ways in which established political actors orient themselves both to mainstream politics and to both established and rising constituencies. It's important to think of opportunities as not open or closed, but as sometimes somewhat available or screened or channeled. If we think about the broad structure of political institutions established by the Constitution as a constructed house, we can think about political space as being shaped by the positioning of furniture and actors within that space. Infrequently, someone knocks down a wall or puts up an extension. More frequently, someone pulls a chair up and sits on it, blocking and redirecting traffic. And continually people cluster in groups, standing back from the entry of new people, seeking out new conversations, and blocking doorways.

Importantly, insurgents create their own new institutions and relatively permanent fixtures on the political landscape. The establishment of a new legitimate actor on the landscape affects the prospects for everyone who follows, monopolizing some claims, crowding out others, and taking up space in mainstream institutions and mass media that is no longer easily accessible to new groups. Indeed, because well-established groups have their own routinized relationships with authorities, new movements frequently take off when activists organize outside those groups, seeing possibilities that others long versed in the issues would ignore or being willing to take risks that are less attractive to those with more to lose.

The existence of well-established organizations is only one element of the political alignments that activists face. How necessary or potentially effective social activism appears is partly a function of which people are in political power, their political positions, and their vigor in pursuing them. The jigsaw puzzle of power that Madison and the founders established makes it difficult for any unified faction to gain complete control of government and use it to effect major policy changes. If we take the civil rights case, for example, even though the Democratic Party controlled all major national political institutions, it included both civil rights supporters and opponents. Indeed, in looking at the origins of New Deal welfare policy, Amenta (1998) argues that rather than focusing on parties, it makes more sense to look at the disposition of elected officials toward federal spending. Social movements, he contends, are likely to mobilize effectively only when the institutional context, defined by a working majority of social welfare spenders, controls Congress.

Because social protest movements are closely related to institutional politics, the preferences and commitments of those in power matter, as do their faction's margin of dominance over challengers. Just as theorists of democracy would suggest, people in power are generally less likely to embrace new ideas, to take risks to win new constituencies, or to abandon the policies and political coalitions that put them in power. Similarly, it is generally harder for activists to mobilize protest outside political institutions when perceived allies have control of politics inside those institutions. The existence of sympathetic majorities in power makes it less attractive for people to take to the streets, unless it is to generate state action against other threats. In contrast, being able to target enemies in office presents a clear necessity of mobilization to activists and enables challengers outside mainstream politics to offer something—the promise of committed and vigorous support—to entrepreneurial allies in mainstream politics.

This feeds into the availability of sympathetic elites for mobilization. These allies can include disgruntled elected officials or candidates for office, experts cut out of the policy process, or cultural figures who can bring visibility, if not always expertise and credibility, to insurgent efforts. Indeed, they usually come together. Although the cultural figures may be the most visible, they are likely to be the last to enter into social mobilization. Here, too, people in this broadly defined "elite" category make their own calculations about significant issues, potential gains, and risks of participation. Their conduct can legitimate and encourage dissident mobilization—or dampen it. Elites are less likely to abandon a social movement than to channel it, throwing in their lot with institutional actors as a mobilization continues.

Taken together, we've reviewed the range of factors that affects the prospects for activists to succeed in mobilizing on a particular set of issues at a particular time. Whereas the basic rules of American politics are reasonably constant, attention to particular issues or constituencies is extremely volatile. Some activists are always pursuing the same set of issues and enjoy substantial success only at the odd time when opportunities align in their favor. Others, however, are more like prospectors, operating with a broad political and social agenda, experimenting and watching for signals about which sets of issues to work on at any given moment. To understand how this takes place, we need to look at political and social movement organizations.

ORGANIZATIONS

In a small lake town in rural Michigan in 1962, a group of student activists gathered with leaders of several old left organizations to chart a course for progressive politics in the future. The student activists were uninterested in refighting the battles of Communism and anti-Communism but were interested in developing a vision of democracy that might speak to the concerns of young people. Together they worked over a draft of a manifesto that Tom Hayden, a student journalist from Michigan, had produced (Miller 1987). This Port Huron Statement, which called for "participatory democracy," that is, a new political system in which people would be actively engaged in making decisions about all the things that affected their lives, became the ideological centerpiece of the student movement of the 1960s.

The statement circulated in activist circles, particularly on college campuses, and similar groups of students formed chapters of a new organization, Students for a Democratic Society (SDS). Often these chapters were based around the fading infrastructure of campus chapters of the Committee for a Sane Nuclear Policy (SANE) as mobilization on nuclear weapons issues seemed both less promising and less urgent at this point. And promoting democracy was a broader and more inclusive goal—so broad that it was actually hard to get a handle on. Student members of SDS engaged in a number of issues, some directed to local campus politics. Some used the campus politics of free speech to raise broader political claims in society. And many participated in the growing civil rights movement. SDS was a multipurpose and diverse organization that fed into and aided a number of campaigns— until 1965.

SDS was a key organizing force in the first demonstration against the Vietnam War, a march in Washington, D.C., that challenged an early escalation of the war. SDS had organized the initial efforts for the demonstration as opposition to the war grew, particularly on college campuses where young men were subject to the draft. SDS organizers wanted to make the most of this opportunity, and new activist students were eager to find a place to voice their opposition to the war in general and to the draft in particular—even if the explicit connections to the broader political agenda were unarticulated. They flooded into SDS, which, explicitly targeted to students and on record early against the war, was well positioned to recruit.

But SDS was based on participatory democratic rules and structures as well as explicit political claims on government. The new members, committed to SDS out of opposition to the war but often with little developed political analysis or experience, would soon be able to exercise as much influence as the old-time organizers steeped in both political theory and practical politics. The organization, as histories report, was unprepared for the influx of recruits with their own ideas about how to manage a social movement, and the results were chaotic. Within a relatively short time, an organized faction devoted to the ideas of Mao Zedong and Chinese Communism was able to use disciplined action within the chaos to take over SDS, and it disappeared shortly thereafter.

Making sense of SDS is a way for us to examine important issues in social movement organizations. In beginning with the postmortem, SDS's record is obviously mixed. On the one hand, without doubt, SDS was responsible for uniting students opposed to the war on campuses all over the United States. It was also an important coalition partner of other groups that staged large national actions against the war in Vietnam. SDS contributed activists to other movements and served to train and politicize thousands of students across the United States, many of whom continued political action for decades after its demise. It also produced several notable academics, some of whom wrote about their history in SDS (Flacks 1988; Whalen and Flacks 1989; Gitlin 1980, 1993).

On the other hand, SDS disappeared rather quickly, its entire political history limited to less than a decade. It's hard to trace the influence of this organization to any particular policy reforms, and the broader thinking and aspirations of participatory democracy were lost in a wave of chaotic action, some of which did more to discredit than build the movement and made it more difficult to convert policymakers or build allies in mainstream politics. Although SDS generated actions and activists, the ideas around which it was initially organized never again received the comprehensive articulation promised in the Port Huron Statement.

How we evaluate SDS is dependent upon what we think social movement organizations are supposed to do. In fact, social movement organizations, like other political organizations, must serve different audiences and constituencies, sometimes in ways that lead to gross contradictions. To the extent that organizations try to effect political change, they need to offer policymakers the appropriate (and undefined) combination of persuasion and threat to gain attention and respect. To the extent that they are concerned with maintaining their members and the flow of resources into their efforts, they need to serve their constituents. Although these goals are certainly interrelated—a strong, stable, and well-resourced organization is in a better position to bargain with people in government—the demands of different functions often push in different directions. In trying to effect policy change, for example, it makes sense to cooperate with other organizations that share similar goals. In trying to maintain a flow of members and resources, it's necessary to carve out a distinct organizational identity and politics, in other words, a distinct niche that allows the organization to maintain its existence (McCarthy and Zald 1977; Wilson 1995; Zald and McCarthy 1987). Polemical rhetoric that emphasizes great threats and extraordinary achievements helps to inspire participation—at least for the short run—but makes it hard to talk effectively with elected officials or bureaucrats.

All organizations must balance these conflicting pressures, but there is no magic formula for success. Indeed, the range of groups concerned with a particular set of issues comprises an organizational field, with each carving out a distinctive balance of claims, tactics, constituencies, and alliances. We will examine these issues as we discuss social movement organizations.

First, why organize? In fact, setting up a structure that routinizes the process of making claims and mobilizing action carries with it significant risks for a social movement. Scholarship on social movements that focused on riots and large-scale disruptions deemphasized the role of organizations altogether, viewing social protest as a spontaneous outbreak of large numbers of individuals in response to some external pressure. Seeking to quell dissent, at times of great disruption authorities may respond by offering concessions in terms of policy reforms. Formal organizations may actually play a role in stifling protest, thus undermining the influence of social movements.

The strongest version of this argument has been offered by Frances Fox Piven and Richard Cloward (1977). In their examination of movements on behalf of poor people, they offer four case studies in which insurgency erupted in response to wholesale changes in the economy, authorities started to respond, and formal organizations, both established and new, used an extraordinary moment of potential influence to develop their organizations, wasting an opportunity that would always be limited.

This is an important argument, articulated with careful examination of the historical records of extraordinary times in American history. And there is certainly strong evidence to support the idea that organizations often stifle and smooth out disruption, routinizing collective action in ways that protect themselves. At the same time, meaningful and powerful dissent is not something that occurs spontaneously. Indeed, Piven and Cloward note the important role that what they describe as "cadre" organizations played in promoting dissent. Communist-led unions in the 1930s organized workers to strike and to engage in community politics, and thirty years later young activists in the Student Non-Violent Coordinating Committee provoked and coordinated political action against segregation, action that proved to be very disruptive.

Looking at very different sorts of movement organizations in a different period, Suzanne Staggenborg (1988) has found that leaders of abortion rights organizations tended to be more committed, more radical, and far more active than the rank-and-file members of their organizations. Moreover, established organizations were able to maintain vigilance on potential changes in reproductive rights that might not be so salient to a broad public—at least not unless packaged, cultivated, and promoted by activists. They could maintain a long-term presence in both Washington and national politics that constrained their opponents. They could also survive during difficult political times, providing a safe space for unpopular ideas or constituencies (Taylor 1989). In short, the story of organizations is a complicated one, laden with potential contradictions. Social movement organizations can represent the institutionalization and pacification of a social movement, or they can represent a movement's formal and continuous presence in American life. In fact, both of these statements are true.

Social movement organizations form to coordinate the process of turning inchoate grievances into issues and apathy or dissatisfaction into political action. These events don't happen automatically, nor do organizations form without the dedicated efforts of people committed not only to achieving change on a set of political issues, but also to building an organization. The pressures of building and maintaining an organization, however, sometimes work at cross-purposes with the processes involved in making strong claims on issues politically.

In order to sustain an organization, leaders need to maintain a reasonably stable flow of resources, including money. Social movement organizations hire professional organizers and staff, people who will devote their full efforts to the cause but need to earn a living at the same time. Organizations also need to pay rent on office space, hire support staff to answer phones—which also must be paid for—photocopy materials, and file reports with the Internal Revenue Service (McCarthy, Britt, and Wolfson 1991). They also must raise money, which itself comes with costs of time and money. When you send a check to an organization in response to a direct-mail solicitation, only a small portion of your contribution actually goes directly to the political work you've been asked to support. Some portion, depending upon the organization's size and success at fundraising, must go to the printing and mailing costs of the appeal, to someone who wrote the letter (often a professional consulting firm), and to all of the infrastructure that supports the political work. As with an aircraft carrier battle group, the ratio of support to political action is surprisingly high.

Organizers can find different ways to deal with the funding and stability challenges. Some organizations are able to cultivate powerful and well-heeled sponsors, including wealthy individuals committed to a particular cause. The American Friends Services Committee, for example, is central to the hearts of some people who leave their estates to it. Some groups provide services that generate money, for example, Planned Parenthood of America, which operates women's health and reproductive clinics around the country, or apply for grants. Some become accomplished at producing events, such as concerts featuring musicians committed to the cause, which can be profitable. And most also depend upon financial support in small donations from members.

The process of ensuring stable resources naturally affects how organizers think about politics and political activity. They must be concerned not only with their judgments about what issues are important, urgent, or amenable to action, but also with how their supporters will view engagement on the issues. People for the Ethical Treatment of Animals, for example, which espouses a broad reconception of the relationship between humans and animals that includes promoting vegetarian diets and the end to scientific experimentation on all animals, found that its fundraising letters generated the greatest response when they featured pictures of chimpanzees, kittens, and puppies rather than lab rats. The pressures of maintaining the organization led to putting the more controversial aspects of its agenda on the back burner— at least in public. Other groups, such as the Public Interest Research Groups founded by Ralph Nader, raise money by conducting door-to-door canvassing or soliciting fees from student governments on college campuses. Obviously, in order to be successful, they need to maintain among their political profile issues that will appeal to such constituencies.

Organizations also tiptoe warily around issues they think will compromise the vigor of strong donors. The American Civil Liberties Union (ACLU), for example, suffered a serious decline in both membership and financial support when it defended the rights of American Nazis to march in a predominantly Jewish suburb of Chicago (Neier 1979). Although taking the case was no stretch in terms of the ACLU's explicit commitment to defending the Bill of Rights, it was challenging, and perhaps courageous, for an organization that needs to keep its doors open and its photocopy machine in working order.

There is an alternative model of organization, represented by organizations such as the one founded by Dorothy Day, mentioned at the beginning of this chapter. The Catholic Workers never managed a large budget but rather depended upon the moral and religious commitments of determined individuals, many of whom, like Day herself, viewed making a commitment to social action much like following a vocation to the ministry and took a vow of poverty. In a similar way, the Student Non-Violent Coordinating Committee did not ask its volunteers to take a formal vow of poverty, but it paid them wages that ensured that outcome: $10 a week. Such groups are less vulnerable to pressures from donors, for obvious reasons, because they make up for financial deficits with intense commitment from members. But such intense commitment, difficult for individuals to sustain, is also an unstable base around which to build an organization. Organizations that don't routinize and professionalize (Staggenborg 1988; Wilson 1995) disappear when the issues they represent no longer seem so urgent or promising to a broad public or when a charismatic and committed leader leaves.

By affording tax-exempt status to educational organizations, the federal government has offered a clear path toward institutionalization to social movement organizations (McCarthy, Britt, and Wolfson 1991). Accepting 501(c)3 status means that politically oriented groups can legally raise tax-exempt funds, but they must develop an organizational structure that makes sense to IRS auditors. They file legal documents, develop a board and formal organizational structure, and restrict, somewhat, their actions to primarily explicitly educational—rather than political—efforts. This path has proven to be attractive for activists, and the number of political and social movement organizations across the country, though mostly based in Washington, D.C., has expanded steadily over the past forty years.

Activists and organizers struggle to develop organizational forms and structures that allow both for sustained mobilization and for political impact. The decisions about how to organize are rarely easy, and not necessarily permanent. For example, in the summer of 2005, leaders of two large unions, the Teamsters and the Service Employees International Union, announced their intention to leave the AFL-CIO, the dominant voice of American labor for at least fifty years. The AFL-CIO itself resulted from a change in organizational form, when the Congress of Industrial Organizations negotiated a merger with the larger

American Federation of Labor in 1955, when both groups faced a difficult political climate (Stepan-Norris and Zeitlin 2003).

In 1955, labor organizers had argued that bigger was better, that the broad base and extensive resources of a dominant national organization of labor unions would be more effective in representing the interests of American workers. The AFL-CIO, they hoped, would be able to influence national politics through elections and simultaneously present a large and unified front for American workers.

On the occasion of the fiftieth anniversary of the merger, however, leaders of several large unions, recognizing American labor's steady decline over decades, argued that the AFL-CIO no longer represented labor's best hope. Forming a new coalition of unions, Change to Win, advocates of the split argued that a competitive coalition of unions would be more effective in recruiting new workers, targeting large employers, and in creating a strong and effective labor movement. Change to Win's leaders promised to devote a larger share of their budget to organizing drives, arguing that the AFL-CIO spent too much of its money, ineffectively, in supporting Democratic candidates for office.

John Sweeney, president of the AFL-CIO, was understandably unhappy, announcing that the split was ". . . a tragedy for working people. Because at a time when our corporate and conservative adversaries have created the most powerful anti-worker political machine in the history of our country, a divided movement hurts the hopes of working families for a better life" (quoted in Greenhouse 2005). Sweeney himself had been elected president ten years earlier, heading a reformist New Voice slate that promised to reinvigorate labor by emphasizing organizing. Without doubt, organized labor as a whole had declined in both size and influence during the Sweeney years, but it is not clear whether this was the result of the policies of the AFL-CIO or larger forces, including defeats in the political arena and increased economic globalization. It is also not clear whether the promised invigoration of the labor movement through competition will improve the prospects of American workers. The influence of organizational form on political action, however, is of critical importance and will remain a matter of debate within social movements, including American labor.

At first glance, it appears that there are only bad choices to make about organizational form. An organization that depends on ideological commitment will be unstable, subject to schism, and dependent upon something inherently volatile. An organization that takes the path of routinization will moderate its goals and tactics so it can maintain its survival and support its staff, whose sustenance will take up an increasingly large share of its efforts. In reality, however, things are always more complicated. Professionalized groups can be more radical politically when a staff is able to focus on issues; redemptive groups can initiate important waves of collective action and exert great influence on political movements. Finally, some groups are able to balance satisfying members and affecting political action. Greenpeace, for example, uses dramatic actions against whaling, featuring activists in small fast boats trying to interfere in commercial whaling operations, to bolster its fundraising letters and support its Washington lobbying effort.

The point here is that social movements are not spontaneous but rather are organized, even in terms of the chaos and confusion they may sometimes create. The existence of organizations committed to a set of issues presents activists with both opportunities and constraints, as existing organizations can channel dissatisfaction in less disruptive ways, taking the steam out of an incipient social movement. At the same time, these organizations can provide the infrastructure of a movement when a new set of claims emerges strongly, offering not only material resources, but also connections to government, issue expertise, and hard-earned experience in the nitty-gritty of organizing. We now turn to understanding how issues come and go, pulling organizations up in their wake.

IDEAS AND SOCIAL MOVEMENTS

If we've established that collective action in social movements isn't a spontaneous reaction to something unfathomable, such as sunspots, and that issues that emerge are in some serious way related to mainstream politics, we now must turn to understanding how issues come and go, why an issue's time comes when it does. In discussing political opportunities, we've emphasized grievances and the alliance of mainstream political actors. At the same time, we need to confront the notion of ideas driving social movements in some way. Certainly, the history of social movements is full of stories of people who receive credit for offering new ways of thinking about politics and political issues and then spurring action.

In fact, I want to suggest that the notion of ideas generating social movements provides a too-comforting myth that takes the onus off political organizing. If only people could see that . . ., they surely would organize to do something about it. Indeed, American history is replete with such tales, about how Harriet Beecher Stowe's *Uncle Tom's Cabin* pricked the conscience of a nation, ultimately precipitating the Civil War; or about how Upton Sinclair's novel of the meat-packing industry in Chicago, *The Jungle,* led to the first federal regulations on food processing. Much later, Susan Brownmiller's *Against Our Will,* an analysis of rape and other sex crimes, was credited with spurring a successful feminist campaign against rape that led to massive reforms in criminal law around the country.

This is a comforting myth because it implies a responsiveness in mainstream politics. It implies that once enough people are alerted to an issue, meaningful political action and then reform will result. It reinforces a vision of democracy that essentially endorses the openness of the political system and the goodwill of those in it. It suggests that what must be done is to articulate a problem clearly and to offer some possible solutions. If, however, awareness of social ills is neither necessary for a social movement nor sufficient to generate mobilization or reform, well, that raises other issues. But this myth may not be true.

To confront this myth, I want to examine a time of recognized political mobilization on a variety of issues: the decade of the 1960s. Indeed, in this time, four books are commonly credited with spurring large and influential social movements.[3] Michael Harrington's *The Other America* is credited with awakening both ordinary citizens and politicians in the United States to the extent and costs of poverty, promoting government action ultimately described as a "war on poverty." Rachel Carson's *Silent Spring,* an exposé of the prevalence of and damage done by pesticides in farming, is commonly credited with the rebirth of the environmental movement. Betty Friedan's identification of "the problem that knows no name" in *The Feminine Mystique* gets credit for the revival of the women's movement in the 1960s and 1970s. And Ralph Nader's exposé of General Motors, *Unsafe at Any Speed,* is used to date the emergence of the consumer movement in America.

---

[3] This section draws on work with Deana Rohlinger, and I'm grateful for her help and insights.

Before examining these stories, I want to stress how attractive the myth of "big books" is. It implies that the statement of an issue, if articulated with sufficient power and clarity, will find a responsive audience that can then mobilize effectively and spur meaningful reform. It belies notions of purposive injustice and permanent inequality and encourages the social critic to spend time in the study, rummaging through the Internet doing research and sitting at the keyboard trying to craft the right phrase. But this isn't likely to be enough. Although social movements carry ideas, ideas themselves do not provoke political action, and the political context determines which ideas appear attractive to both organizers and to broad audiences.

We can start with the story of *Silent Spring*. Rachel Carson, a veteran of the U.S. Forest Service, became a writer when she retired and focused her efforts on the world around her. A gifted writer, she decried the damage that DDT, a pesticide then commonly used, did to the environment as well as its health effects. Published first in the *New Yorker,* her warning drew a tremendous amount of attention, spurring news articles, profiles, and analyses almost immediately. The book was on the *New York Times* best-seller list for more than thirty weeks, and most histories of the environmental movement credit the book with reviving and redefining a social movement that dated back to the beginning of the century.

In fact, however, the timing didn't quite occur this way. Congress had commenced hearings on pesticides in general and DDT in particular nearly a decade earlier, and Carson's own knowledge was based in government research. Her ability to spread the word was also contingent not only on her prose style, but also on her strong contacts within the Forest Service. And the origins of mass action, commonly pegged to the first Earth Day, took place nearly a decade later, in 1970, when the environmental movement began to command broad attention. It must be said, however, that the case for Carson's *Silent Spring* being the big book that spurred a social movement is stronger than that of the other three books.

Michael Harrington's *The Other America* was also written with the express intent of provoking mass action. Harrington was a long-time activist, having developed his politics in the Catholic Worker movement that Dorothy Day founded. The book focused on rural poverty in the United States, written as an indictment of a society that allowed people to suffer so. The popular story was that President Kennedy read the book—or, more likely, Dwight McDonald's long review of the book in the *New Yorker,* and decided to add something for poorer people to his budget, which was predicated on tax cuts for the wealthy. When Kennedy died, his successor, Lyndon Johnson, carrying on the style and commitment of the New Deal, inflated Kennedy's program into a "war on poverty," based around a series of social welfare programs he termed "the Great Society." Government action and citizen mobilization fed off each other until urban unrest undermined political support for the programs while the war in Vietnam robbed the budget for them (Katz 1989).

In fact, Harrington's book appeared while the civil rights movement was already well underway. Indeed, the famous march on Washington was planned well before *The Other America* appeared in print and took place just weeks after its publication. Although the book certainly became a touchstone for public discourse about poverty in the United States, it was less a spur for action than a rationale and cover. Particularly, Harrington's treatment allowed the Kennedy administration to respond to the civil rights movement less explicitly, whitening the political face of poverty and encouraging the expansion of some universalistic programs. Importantly, Harrington himself was always an activist and organizer, even more than a writer. He was involved in the initial meetings that formed Students for a Democratic Society and was the guiding force behind the formation of Democratic Socialists of America as well. He never depended on the word alone to get his concerns out.

Also an organizer by temperament and background, Betty Friedan was an experienced labor journalist with a history in the American Communist Party. Her tale of a shallow, barren, and deeply unsatisfying existence as wife and mother in sterile suburbs described a life she'd never really led. In response to entrepreneurial action by a few women in Congress, gender discrimination was grafted onto the first few civil rights bills in the 1960s, sneaking in with minimal debate because majorities didn't see it as likely to be important. Friedan herself founded the National Organization for Women (NOW), which promoted a broad women's liberation agenda that extended far beyond her book.

Finally, Ralph Nader's *Unsafe at Any Speed,* published in 1965, did provide the infrastructure of the modern consumer movement, but largely because of General Motors' foolish reactions to it, in conjunction with Nader's tireless organizing. Written as he was establishing himself as a young crusading attorney on the Department of Labor's payroll, Nader's well-researched book documented General Motors' design and production of the Corvair, charging that General Motors knowingly neglected safety in design in order to maximize style and minimize costs. Nader called for government oversight of the automobile industry, as well as business in general, and tried to establish buyers of products as a constituency that merited government protection.

General Motors made a colossal mistake, commencing surveillance of Nader in an attempt to get information to discredit him rather than the details of his report. Nader sued and received a cash settlement of more than $400,000. Of course, the publicity further undermined General Motors' public credibility, and Nader plowed the entire sum into further organizing and research efforts, establishing a number of public interest groups based in Washington, D.C., and inspiring others to take on similar projects. His first organization, the Center for Study of Responsive Law, established in 1969, used the cause of consumer rights to examine interstate commerce, food safety, corporate welfare, and government procurement. Nader's efforts spawned similar groups, including the Public Citizen, the Center for Auto Safety, the Disability Rights Center, the Freedom of Information Clearinghouse, and the Congressional Accountability Project, as well as the Public Interest Research Groups, with branches established on private and public college campuses across the United States.

The regulation of the automobile industry, beginning with what would now be considered rudimentary safety requirements, including seat belts in all cars, provided a model for both citizen and government action that inspired other activists to take on other industries. At the same time, it's important to recognize that Nader had identified a wedge issue that government was already working on. Congressional oversight hearings of automobile safety had taken off during the 1950s in response to an increasing number of traffic fatalities with the completion of the interstate highway system. Nader responded to government openings, intensifying and challenging government to take greater initiative and alerting a broader public at the same time.

The attractions of the big book myth aside, it should be clear that it's not the books themselves that spur action.[4] Many well-written books on important social problems haven't

---

[4]Nor is the quality of the writing critical. Although Carson's writing is poetic, it's much harder to make that case for Nader's book, the only one of these big books no longer in print.

generated comparable movements and government action. Indeed, Jonathan Kozol, a powerful writer whose first book appeared shortly after this period, in 1968, has dedicated his writing to achieving an effect comparable with that of those earlier four books. His first book, a memoir of his year teaching in an inner-city school of Boston, *Death at an Early Age*, won a National Book Award yet did not spur a massive school reform movement. In subsequent works, even more powerfully written, Kozol has addressed other inequalities, including homelessness, school funding, and urban life more generally, without producing the social impact of these earlier books. Clearly, it's not about the writing.

What's more, the largest social movements of the 1960s, the civil rights movement and the antiwar movement, are not similarly tied to big books representing their ideas. Although proponents of civil rights and opponents of U.S. participation in the war in Vietnam often had far broader analyses of social ills, the essential claims of each movement spread quickly and were easily understood: stop legal discrimination based on race; remove American troops from Vietnam.

It seems clear that the quality of an idea is not what makes its time come. Nader's claims about corporate greed and Carson's warnings about DDT were not the first time in American history that such claims had been made, nor were they necessarily the best representations of those claims. This is even more true for Harrington's portrait of poverty in an affluent society or Friedan's indictment of sexism in America. Indeed, periodic reform movements and moments involving exactly those issues have animated American politics. Certainly the reception context of a big book is critical to any influence it has.

If the books and the ideas they embody are neither necessary nor sufficient, then just what do they do? At the base level, certainly some people read a book and find their lives changed, now suddenly aware of a new set of issues or a condition. But this view neglects the social aspect of social movements and the politics of organization. Books provide a symbolic touchstone for a movement and its ideas and a means for uniting people. On one level, carrying around or quoting a book can become shorthand for expressing sympathies and identification with a cause or group of people. It provides the appearance of intellectual ballast and sometimes evidence at the same time. It offers communication in itself but also becomes a vehicle for communication. In their treatment of the animal rights movement, for example, Jasper and Nelkin (1992) note that organizations commonly gave Peter Singer's *Animal Liberation,* originally published in 1975, to new recruits. The language, the argument, and the book itself provided a connection between an individual and a larger movement. It's less that a book spurred a movement than that the book provided a resource to organizers.

In this chapter, however, we've seen that the reception context, comprised of opportunities and constraints in the larger social and political world, determine which ideas are likely to take off and which are likely to simmer on the back burner or to cool off altogether. A meaningful conception of agency, that is, the difference individuals can make, comes only when we consider the influence of context, that is, a sense of what's possible at any given time.

BECOMING
AN ACTIVIST

It was a Sunday evening, January 31, 1960, when four freshmen at North Carolina Agricultural and Technical College stayed up, talking late into the night about ending segregation in the South. They were extraordinarily poorly positioned to effect political or social change on campus, much less in the United States: young, black, by no means affluent, and far distant from the major centers of social and political power in America. All had been involved in NAACP youth activities and had grown frustrated not only with the slow pace of change, but also with the NAACP's relatively moderate tactics; they saw a time for change. On Monday morning Ezell Blair Jr., Franklin McCain, Joseph McNeill, and David Richmond, dressed in their best clothes, walked into the Woolworth's in downtown Greensboro. (Woolworth's was a national chain of low-cost dry goods stores, most of which also included lunch counters with limited menus and modest prices.) They bought some school supplies, then sat at the lunch counter and waited for service. They spent the rest of the day there.

The following day, twenty-seven other black students joined them and on Wednesday, twice that many. By Thursday, a few sympathetic white students from nearby schools had joined and, having filled the lunch counter at Woolworth's, activists started a sit-in at another lunch counter down the street. By the end of the week, city officials offered to negotiate a settlement and, on Saturday night, sixteen hundred students rallied to celebrate this victory (Sitkoff 1981). News of the sit-in campaign spread throughout the South and then elsewhere across the United States, spurring other activists to emulate the effort. Sit-ins to desegregate lunch counters and restaurants, stores and libraries, and even buses swept the South. A new organization, the Student Non-Violent Coordinating Committee (SNCC), was formed in April 1960. SNCC would become a leading force in the civil rights movement, setting much of the agenda for liberal politics in the United States during the early 1960s, precipitating passage of the Voting Rights Act of 1965 (Garrow 1978), and politicizing student activists across the United States (Morris 1984).

The story of the student protesters in Greensboro is frequently told, perhaps trailing only the story of Rosa Parks and the Montgomery bus boycott in popular lore of the civil rights movement. But how are we to make sense of these young men taking on a great risk in order to promote ideas that were unpopular among the governing majority in Greensboro? And why did these young men take on this risk when most of their classmates would not? Social movements rarely actively engage more than a small fraction of the population, although their efforts can have consequences for everyone.

WHO PROTESTS? DIVERSITY IN SOCIAL MOVEMENTS

Although circumstances and opportunities are critical in explaining why particular movements or issues emerge and why activists try the tactics they do, they do little to describe who the activists will be. Circumstances matter, of course, but people respond to the same issues, arguments, and events differently. In this chapter, we will examine the factors that lead someone to participate. The character, background, and interests of activists are frequently the subject of critical commentary and dismissal; it's great to be able to say that the people working on issues we don't like are the products of fractured families or the victims of mental illness or that the leaders in social movements we admire are heroic individuals, seemingly out of time.

In truth, movements are always comprised of a wide range of people—people who have an equally wide range of reasons for engaging in social action. The larger and more visible a movement is, the greater the diversity of people likely to be participating in it. Unlike vanguard political parties or exclusive clubs, however, few movement organizations want to filter out willing participants, and so the diversity increases. And analysts who look at social movements can find the committed hero or crazy fool in any social movement, proving whatever point they want to make. The point is that a journalist or analyst, by selecting a particular subject within a movement, can tell the absolute truth and still provide a misleading picture of who is inside that movement.

We can see how reporters use an emblematic set of characters to describe a movement in competing accounts of a volatile protest action, the "Battle in Seattle," a series of disruptive protests against the World Treaty Organization in November 1999. The protests featured a broad coalition of groups that often don't work together, including religious activists calling for the forgiveness of third world debt, human rights activists, organized labor, feminists, crusaders against biotechnology, animal rights protesters, and "black block" anarchists. Encounters with a police force unaccustomed to national-level protests and unprepared for such protests led to violent confrontations in the streets, broken up—and exacerbated—by tear gas and rubber bullets (Thomas 2000). The events gave analysts plenty of raw material with which to work.

Shortly after the antiglobalization demonstrations, two journalists published conflicting accounts of the activists who animated them. Writing in *Harper's,* David Samuels examined some of the residents of Whiteaker, a neighborhood in Eugene, Oregon, which he reported was filled with alienated young people with little clear ambition or direction except to act out. Careers, as such, were undeveloped, as was personal hygiene, and virtually all were seriously deprived of protein reflecting and producing, the journalist reported, impaired judgment.

For Samuels, participating in the demonstrations was one step in making a commitment to a meandering and marginal life. "Life as a frontline activist requires a kind of personal migration," he writes (2000: 40), "beyond the boundaries of work and school, beyond the reach of the thousand-fingered massage of brand names and logos, well-designed toasters, and television ads. You change your name. You stop eating meat. You stop drinking milk. Everything you own fits comfortably in the pack that you carry from town to town and from apartment to apartment. The apartments you live in have no furniture . . ." These people, he reports, were in Seattle for the demonstrations and planned to undertake great expense and risk to go to other antiglobalization demonstrations, although their analysis of global trade—or almost anything else—was almost nonexistent. In Samuels's tale, the issues are virtually irrelevant, and the demonstrators are just acting out.

In sharp contrast, at just about the same time, William Finnegan published a shorter piece, revealingly entitled, "Anarchists Get Organized," in the *New Yorker*. Finnegan profiled a few young organizers, focusing on Juliette Beck, formerly an environmental engineer, described by one of her professors as "One of these new Renaissance people, so smart they could be almost anything" (Finnegan 2000: 40). "Intellectually insatiable," she began studying economics and international trade and grew convinced that the emerging free trade regime led to economic inequality and environmental degradation. Beck and her allies worked with activist organizations to conduct public education and to participate in political demonstrations to draw attention to their concerns. Finnegan emphasizes not only their commitment, but their also intelligence and the substance of their concerns. Finnegan's subjects were driven by deep concern about social justice and the environment, well informed on the issues, and thoughtful about how to exercise political impact. They were also all keenly attuned to mainstream politics.

There is every reason to believe that all of the facts reported in each story were correct and that the reporters presented quotes and profiles accurately. Each view provides a partial picture of the reality of the movement against corporate globalization coming out of Seattle, with the selection of facts and subjects the result of each author's predisposition. And the bigger message that each journalist offers is very different: Samuels's readers will want to understand how young people grow alienated and disconnected from mainstream society and spend little time thinking about what they're protesting about. Finnegan's readers will be thinking about global trade, the World Trade Organization, environmental protection, and thoughtful activists trying to find a way to affect institutions designed to be insulated from their efforts. Whereas Samuels's piece denies politics, Finnegan's connects the protests closely with mainstream politics and contemporary policy issues.

Every social movement is composed of both committed and informed organizers and nutty hangers-on, although the share of each varies from movement to movement and event to event. If this is true, how can we really begin to understand who becomes an activist and how? In fact, this is a topic that has been subject to empirical research—as well as idiosyncratic reporting and gross generalizations—often politically motivated.

THE ACTIVIST

Activist is a catch-all term that covers a broad range of commitments, ranging from someone who might sign petitions, make phone calls, and donate money from time to time to someone who routinely shows up at demonstrations, lobbies elected officials, and sometimes risks arrest. In fact, the level of participation for most people active in politics fluctuates, affected by both the pressing political issues of the moment and the extent of commitments in the other aspects of their lives: career, family, health, and relationships. The most important people to watch in understanding social movements are not the hardest working or the busiest, but rather the ones who come and go; their shifts in participation, intensity, and issues define the volatility and potential influence of a movement. But they don't appear spontaneously; instead, more experienced, professionalized, and committed organizers recruit them. Here, we'll discuss first the activist and then other categories of participants in movements: *movement professionals, entrepreneurs,* and *anomics.* There can be some blurring among these categories as activist lives develop and change and as political opportunities change. But by distinguishing these categories, we can begin to sort out the range of factors that leads someone to participate in social movement politics.

Although all of these categories of people are involved in every social movement, we get less insight in understanding a movement by focusing on the odd case and more insight by looking at the sometime activist drawn in by issues of the moment. Scholars have been oddly slow in recognizing the diversity of characters in social movements, first embracing, then reacting against, the myth of the "true believer" (Hoffer 1951). In popular books of the 1950s by both scholars and popular writers, participants in social movements were commonly described as crazies, anomic individuals who desperately search for some kind of human connection to make sense of their disjointed and disappointing lives (Kornhauser 1959). This view was premised on a notion of fundamental openness of American society, a belief that a rational citizen wouldn't protest or join a social movement when there were plenty of other opportunities for connecting with other people and/or influencing government policy. This view conveniently exempted important movements and events of the past, such as the American Revolution and the Boston Tea Party, reclassifying them from social movement actions into justifiable and explainable revolts against authorities who did not offer more reasonable means of political influence.

The social movements of the 1960s led to a reexamination of the basic tenets of the earlier faith. Even while politicians tried to dismiss the claims of the student movement about civil rights, peace, student rights, or democracy more generally by charging that the student activists were the products of bad parenting, scholars were using a variety of methods to investigate the people who animated the new social movements. Social psychologist Kenneth Keniston (1968) interviewed the leaders of the new student movement and found that they were better educated, more informed, and more connected to organizations and established politics than were their less-activist classmates. What's more, they got along better with their parents and achieved better grades in school. In other words, none of the assumptions of disconnection or disaffection stood up to the facts. Keniston's research focused on young *activists,* the category that covers most participants in most movements.

Keniston's findings allow us to start a review of the key elements affecting who will become an activist and how. When we recognize that participation in a social movement has more in common with participation in more conventional politics, such as joining a political party or interest group or voting, we won't be surprised by what we see. Activists in social movements are disproportionately advantaged in terms of education, resources, familial support, and social connections. At the same time, this situation varies across movements. Let's figure out why.

First, the best predictor of why anyone takes on any political action is whether that person has been asked to do so (Rosenstone and Hansen 1993). Issues do not automatically drive people into the streets. Rather, organizers *mobilize,* that is, induce people to undertake activity directed to achieving some kind of outcome, be it changing welfare policy or achieving a large turnout at a demonstration or raising money to charter a bus to Washington, D.C. Because being asked is so important, people who are active in a variety of social contexts are most likely to encounter organizers. People who attend a church are most likely to hear about an upcoming demonstration on abortion and to be asked to join it. Students on a college campus are most likely to be contacted by organizers trying to recruit students, and people who go to Parent Teacher Association (PTA) meetings are most likely to hear about collective action against cutting funds for schools.

The dictum about trying to mobilize the organized has several reinforcing components. At the personal or psychological level, people who are active in political organizations are already likely to see themselves as potentially effective. They have at least some familiarity with political issues and participation and are therefore much likelier to join a new campaign or line up with a new cause. In short, the recruiter who goes to a political or social organization to find new activists finds people who are already active. Persuasion is about only the importance of the issue and the prospects for effectiveness, not about personal empowerment.

Second, those active in community groups will be able to find a zone of personal security by engaging in new commitments with some of the same people. Going to a political meeting or attending a demonstration, one is with acquaintances or friends, providing a feedback loop of information and affirmation. Colleagues share at least some concerns, grievances, and beliefs about meaningful action.

Third, people who are engaged actively in social and political life are more likely to be *asked* to do more. Community meetings are a primary site for recruitment to all sorts of political causes and social movements. Opportunities to mobilize come to those who are already mobilized. Dense social networks among activists provide for ongoing recruitment to new issues and campaigns.

Fourth, a person's community connections, feelings of efficacy, and even basic political attitudes begin developing very early in life, influenced not only by the broader American political culture, but also by religious traditions, community values, and family (Rohlinger and Snow 2003). Although the popular image of protesters as rebels holds true in the larger universe, activists frequently follow the lead of those around them. McAdam (1988) found that Freedom Summer volunteers generally shared the same liberal and integrationist values of their parents. Klatch (1999) found that leaders of student movements on the left and the right generally pulled in the same political direction as their parents, albeit sometimes with more vigor. In addition, families themselves are not insulated from other influences. Some religions and congregations teach very strong moral values, for example, against war or abortion or for social justice or charity. These churches or activist communities can also provide the social connections and organizational support that aid in the development of activism.

For these reasons, it's not surprising to learn that the basic demographic profiles of activists are similar to those of people who engage in other kinds of social and political activities: the *relatively* well off, well educated, and active. These are exactly the same people who are most likely to engage in more conventional political participation. Social movement participation is most frequently an addition to, rather than a departure from, more institutionally oriented politics. Social movement activists are more likely to vote, to contribute money to causes, and to be aware of other political issues. They continue these more conventional activities even when the peaks of mobilization have passed. Social movements are animated by the connected and the comparatively well off psychologically and economically.

Indeed, it's critical to realize that even movements representing the poor, the powerless, or the unconnected are spearheaded by people disproportionately advantaged. The four young men in Greensboro were college students, a position of relative privilege among African American youth in the 1950s—and even today. Their attendance at North Carolina Agricultural and Technical College afforded them more exposure to the significant issues of the day, more information on political actions taken by both activists and institutional politics.

It also made them the target of political organizations, including the NAACP. Their connections to each other gave them a supportive group and solidarity; together, it was possible for each to take a brave and risky step. Although narratives of the civil rights movement often portray brave activists as solo performers, in reality, most were already engaged in civil rights politics. Reverend Martin Luther King Jr. was the son of a minister, the graduate not only of college, but also of theological school. Rosa Parks was a local official in the NAACP and well connected to other activists across the country. Indeed, earlier in the year of her famed defiance of segregation laws, her NAACP chapter had sent her to a summer leadership training session at the Highlander Folk School in Tennessee. Social organization and political exposure present the opportunities for greater political exposure and more extensive social ties.

The relatively privileged enjoy the education and affirmation that afford them the belief that they might make a difference, what social scientists call "personal efficacy." Education and affirmation also are likely to afford them the relative economic, social, and psychological freedom to commit to larger issues and distant actions. Take, for example, Freedom Summer, a 1964 civil rights campaign that sent mostly white college students from the North to Mississippi to engage in voter education and registration. In his landmark study of the campaign's volunteers, Doug McAdam (1988) compares those who volunteered their summers to the cause of civil rights with others who shared similar political views but chose not to go south. He found that people who had others depending upon them for financial or emotional support were far less likely to volunteer than were others less encumbered. He terms this "biographical availability." For this reason, students and young people have frequently been the leading edge of social movements for change, dating back even to the American Revolution.

The issue of biographical availability also applies to the professional lives of activists. Some jobs afford people more flexibility in scheduling their lives, even if that flexibility is accompanied by increased demands. Thus, ministers, educators, and attorneys, for example, often enjoy sufficient wiggle room in their schedules to take up the extra commitments of social movement action. And, of course, there is the self-perpetuating process of asking people already active in one cause to take on another one. The important recognition here is that intense participation in social movements is highly concentrated among relatively few people. Those who are engaged in one movement are likely to be engaged in another, with the vast majority not routinely engaged in the larger political struggle.

MOBILIZING SOCIAL MOVEMENTS

It's a mistake to apply a blanket notion that social movements are comprised exclusively of younger, well-off, and well-educated people, connected to their communities in multiple ways but not so tied into family or professional obligations that they can't spare the time and take some risks. This notion does give some insight into contemporary social movements focused on general "collective goods," that is, benefits that accrue to all of society, rather than more concentrated benefits focused on a constituency. For example, cleaner air and more comprehensive food labeling affect society as a whole—at least everyone who breathes and eats. Movements on such issues tend to be full of people from the middle class and above.

At the same time, we know that American history is replete with important social movements of the less advantaged—not only the civil rights and ethnic identity movements of the

1960s and since, but also the important labor movement that has waxed and waned in mobilization and influence over the past 120 years. Such movements are not animated by the most advantaged people in society at large, but they are led by people who enjoy disproportionate advantages within their communities.

But these people don't spill into the streets on their own. Rather, they can be mobilized by committed and creative organizers seeking to engage them in political action—sometimes. To a large degree, organizers need to offer people something for participation. An old axiom in scholarship on social movements and interest groups points to the "free rider" problem (Olson 1967), based around an economic understanding of personal action. Here it is:

Your time and efforts are worth something to you, but the value of any individual's participation in a social movement effort is relatively small. Thus, you must offer something to participate in a social movement, but you will benefit from its (potential) success whether or not you do. In these terms, participation is rarely economically "rational," at least when considered a trade of your efforts for the potential of some kind of general effect. This obviously incomplete understanding still helps us highlight why the people who are most likely to participate in social movements are relatively advantaged.

First, slack time is more likely to be found among people in certain professions and among people who aren't living paycheck to paycheck. Because they have more money and more flexibility in the organization of their time, the "costs" of participation are more variable for them. Second, because they have more education, as well as political, social, and cultural connections, their participation in a social movement may, in fact, be more valuable, more liable to bring others into the movement or to gain access to other social and political institutions. They are thus likely to receive more intense recruiting. Third, the development of a middle-class ethos allows for some delayed gratification in terms of an investment in anything, be it an education or a cause. They are likely to be not only more able, but also more cognizant of the possibility of making a substantial investment over a long haul for an important payoff.

When we start to open up the economic analysis, we see a great deal more. The modeling that economists and rational actor theorists offer in understanding collective action misses some of the goods that motivate people to participate. Not the least of these is an ethical sense of what's important in a life. Whereas some portion of human behavior is instrumental, that is, directed to generating an outcome, such as putting money into a vending machine, another portion is based on an ethical sense, regardless of the likely payoff. In contrast, people undertake all kinds of actions every day without thinking of the likely instrumental payoff. But people witness or act on behalf of their beliefs, even if they are pessimistic about the political battle, particularly when we talk about some perceived greater moral good—stopping abortion or slavery or the death penalty—of keeping any of these practices available against the committed actions of others. Acting on behalf of one's deeply held moral and ethical beliefs is a good in itself.

Next, participating in ethically motivated social action is a way to define yourself as who you imagine you want to be, to take a stand and find pride in doing what you think is right. Recalling his initial encounter at the lunch counter, for example, Franklin McCain reported, "I probably felt better that day than I've ever felt in my life. I felt as though I had gained my manhood, so to speak, and not only gained it, but had developed quite a lot of respect for it" (quoted in Sitkoff 1981: 81). *Manhood,* in this case, meant asserting himself *as a person* in a context in which black men were not seen as autonomous social actors: being a "man" meant being a person. McCain and his allies not only forced whites in Greensboro to see color differently and to consider again the daily practices of segregation, but also helped the four young men see themselves differently, as potentially powerful actors, rather than as victims. Taking a risk to feel this way about yourself and your action hardly seems best expressed as a "cost."

Further, acting collectively means acting with other people who share some of your beliefs. The feeling of connection with other people is also a good. You join in a social movement action to work with people who, you think, represent your deepest beliefs, who are what you are or could be—or to meet such people in the first place. The deep human connections forged in the context of a social movement are long-lasting and important in forging and maintaining an individual's identity.

If we start thinking about the process of generating mobilization, the "free rider" problem, despite its obvious limits, is a useful place to start. The mobilizer or recruiter thinks about what it takes to get someone involved in action, and thinking of incentives is a good place to start. Following Olson (1967) and others (e.g., Wilson 1995; Salisbury 1970), we can think about categories of incentives. The first distinction, represented in following table, is between those benefits that are offered only to those who participate in collective action of some sort and those that accrue to all people, regardless of their efforts. The second distinction leads to a set of categories for incentives: "purposive" refers to the substantive political goals of a social movement; material incentives are concrete goodies provided to those who are active; and solidary incentives are the feeling of connection and satisfaction that comes from being with others who share your beliefs.

Incentives	Purposive	Material	Solidary
Collective	x		
Selective		x	x

We can think of the purposive incentives as being impossible to earmark directly for those who actually do the work of organizing, even when the mobilization is on issues that are targeted to particular constituencies. But even something as targeted as quicker federal approval for AIDS drugs, for example, affects all patients, not just those who demonstrate and hold die-ins. For this reason, purposive incentives alone are unstable bases for mobilization, dependent upon the political environment to make some grievances or issues more salient and attractive for mobilization.

In contrast, material incentives fluctuate less in response to political circumstances and are those that are limited to those who participate. An easy example is some of the well-established advocacy organizations in the United States that provide goods, such as magazines or calendars, or benefits, such as discounts, to their paying members. Here it's important to note that the discounts and benefits can be so good that potential members of, say, the American Automobile Association or the AARP (formerly American Association for Retired People) make the membership decision largely unaware of the political agendas of these groups. Also, obviously but importantly, groups that serve well-heeled constituencies are far better positioned to offer attractive material incentives than are their counterparts. New initiatives on Social Security or highway construction don't affect membership much.

Finally, solidary incentives affect only those who participate. The sense of stepping into history as a force, in conjunction with people who share your beliefs, is a powerful motivator. It's hard to imagine from a distance, but participation breeds more participation as the first tentative step toward engagement that can change one's life. An effective organizer knows how to appeal not only to the intellect of potential participants, but also to their sense of justice and influence (Gamson 1992).

Mixing all of these incentives, organizers who mobilize must work to convince both the heads and hearts of potential activists to join them by participating in a social movement. At one level, they must convince potential activists that collective action is necessary, possible, and at least potentially effective and that each individual's role *might* matter. For some people, this means emphasizing that many others are involved and that the movement effort will be large enough to generate attention and responses; for others, it means suggesting that few others are sufficiently engaged on these critical issues and that the individual efforts will therefore be critical.[1] But these arguments are usually made in a shorthand fashion that assumes many shared interpretations and goals. Beyond this, however, organizers must work to build a culture of activism and collective efforts, which grows out of, and reinforces participation. Activists begin to hang out more with other activists, finding reinforcement not only for their positions on issues, but also for the very acts of movement involvement. Both less and more than formal organizations, social movements develop a movement community that embodies and shapes their values. Activists in the community develop a shared vocabulary that extends well beyond particular political issues; it includes ways of socializing, styles of dress and presentation of self, and often unarticulated, but shared, beliefs in a range of issues (Meyer and Whittier 1994; Taylor and Whittier 1992; Whittier 1995). In participating in such communities, people create and maintain the components of civil society and create a sense of belonging for themselves. Organizers build these communities and try to take advantage of them when they find them.

An organizer's job is to persuade significant numbers of people that the issues they care about are indeed *urgent,* that alternatives are *possible,* and that the constituencies they seek to mobilize can, in fact, be invested with *agency.* We can think about crafting appeals that invest audiences with the components of collective action as creating a *collective action frame* (Gamson 1992; Snow and Benford 1992). The frame connects the political issue with a personal viewpoint and political action; in effect, it acts as a cognitive and/or emotional bridge to social and political engagement. Organizers construct these frames in direct opposition to a prevailing political rhetoric that emphasizes the risks of social movements: the *futility* of collective action; the *jeopardy* of changing the status quo because things could get worse; and the potential of unanticipated *perverse effects* of social movements (Gamson and Meyer 1996). A collective action frame answers the objections to participation in collective action, engaging an individual in something larger than himself or herself and in opposition to some elements of mainstream politics.

But organizers do not construct these frames in a vacuum, nor do potential activists interpret each new appeal solely on its own terms. Both operate in a larger political environment, a crucible in which their values are tempered. Critical to the successful

---

[1] In studying local community action in Detroit, Pam Oliver (1984) found that the perception that others would not act drove some to dedicate their time to activism, believing that if they did not, the effort would not take place altogether.

emergence of protest movements is a positive feedback loop through which well-positioned elites reinforce both an alternate position on issues and the choice of protest as a strategy. In the case of civil rights in the United States, for example, the Supreme Court's 1954 decision, *Brown v. Board of Education,* legitimated criticism of segregation and offered the promise of federal government intervention as a powerful ally against southern state and local governments. The *Brown* decision suggested new possibilities for social organization, and organizers and activists responded. The Highlander Folk School, an activist training center rooted in labor, shifted its emphasis to civil rights and created leadership training sessions that people such as Rosa Parks *could* attend and study both the *Brown* decision and civil disobedience as a political tactic. Organizers draw from and respond to the larger political culture, creating a community of struggle in which to nest social movement efforts.

Take, for example, the Communist Party in the United States. It was a movement organization that never approached significant influence, and its members found support for their efforts not only in a distant and abstract ideology or instructions from another party, but also in the lives and commitments of their neighbors. Organizers shared meals and child care with other Communists, played cards on weekend nights, and argued about sports as well as politics. Politics and social movement action became part of a larger internally coherent life.

This sense of commitment varies by degree across organizations and movements but unites all sorts of movements, often more deeply than do explicitly expressed political commitments. Kathleen Blee (2002), for example, interviewed women involved in hate groups and identified four distinct subcultures that were easily identifiable by styles of dress, preferred music, and styles of socializing. The strength of a movement culture, as developed, provides an infrastructure of belief that allows activists to see commitments and take risks, even if they can't always articulate a political strategy or a viable political alternative.

In any collective action there will be a range of people with a range of motives and understandings of what's going on and of what their goals might be. Social movements, for this and other reasons, are therefore always relatively sloppy affairs. Organizers are faced with the challenge of harnessing the energies of diverse people and styles of action into a whole that can be presented coherently to a broader world and of managing the inevitable tensions within (Benford 1993a).

The American setting provides a special context for trying to mobilize participation. Despite a long history of relative political openness, there is also a long history of weak movement cultures, particularly for working-class organizations. Tocqueville, writing more than 150 years ago, identified the challenge as the problem of "self-interest, rightly understood." The essential question in American politics, he reported, might be summarized as "what's in it for me?" The lack of a long history and embedded social relationships and the relative openness of the government and the economy encouraged a strong ethos of self-interest bordering on selfishness; everyone is on the make, and no one anticipates someone else helping. But the same openness, in conjunction with Madison's fragmentation of political power, means that citizens need to work with others in order to look out for themselves, that they must, in effect, temper their own pursuit of interests to join with others. Although political circumstances can encourage this kind of cooperation, particularly in times of heightened crises, when the threat of loss combines with the promise of opportunity, the very volatility of circumstance makes such coalitions and campaigns limited and unstable. Sustaining mobilization and participation is an ongoing challenge for organizers.

Establishing organizations is one viable way to do this, to routinize the process of mobilization and to allow for a consistent presence in political action. Let's return to the four students in Greensboro. The young men who started the sit-in campaign had all been involved in NAACP youth councils and had been influenced by the efforts of well-established organizations taking on civil rights, including the NAACP and the Southern Christian Leadership Conference (SCLC). After a few months of student protests directed to desegregating the South, Ella Baker, one of the activists who created the SCLC after the successful bus boycott in Montgomery, persuaded that group to sponsor a national conference to create a new student-based organization, the Student Non-Violent Coordinating Committee, which would coordinate activity as an adjunct to SCLC. Of course, SNCC took on its own life as the movement grew (Zinn 1964).

The organization, like others, built up a culture not only of politics and participation, but also of shared values and communities that could, at least theoretically, sustain participation over a period of time. Importantly, SNCC differed from more conventional political organizations in explicitly eschewing professionalization. Field organizers were paid salaries that could only charitably be described as "subsistence," so that the moral and political incentives had to remain strong. Although such an approach guarantees a high level of commitment from current participation, such a passion has a double edge that can rip apart organizations over time as individuals are unwilling to broker compromises about their lives.

Activism itself generates its own commitments because after someone has begun the process of taking responsibility for the larger world and acting purposefully in concert with others, lives change and possibilities open. Activists come to see themselves as members of a group differentiated from outsiders. They interpret their experiences in political terms and politicize their actions both in movement contexts and everyday life. Collective identities constructed during periods of peak mobilization endure even after protest dies down. One-time movement participants continue to see themselves as progressive activists even after organized collective action decreases, and they make personal and political decisions in light of this identity. Veterans of Freedom Summer, for example, became leading organizers in the peace and student movements of the 1960s, the feminist and antinuclear movements of the 1980s, and beyond (McAdam 1988; Meyer and Whittier 1994). Engaging in political activism changes the lives of participants, making subsequent activism more likely.

MOVEMENT PROFESSIONALS

Activists who start by making a space in their lives for social movement participation sometimes come to support themselves through their political efforts. When you begin to see activism as not only a way of life, but also a source of livelihood, your considerations must change, at least somewhat, in response to the exigencies of making a living. It's not that movement professionals will take on causes they don't support for money, but rather that the filter of livelihood also affects the movements they join. Although the path toward becoming a professional is relatively clear, it's not one that many people take.

Activists engaged in social movements always discover an unending supply of things to do. Because social movements are the effort of those who want to effect—or prevent—substantial political changes, there is always room to do more: make another phone call, write another letter, lay out another flyer, and on and on and on. The activist who needs to make a living doing something else will face a time squeeze that puts pressure on all other aspects of life and still will feel as if there is more to be done for the cause. Activists who can make a living from their efforts can focus on what needs to be done for a social movement, and their understanding of what needs to be done will expand. Most particularly, professionals develop a stronger vested interest in the survival and well-being of their organizations than will the rank-and-file activist. First, their livelihood depends upon it; second, preserving organizational infrastructure entails mostly detail-oriented work that isn't intrinsically satisfying and that few amateurs want to put at the center of their social movement efforts.

Professional activist careers vary across issues because the prospects for paid employment in social movement organizations change with the ebbs and flows of politics. Thus, it is not uncommon to see professionals move among several causes as campaigns come and go. An activist for working women may find better employment prospects working for abortion rights and then later working for a labor organization. An antinuclear activist may move to environmental causes, and an antiabortion activist may turn to campaigns against gay and lesbian rights. Their movements among movements don't signify a mercenary attitude toward social movement politics, but rather a pragmatism about professional activism. Activists may also run for office or engage in mainstream partisan politics. All of this is part of a professional and political whole, with different emphases at different times. Indeed, carrying the lessons, tactics, values, and contacts from movement to movement can invigorate new social movements and revive faltering old ones. As example, Kim Voss and Rachel Sherman (2001) found that local union chapters most likely to revive included activists who cut their teeth in causes other than labor.

The role of the professional in a social movement is something that has been a matter of important dispute within scholarship. On one hand, Frances Fox Piven and Richard A. Cloward (1977), writing about the movements of poor people in American history, are deeply skeptical about how helpful these professionals are. The professionals, they observe, are good at building organizations, securing resources, and setting up stable institutional structures. At least for poor people, Piven and Cloward observe, this is problematic because the disruption of the poor is their primary resource in effecting political change. The routines established by professionals, at best, waste the critical moment when mobilization is possible on less critical activities. At worst, they channel dissatisfaction into routine and less disruptive modes of action.

On the other hand, Suzanne Staggenborg (1988) looks at the professional organizers in the pro-choice movement. She observes that the professionals are, in fact, more radical in their analyses and their tactics than are the people who make up their organizations. Living from, as well as for, the movement, they are able to monitor politics and policy, calling attention to issues and actions that might otherwise escape scrutiny. By maintaining the movement during periods of slack mobilization, she argues, they keep the concerns alive and can mobilize their constituencies more quickly when opportunities present themselves.

Assessing these different perspectives, it's difficult to make a blanket statement about professionals stoking or damping protest. It's most likely that both are possible, depending upon a number of factors, including the nature of the constituency involved, the character of the issues, and the orientation of the professional activists.

ENTREPRENEURS

The category of professionals blurs around the edges to commercial entrepreneurs, who also make their living from social movements but may offer less of a commitment to the issues involved. Movement entrepreneurs also find something worthwhile in engagement in social movement causes, but it is less a commitment to issues than a commitment to a practice of politics. Start by thinking about someone who sells soda at demonstrations. On a hot day, a demonstration is a great place to do business, largely because of a concentration of people. Entrepreneurs print T-shirts, make badges, compile and sell mailing lists, file legal papers, or rent sound equipment.

They move from active movement to active movement. Although the soda salespeople may turn up at any demonstration, most of these entrepreneurs will stay on one broad side of the political debate or the other. Still, the crowds gathered by political causes provide opportunities for people doing business on other issues. The musicians struggling to find an audience may perform cheaply to find one at a demonstration or fundraiser. The caterer may discount his services to meet those at a fundraising party.

Entrepreneurs cluster around active movements because that is where people, and a potential livelihood or audience, are. In addition to providing valuable services, they may raise the public profile of a movement or help activists do it themselves. The challenge for activists is to maintain a focus on the health and vigor of a movement and its attendant issues and not to get lost in the concerns of the entrepreneurs who will come and go.

ANOMICS AND THE RADICAL FLANK IN SOCIAL MOVEMENTS

The so-called classical paradigm of social movement emphasized the activities of the psychologically troubled and socially disconnected, who find connection, if not understanding, in the life of crowds (e.g., Kornhauser 1959). These people are rarely, if ever, a large share of those in social movements, but they may generate the most visible actions and can also be a serious danger to a movement's cause. Because social movements generally recruit freely, because access to participation comes easily, and because they rarely police their own boundaries or filter out extremes effectively, they are always vulnerable to the passions of zealots from within. The dramatic actions of the intensely committed present both a challenge and an opportunity for activists and their opponents. Opponents can point to the radical actions of a few to discredit a movement; yet, sometimes such radical actions can draw attention to a larger and more moderate group pushing for serious reforms. Take the case of the movement against abortion.

Just after Christmas of 1994, John Salvi, deeply convinced of the evil of abortion, tried to do his part to end it. Dressed in black and packing several rifles and handguns, he drove down Beacon Street in Boston, where three women's health clinics provided abortions. Salvi attacked two of them, killing one worker at each clinic and wounding several others. In flight, Salvi drove to Norfolk, Virginia, where he opened fire from a distance at another clinic.

Police apprehended him in Virginia and extradited him to Massachusetts, where he was tried, convicted, and sentenced to two life terms in prison.[2]

Workers at all the clinics were already familiar with on-site antiabortion protests. Generally, however, it took the form of "sidewalk counseling," in which a few activists would scream at women outside the clinic, attempting to provide information, including graphic photographs of fetal parts, that would dissuade the women from entering. Clinic workers became accustomed to hearing demonstrators quote Scripture and call them and their clients "murderers," a daily occurrence at many clinics that offer abortion services. Less frequently but with some regularity, larger groups staged nonviolent civil disobedience in attempts to shut down the clinics and "rescue" the "unborn children." Such "rescue" efforts often spurred vigils and counterdemonstrations by abortion rights activists, and, indeed, the antiabortion movement effectively set much of the agenda for its opponents (Staggenborg 1991). Abortion rights supporters organized to escort women to family planning and women's health clinics; at apparently even greater risk, activists organized to protect doctors as well. In larger political arenas, abortion rights activists pressed legislatures for more protection at the clinics, including buffer zones in which street counselors would be banned. They called for federal prosecution of antiabortion activists on conspiracy charges and began to file civil suits against antiabortion organizers. With Bill Clinton's election to the presidency and the subsequent emergence of a seemingly solid majority supporting abortion rights on the Supreme Court, the antiabortion movement began to fade. The protests, although disruptive, were familiar, and clinic staff and abortion rights supporters developed their own routines for dealing with them. Still, the antiabortion movement had developed a range of tactics and had become a visible presence in both mainstream politics and the streets in front of women's health clinics.

John Salvi's relationship to this larger antiabortion movement was loose, if not tenuous. He had attended a few organizational meetings of local groups in New Hampshire and had on occasion spoken out against abortion at church services. He carried and sometimes distributed antiabortion literature produced by movement groups. For the most part, however, Salvi viewed the movement as too weak and tentative in the face of what its supporters described as a great evil. After Salvi's attacks, most antiabortion activists were quick to disavow him personally; most condemned the murders. With certainty, Salvi's actions terrified both opponents and supporters of abortion rights. He injected an element of danger into the abortion debate that most activists on both sides didn't welcome, and his cause became a burden for abortion opponents.

It is important to recognize that social movements are *not* primarily the work of the psychologically troubled and socially maladjusted, but it's also important to recognize that mentally unbalanced people may also be engaged by the rhetoric of promise and social change and may take on the mantle of a social movement to justify their own activities. Take, for example, John Brown. In 1859, Brown, who believed that God was speaking to him, decided to take responsibility for ending slavery, which had been a recurrent—and seemingly irresolvable—issue on the national agenda since the founding. Fearful of the

---

[2] A summary of Salvi's itinerary can be found in *The Boston Globe*, January 1, 1995, p. 1+. The account that follows is drawn from the *Globe* and other media accounts of the attacks. Salvi, deeply disturbed about many things, killed himself in prison.

political consequences, members of Congress representing free states had negotiated compromises with slave states that virtually ensured a permanent deadlock. The Supreme Court, in *Scott v. Sanford,* had ruled in support of the Fugitive Slave Law, which provided for the return of slaves in free territories and states to their owners in slave states. In effect, this negated Congress's compromise to stall the expansion of slavery—and slave owners started moving to Kansas with their slaves.

In the face of the evil of slavery, now expanding to his home territory of Kansas, John Brown knew it would be immoral to wait for government to act. Indeed, based on all the available evidence, government would not act effectively to stop the spread of slavery. He took the matter into his own hands.

On October 16, 1859, Brown led a small army of twenty-one, including his son, to begin to free the slaves. Thinking their efforts would bring about massive slave rebellions in the South, the crusaders—and this is an apt term—seized an armory at Harpers Ferry, West Virginia, and began executing men with swords. Brown wanted to arm the slaves and, really, to start a civil war. The rebellion lasted only two days; Brown and his band were captured, tried, and, unrepentant, hung on December 2, 1859. The raid on Harpers Ferry and its aftermath were more fuel on the fire that soon erupted into the Civil War, with abolitionists around the country valorizing Brown's courage as well as his cause. From a historical vantage point, it's impossible to question the justice of his cause; at the same time, from a modern viewpoint, it's also hard to think that John Brown was sane.[3] He heard God speaking to him and was dismissive of any arguments about not only the justice of his cause, but also the wisdom of his tactics. Taken altogether, it's far from clear that his bold raid on Harpers Ferry actually helped the cause of abolition.

Except, perhaps, for what others did with the raid afterward. Once dead, Brown could not speak for himself, and subsequent slavery opponents could construct a more appealing figure for their own purposes. Henry Thoreau, now best known as a nature writer, living in Concord, Massachusetts, where there was little sympathy for slavery, used Brown's trial and execution to mark one of his few interventions in political life. In a well-attended talk on October 30, 1859, at the Concord Athaneum, Thoreau read a lecture, "A Plea for Captain John Brown," to the residents of Concord. Thoreau's John Brown was also a moral crusader, albeit somewhat less bloodthirsty and not hearing the voice of a vengeful God. For Thoreau, Brown's act was really an indictment of other abolitionists who gave voice, but little more, to arguments about slavery. "Such were his humanities, and not any study of grammar," Thoreau said, "he would have left a Greek accent slanting the wrong way, and righted up a falling man." (quoted in Thoreau 1975: 829). He concluded with a call for unspecified action, likening Brown to Jesus Christ. Surely the myth of John Brown is part of what inspires people such as John Salvi.

These tales are not unique. Caught up in the moment of a movement, impassioned by the rhetoric that animates movements—polemical, inflammatory, uncompromising— some people see a mismatch between talk of moral apocalypse and the day-to-day activities even of movement politics. Unlike the overwhelming majority of social movement activists,

---

[3]David Reynolds (2005) disagrees. In a recent biography, Reynolds argues that Brown had a reasonably accurate view of what it would take to end slavery, envisioning his trial and execution as necessary steps to a greater social good.

these people are not likely to be engaged in community action or more conventional activity because the routine and compromise necessary for the day-to-day practice of both mainstream politics and most movement politics can't sustain the craving for drama and action; they seem a mismatch for the strong moral claims and fiery rhetoric that organizers use to generate attention. These troubled people taken up in the wake of a social movement take action into their own hands, leaving those who might agree with them to manage the political fallout. Movement opponents will try to tar the larger movement with the activities of its most troubled and zealous supporters. Journalists understand that the focus of their attention will shape the public perception of a movement, comprised of "regular people," ideological activists, or the lunatic fringe (Gitlin 1980; Rojecki 1999). And activists have the challenge of managing the public discussion of people who, through the drama of their efforts, command public attention in a way that more restrained—or thoughtful—efforts cannot.

In 1983, a man named Norman Mayer, with no history with the nuclear freeze movement or apparent connections with other activists, drove a truck he said was full of explosives to take the Washington Monument hostage and demanded that the United States conduct a serious debate on nuclear weapons issues. Mayer had operated something of a one-man vigil outside the White House, calling for such a debate. In fact, at the time of his action, when the nuclear freeze movement was sweeping the country, the United States was probably as close as it had ever been to such a debate (Meyer 1990). Although Mayer didn't claim allegiance to the freeze movement, his action fed an image of danger and irresponsibility of the movement that its political opponents had been trying to project. It undermined the very notion of regular people getting involved in issues of national security, and it implicitly strengthened the position of mainstream politicians, who didn't need to do such things. At the same time, far more dramatic and dangerous than anything that antinuclear activists were doing, it proved much more attractive to mass media to cover in great detail. Within a day, specially trained police officers shot and killed Mayer as he tried to drive his truck, which turned out to be empty.

The drama, rhetoric, and uncertainty of a social movement can attract people who crave exactly that drama and sense of possibility. Movement activists and leaders must manage the tension between inclusiveness and maintenance of goals and image. It's not an easy task.

In summary, we see that social movements are diverse affairs, with loose boundaries, and that they offer opportunities for all sorts of people to get involved for all sorts of reasons. The classical paradigm had things backward, devoting most attention to those groups that are actually the least prevalent in social movements. The rank-and-file activist is best understood as someone who is trying to achieve conventional political goals, albeit by somewhat unconventional means. Sorting out cooperation, competition, and politics among movements and those they challenge will take us to a somewhat broader level of analysis in the next chapter.

CHAPTER 4

INDIVIDUALS, MOVEMENTS, ORGANIZATIONS, AND COALITIONS

When the World Trade Organization met in Seattle in 1999, more than two hundred thousand people assembled to protest its participants and their work. Protesting corporate globalization, teamsters, "black block" anarchists, environmentalists, vegetarian fundamentalists, lesbian feminists, and white nationalists marched together in an alliance that must have been uneasy. Although all opposed "globalization," these groups differed on what this meant and on what could—and should—be done about it. For some, globalization meant increased economic and social integration with the rest of the world and, as such, represented a threat to American life—or American wages. The remedy was some kind of isolationism, limiting American engagement in foreign affairs and economies generally and perhaps ending immigration. For others, globalization increased corporate dominance of all elements of life, undermining the authority of democratic governments, both in the United States and abroad. The remedy was increased citizen globalization: better coordination and transnational agreements to protect the environment, ensure minimum work standards and wages, and enhance human rights (Thomas 2000).

Only the shared enmity to the powerful people meeting in Seattle held these disparate groups together, and tensions could be seen on tactics as well as ultimate goals. Whereas some groups were committed not only to nonviolence, but also to orderly demonstration in accordance with Seattle's police, others wanted to maintain and exploit their unpredictability, trying to create as much disruption as possible. Seattle police were overwhelmed, and activists, using cell phones, were able to coordinate the movement of demonstrators to places where police forces were understaffed, creating a maximum of havoc and disruption. The "Battle in Seattle" was the most dramatic shot in the emerging war against corporate globalization, whose effects are still working out for both authorities and their opponents.

At the same time, in looking at both that battle and the larger war, it's clear that holding together the broad coalition of interests and groups will be extremely difficult. Any government response, ranging from violent repression to negotiation and conciliation, will present dilemmas for activists and organizers. The demonstration is a particularly sharp illustration of an important dynamic of social movement politics: the coalition, that is, a collection of distinct groups and often unaffiliated groups whose members cooperate on some issues in order to have political influence. Because groups join movements for different reasons, their responses to changing circumstances also differ. Yet, understanding the development of a social movement, it is difficult to untangle the various trajectories of participating organizations in a larger movement cycle of mobilization and decline.

We will revisit the issues attendant on social movement organizations and their relations with the outside world, including supporters, authorities, and other social movement organizations. We'll look at the different strategies that organizations employ to survive and the risks of various strategies. We'll then look at coalition dynamics to see how social movement organizations relate to each other as allies, as competitors, and as opponents.

SOCIAL MOVEMENT ORGANIZATIONS AND SURVIVAL

A key recognition in the literature on social movements was that the translation of a grievance into collective action isn't automatic or unproblematic. This means that people rarely recognize actionable grievances on their own or spontaneously. Organizers help them do this and direct the efforts of recruits toward an extremely broad range of potential activities, including donating or raising money, working in campaigns, showing up at events, chanting slogans, writing letters, and breaking windows.

Whenever we look at any event, we need to think about who is organizing it and why. Looking at events exclusively and reading back causes through opportunities, misses the important shaping of both grievances and collective action that organizers do. Without looking at the organizations, we miss understanding political alternatives, strategic decisions, missed opportunities, and the real successes of dedicated efforts at mobilization. Indeed, the dramatic events associated with protest are a tiny fraction of social movements' activities. Social movement organizations arise to coordinate efforts in the service of a set of issues or a constituency. Although dedicated organizations are a critical component of any ongoing social movement, they also consume some share of a movement's resources, including money, time, and passions. In one way, organizations provide the primary vehicle for collective action. Extending this vehicle metaphor, we can see that although people can move faster down a track when in a car, the car itself demands attention, maintenance, and fuel and creates its own drag. Different sorts of organizations offer distinct combinations of energy, action, focus, and drag and consume different mixes of resources. For this reason, it's a mistake to make generalizations about the role of organizations in social movements, be it tempering action (e.g., Piven and Cloward 1977) or coordinating collective action.

We can start with basic premises. A social movement organization operates in the service of at least three distinct, but interrelated, goals: to pressure government to affect the policy changes it wants; to educate the public and persuade people of the urgency of the problems it addresses and the wisdom of its position; and to sustain a flow of resources that allows it to maintain its existence and efforts (Zald and McCarthy 1987; Wilson 1995).

What is useful for achieving one objective isn't always helpful for achieving another. For example, the literature on lobbying (e.g., Berry 1999; Schlozman and Tierney 1986) suggests that moderation, credibility, and restraint are key to influence on Capitol Hill. At the same time, those very qualities are anathema to maintaining a high public profile and thus publicizing ideas and may make sustaining a flow of resources for a citizen group more difficult as a result. In contrast, a politics of polemic, characterized by dramatic action, may be useful in maintaining a public profile, but the action may supercede the analysis (for example, a dramatic civil disobedience action, such as one staged by Operation Rescue). Although satisfying supporters, it may reach few others—or may even mobilize the opposition (Meyer and Staggenborg 1996). Organizations then must balance a profile that contains some mix of these three dimensions, mindful of maintaining a balance that works for them. We need to see every choice of issue, tactic, and alliance as something that offers advantages and risks along these three dimensions.

Once established, groups develop devoted constituencies, ways of doing business, professional staffs, permanent office space, fixed places in the contact lists of reporters, and relatively routine patterns of cooperation with other groups. They also develop elaborate ways of making decisions that enhance their prospects of survival. In most cases, rank-and-file members vote with their feet or, more accurately, with their annual membership dues. Like a company, groups need to adapt to changing political circumstances in order to ensure their survival. This means adapting not only organizational structures, but also goals and tactics in order to continue to service members (Clemens 1997; Hansen 1991).

There is a virtually unlimited repertoire of organizational forms, mixes of political claims, and combinations of political tactics that organized groups of people can employ to manage the conflicting pressures of influence, service, and survival. Every choice carries with it serious constraints and opportunities for everything else. In the next chapter, we will consider tactical choice; we begin here, however, by looking at the implications of possible organizational choices. We will then consider governance within organizations, a function of form, and organizations of organizations—social movement coalitions.

The field of social movement organizations includes a great deal of diversity, a diversity that gets washed out in broad generalizations by both activists and academics about organizations more generally. Thus, arguments that organizations spur radical action, political efficacy, and moderate tactics or stifle activism in the service of their own survival all oversimplify. At the same time, some kinds of organizational forms have dominated in the United States, being more suitable for survival over a long haul.

As we discussed in previous chapters, large numbers of people are not engaged in politics most of the time. External circumstances lead them to be committed to social movement activism on a given issue at a particular time. But these commitments are fleeting. The resolution of a political grievance, by victory or defeat, makes the pursuit of private life more attractive than political mobilization (Hirschman 1982). Because most people shift in and out of various degrees of political engagement, organizations that seek to survive need to find some way to keep supporters engaged, either by nurturing long-term commitments or constantly recruiting new members. In fact, most organizations do both.

So what is to be done when the issues are resolved? A group such as the Woman's Christian Temperance Union, which first won and then lost its central demand (the prohibition of alcohol production and distribution) is nowhere to be seen in American politics today (Szymanski 2003). Like a business, an organization that has seen its central mission disappear can try to find a new mission, one with a longer life, or develop another source of recruitment that provides a more stable base of support. We can call this "goal shift."

The classic study on this sort of organizational adaptation was a detailed look at the Young Men's Christian Association (YMCA), which began as an organization devoted to spreading the Gospel (Zald and Denton 1963). In order to carve out a stable existence, however, the organization had to develop a reliable stream of revenue. It did so by setting up gyms, dormitories, and health clubs that charged those who used them. To be sure, the organization has continued both religious and political work, but this fact is generally obscured by the daily services, which consume a large portion of the organization's activities. In effect, services are a selective incentive that help recruit and retain members.

Similarly, the American Automobile Association's ongoing political efforts, lobbying for funds for highway construction and maintenance, are low on the agenda of the lion's share of members, who join for free towing or maps or store discounts. Similarly, the National Rifle Association (NRA), which lobbies to maintain free citizen access to firearms and donates money to supportive candidates, maintains a large membership by providing gun safety classes, discounts, and a monthly magazine. Of course, none of these groups, nor the AARP, can be considered a social movement organization.

Services are one way of maintaining a flow of resources but not one that is easily available to most explicitly political groups. Indeed, the services can get the best of these groups, obscuring their own political aims. This isn't the only kind of shift that's possible, however. Groups that have completed a political battle can turn to other battles, generally related to what they've done in the past.

INFACT (Infant Formula Action Coalition) is a good example. INFACT developed to coordinate a worldwide boycott of Nestlés targeted at stopping the company from deceptive marketing of infant formula in poor countries. After a campaign of just six years, in which it called upon people to buy alternatives while pressing a strong case against bottle feeding when alternatives were available, INFACT negotiated a compact with Nestlés. Nestlés agreed to stress that breast feeding is best and to stop using deceptive means (e.g., dressing salespeople in nursing uniforms) to market its products; INFACT called off the boycott (Sikkink 1986). At that point, although there was surely some work to be done in monitoring compliance, INFACT's organizers could have declared victory and turned to other pursuits. But the organization had established a successful set of tactics, a reputation, and a set of procedures that had worked—at least once. Organizers decided to shift concerns to nuclear weapons and nuclear power and to launch a boycott against General Electric, which turned out to be less successful. The shift in issues and targets cost INFACT some of its supporters, but the organization continued. Now, twenty-five years after its first campaign, it has restyled itself as a group that "will lead the *grassroots challenge to unwanted corporate influence* for years to come" (emphasis original) (www.infact.org). In 2003, it proclaimed new campaigns against Philip Morris and Kraft Macaroni and Cheese and soon retitled itself "Corporate Accountability International" (http://www.stopcorporateabuse.org).

We can identify different motives for such a shift—maintaining an organization and a set of jobs and relationships for personal stability; deploying a newly available vehicle that had apparently proved successful in redressing one kind of social injustice toward another one. I'm less interested here in judging motives than in identifying processes that support organizational survival. Organizers presumed that the shift in goals, but not tactics or organization, would maintain their members' commitment and the organization's continued survival and influence.

There are numerous other ways to maintain the flow of resources, particularly the necessary commitment of members of time and/or money. Some groups, primarily those with a strong religious orientation, benefit from influential angels (large donors) or large posthumous grants from devoted supporters. (This is the case with the American Friends Services Committee.) Others win grants from foundations, many with an explicit political bent. Indeed, some foundations are expressly dedicated to funding social causes, and some wealthy individuals have made a practice of funding groups that agree with their political perspectives. Others, including those who earn a great deal of money relatively early in life, are able to dedicate their efforts and their money to causes they believe in.

Such is the case with Moveon.org. Founded in 1998 by software entrepreneurs Joan Blades and Wes Boyd, who contributed not only their own efforts, but also $5 million, Moveon.org has developed a lean organizational structure and a formidable fundraising capacity. Based on Internet connections and e-mail networks, Moveon maintains a small professional staff of ten, minimal office space, and a sophisticated Web site that serves a mailing list of 1.7 million addresses. Moveon started in response to an effort to impeach President Bill Clinton for lies about his affair with a twenty-one-year-old White House intern. Moveon's founders viewed the impeachment effort as a deliberate political distraction offered by conservative Republicans. They circulated an e-mail petition calling for a quick censure of the president and then a return to more substantial political issues.

Their success in raising their own profile and raising money, and the shift to a conservative Republican administration in 2000, led the founders to try to deploy their model and their mailing list to other issues—even as the impeachment effort and President Clinton faded from national politics. Moveon became a promoter of liberal political causes, asking its members to participate by doing as little as signing e-mail petitions, contributing money online, or sending e-mails to the federal government to create a "virtual march" that would shut down the government in protest of a planned invasion of Iraq. Targeting an Internet-savvy, relatively well-heeled, and resolutely liberal constituency, the low-overhead design of Moveon allows for rapid response to new issues and quick mobilization—at least on the Internet. Moveon's design reflects changes in communications technology around the world and reflects entrepreneurial individuals applying their own expertise, commitment, and money to their causes in new ways. As other groups adopt the tactics and form that Moveon innovated, it will need to distinguish itself from new organizations and maintain its own base of support in order to ensure its stability (Abraham 2004). It is one model of organization.

Federal law provides distinct pathways to organizational stability. In keeping with Madison's vision, but far outstripping anything he imagined, government regulates and effectively supports certain kinds of organizational forms. Of course, you and your friends can organize any sort of voluntary association you'd like, but after money is involved, so is the federal government, through taxes. Because virtually all organizations confront the challenge of stability by raising—and spending—money, they must deal with federal laws about organizational forms. Groups associated with churches, for example, enjoy both tax exempt status and the restrictions that come with tax exemption. Groups that engage in electoral politics must work within laws about contributions and disclosure that affect all political campaign groups.

Most notable in the world of social movements is status as an educational organization. Federal law provides tax exemption to nonprofit educational organizations in exchange for compliance with restrictions on organization, activities, and disclosure. Organizations granted 501(c)3 status must have boards of directors, annual meetings, and annual audits, for example, and cannot devote more than 10 percent of their activities to explicitly political (advocating political candidates) activities (McCarthy, Britt, and Wolfson 1991). Simply, the opportunities that come with recognition and nonprofit status also include restrictions.

Another model is that of organized labor. Labor unions also provide services to members, most notably negotiating contracts with employers. In the context of these contracts, a union in most states can require all workers in a given job site to be dues-payers, if not members, by paying a required service fee to the union if one chooses not to join. In the context of negotiated contracts, unions provide for pensions and health benefits and provide a means of dealing with individual, as well as collective, problems. Although established unions enjoy budgets that far outstrip those of most political organizations, they also devote a far greater portion of their efforts and resources to the provision of individual services—quite apart from any political goals. Critics of organized labor have argued that this strategy for survival has turned organized labor from an agitative social movement into a set of service organizations. The debate continues around and within organized labor.

Most groups must subject themselves to the pressures of the funding market, offering a menu of salient issues and a vision of efficacy and putting the message in front of potential members. Some organizations, for example, the Public Interest Research Groups, depend upon a canvass, in which paid fundraisers go door to door seeking signatures and donations. This approach depends on locating neighborhoods of likely supporters, but even more importantly, on projecting issues that are likely to appeal to more than they will alienate. Most groups canvass by mail, targeting a larger population. They are, however, no less dependent on issues that are attractive to their supporters. As in recruiting members, they must convince supporters that an issue is urgent, that change is possible, and that supporting the organization is one viable kind of political action.

DEMOCRACY, EFFICACY, AND THE COSTS OF SURVIVAL

In 1915, Roberto Michels wrote a case study of a German political party that provides one of the few "laws" in social science. Michels argued that the establishment of a permanent organization of any kind inevitably leads to the concentration of political power in the hands of relatively few people. To demonstrate this "iron law of oligarchy," Michels conducted a detailed study of the German Social Democratic Party. His idea was that a party explicitly committed to democracy would provide the hard test for his hypothesis of oligarchy. He found that the leaders of the party ultimately developed interests different from those of the rest of the membership. Most notably, the maintenance of not only the party, but also their own power within it became paramount. To the degree that this encourages leaders to trade off the interests of their members for their own self-interest, Michels's law creates a problem for democracy and a challenge for all social movement organizations.

Organizations approach the problem of democracy in a range of different ways, each way with its own pitfalls. A common approach is essentially to embrace the market of funders, assuming that after an organization no longer suits its members, it will be unable to continue its existence; people will stop joining or giving money. This reality will make professionals extremely sensitive to the needs and preferences of their memberships, like the proprietors of any service-oriented business. In this case, political action is a kind of product, supported by members. The problem here is that communication with members, particularly communicating an image of effective political organization, can become more important than actually engaging in political action—at least to the survival of the organization.

Perhaps more significantly, the professionalization of organizations and their dependence on funding prioritize causes that are useful for fundraising, rather than those that we might judge to be more significant or more in need of representation. Thus, a glance through the phone book of Washington, D.C., finds scores of organizations explicitly concerned with environmental issues but not many concerned with, say, recipients of food stamps. Organizations that work on behalf of economically disadvantaged people need to mobilize support from others who have resources. This situation leads to a distortion in the composition of groups in the "interest group society." To the extent that social movements are dependent on organized groups, they replicate the same biases of the large world of organized interest groups (Berry 1999). Groups that represent the affluent are disproportionately numerous and well heeled. Groups unable to provide services to reasonably committed—and affluent—consumers, particularly those that advocate for poor people, always face an acute survival struggle.

Although significant organizations maintain national headquarters in other cities, most frequently Boston, New York, San Francisco, Chicago, and Los Angeles, having a national central office in Washington, D.C., helps a group to develop access to policymakers and funders. But it can also lead to a distance from the members at the grassroots who follow somewhat different agendas and are hard-pressed to focus on less visible activities in the halls of Congress. In other words, it is hard to keep the members and funders at the grassroots engaged in activity that seems far away. (Indeed, some contemporary groups exist only as platforms for their founders or executive directors to weigh in on the public debate.) Further, national offices are often ill prepared to respond to local political conditions that may be thousands of miles away.

One solution is the development of a federated structure, in which a national office coordinates activities but affords state or local offices some autonomy in responding to local political issues as well as in serving their own members needs. The National Organization for Women is a particularly successful example. Established in 1966, NOW has maintained a federated structure almost since its founding, with local and statewide officers who represent their members and engage in local politics with a great deal of freedom from the national office in Washington, D.C., which is mostly concerned with national politics. Although the national office sends information to locals about ongoing campaigns and political issues, local offices address local political campaigns and pressing issues. This arrangement keeps activists engaged and probably makes the organization more effective at the same time (Barakso 2004).

Even within local offices, NOW has adopted organizational structures that give people with different interests a home in the organization. Jo Reger (2002) has conducted a detailed inquiry into local chapter politics. She found the potential of a divide between women who are most concerned with political action and others who see NOW primarily as a place to work on personal issues. By separating political action from consciousness-raising groups, local NOW chapters prevented the development of a split within the organization. Moreover, they made it possible for women to start with the personal and become more political. Reger found that women sometimes move from the consciousness-raising part of the local organization into the explicit political action wing but remain in NOW. Expressed boundaries within the organization, however, make it possible for members of one group to avoid members of the other—and conflict about goals and analysis—altogether.

The form an organization takes has important effects on its prospects for survival as well as its politics and potential influence. There is a range of different models, each with strengths and weaknesses. We might start with the sort of organization committed to maintaining a clear political program, regardless of the political environment or the pressures of the moment. Take, for example, the National Women's Party, founded in 1913, as described in *Survival in the Doldrums*. It was comprised of well-educated and committed individuals. When the crest of the first wave of the women's movement passed, organizers opted to maintain the clear identity of the organization, even if that meant sacrificing political visibility, recruiting, or even short-term influence. This strategy, Leila Rupp and Verta Taylor (1987) show, helped maintain a tight core of individuals committed not only to each other, but also to the organization and its ideals, and these survivors were able to nurture the development of a second wave of women's mobilization, based in new organizations. Putting ideology and identity first virtually ensures marginality at certain times, but it can help preserve a place in the political spectrum.

We can tell a similar story about committed pacifist groups such as the War Resister's League (WRL) or the Catholic Workers. These groups are essentially organized as vanguard organizations, meant to house and serve the very committed and to inject their clear perspectives into broader movements when they emerge and to try to hold a place in the political debate even in slack times. Organizers within such groups understand that their appeal will be narrow but intense; in essence, it's better to be right than large. Here, too, it's important to acknowledge that such groups make few concessions to pragmatic politics, tailoring neither their message nor their efforts to the issues of the moment and learning how to survive on limited budgets without routine access to authorities.

A variant sort of organization focuses on mobilization in the moment, sacrificing concern with long-term survival for short-term mobilization. A wonderful example is the Industrial Workers of the World (IWW), known as the "Wobblies." Calling for the organization of "one big union" of all workers—in opposition to employers or bosses—the Wobblies were suspicious of organizations that created new hierarchies and vigorously critical of permanent peace and cooperative relationships with class enemies. First organized in 1905, the Wobblies agitated around the country, most vigorously in the West, promoting worker insurgency and generating a historic wave of strikes in 1912. They explicitly called for all workers, regardless of skill, to be represented by the same unions. In their heyday, which lasted until World War I, they tried to organize workers across the United States and were at the center of several highly contested, sometimes violent, strikes.

Today the most famous Wobblie of that time is Joe Hill, an organizer and songwriter who has been immortalized in folk songs and myth. Hill was convicted of murder in Utah in 1916, almost certainly erroneously. Executed by a firing squad, he asked that his ashes be scattered across the United States—except for Utah, where he wouldn't want to be caught dead—and offered these famous last words: "Don't waste time mourning . . . Organize." But organizing, for Hill and the other Wobblies, didn't mean forming a national office or raising money; it meant mobilizing coordinated opposition to capitalism. The legend of Joe Hill looms larger than the presence of the Wobblies in American politics.

Absent a central organization and professional and well-compensated organizers, the Wobblies were ill suited to stand up to two important challenges. Because they refused to sign contracts with bosses, they could offer little beyond ideological incentives to potential members and they flourished in a crisis environment that most workers found dangerous and exhausting. This was especially true when other unions were able to establish formal organizations that satisfied calls for stability and often offered the security of contracts that improved, albeit marginally, the status of the narrower groups of workers they represented. They were also ill prepared to deal with state repression, reluctant to seek protection from any institutions within government, and therefore even more vulnerable to repression from both state governments and corporations. With a strict focus on direct democracy, the organization was able to fully engage those few members who remained. It still maintains this commitment.

But, as the IWW's Web site (http://www.iww.org/index.shtml) proudly proclaims, in contrast to the claims of many historians, the IWW didn't fade away after its impressive wave of strikes in 1912 or with the advent of World War I in 1917, but instead thrives to this day. A sympathetic observer will find vitality in the Web site, in the efforts of small groups of people, and in the very small number of committed activists still affiliated with the Wobblies, but it has become less "one big union" than one holder of a minority perspective in American labor, one that directly challenges both capitalism and bureaucracy. One of the IWW's current campaign issues, for example, is the proposal of a four-hour workday. However attractive this proposal might be to workers, it is not echoed or even criticized anywhere else in the labor movement or in mainstream politics, leaving us to question how relevant the Wobblies are today. Indeed, the IWW Web site emphasizes that a new member should expect little immediate benefit or influence on politics from joining the IWW; it's a small membership. Without extensive resources, however, and with its commitment to direct democracy and member determination, the organization is not likely to move from the margins to the mainstream—especially when all sorts of other labor organizations may have more to offer.

If the Wobblies are unusual among organizations explicitly committed to both direct democracy within and political mobilization outside, it is because they have been able to maintain a presence, albeit a limited one, on the Internet. This doesn't mean that such organizations aren't critical factors in social movement during their peaks of mobilization. SNCC, for example, which depended largely on a volunteer membership, was critical in leading civil disobedience efforts during the early 1960s—and it vanished by the end of the decade. Students for a Democratic Society, founded in 1962 and committed to participatory democracy, was unable to manage the influx of new recruits as the antiwar movement—and their centrality in it—increased. It, too, vanished in a decade after painful political crises within.

The movement against nuclear power, which grew to its greatest visibility and influence during the 1970s, also contained a direct action wing filled by organizers suspicious of their own capacity to coopt their own movement. They established organizational structures designed to limit their own power—and that of any permanent authority within the organizations. Take, for example, the Clamshell Alliance, which grew to coordinate opposition to a nuclear power plant planned for the narrow New Hampshire coast (Dwyer 1983). Activists commenced efforts against the licensing of the plant almost immediately upon its initial licensing, intervening in public hearings through scientific testimony. In 1976, a small group of activists occupied the construction site before being arrested. The following year, a much larger group occupied the site, resulting in 1,414 arrests, with hundreds held by the police in a tent city for nearly two weeks.

Concerned about Michels's iron law and requiring high levels of coordination and commitment, the Clamshell Alliance was organized around "affinity groups" of eight to twenty people often sharing something in common, such as the same community or college. Affinity groups made decisions by consensus and sent rotating representatives to council meetings to make decisions for the groups as a whole.

For authorities, such as the New Hampshire police, the direct democratic structure was infuriating. Although the organization as a whole honored its deals with police, a different person represented the Clamshell Alliance to authorities and to the media in every interaction. This made life difficult for reporters seeking information and police seeking to negotiate actions quickly. For the Clamshell Alliance, although rotation spread responsibilities among the participants, it also made it more difficult for any individual to develop expertise in, say, appearing on television or talking to reporters. The direct democratic consensus process also made the process of making decisions laboriously slow and made innovation incredibly difficult. The Clamshell Alliance ended up fading away, unable to change in response to new circumstances and lacking anyone committed to its survival above all else. Its records are housed in the University of New Hampshire's library, and its history is worth finding and telling.

So, at one end of the spectrum are organizations in which regular members bear primary responsibility for direction and survival. It's disappointing, but understandable, that such groups have a difficult time changing direction or surviving through difficult times. At the other end of the spectrum are organizations that are led by professional staff mindful not only of issues, but also of organizational survival and often looking past the mobilization of the moment.

These organizations must also confront the Michelsian dilemma in one way or another. Seeking survival and the continued flow of money and members, they need to be especially mindful of the markets for interest-based politics. Of course, this is a function of contemporary political circumstances; it is also a product of the sorts of constituencies that an organization serves. Although some organizations provide a direct service, as noted, such as discounted insurance, for only a few organizations is this a fair exchange for money and time donated.

POLITICS AS PRODUCT: MOBILIZING AND MAINTAINING MEMBERSHIP

To the extent that organizations provide members with benefits beyond active politics that represents their interests, such benefits are usually small and targeted: stickers, newsletters, information, and discounts for trips or activities. Because the politics is such an important part of an organization's appeal to its members, and because the political environment is not stable, organizations that survive reposition themselves politically in order to maintain an image of relevance. This doesn't mean abandoning long-term goals, but it does mean having sensitivity to shifts in political circumstances. An environmental organization can campaign for the preservation of wilderness or against nuclear power without compromising its broad environmental mission, but each campaign will have different consequences for the organization at different times. Organizers use modern market research techniques, including focus groups and surveys, careful examination of results from different direct mail appeals, and astute monitoring of the political scene in prospecting for issues. This means always having something to offer in the way of politics to the group's target audience of funders and members and being sensitive to what members are thinking about at any given time.

This also means balancing the prospects of threat with those of opportunity. Emphasizing either danger or possibility can mobilize members at different times, and this varies from constituency to constituency. This also means, in contrast to the IWW, for example, finding the most proximate issue that seems possible for action. In other words, no matter how large the agenda for change, any social movement organization needs to find a viable piece of the agenda to press—or defend. And this will change in response to political circumstance. We can think about this as a matter of prospecting an *issue frontier* (Gornick and Meyer 1998).

For example, look at the movement against rape, which was an offshoot of the women's movement in the 1970s. Activists within the feminist antirape movement saw sexual violence, including wife-beating and rape, as inevitable byproducts of capitalist patriarchy but recognized that the issue of capitalist patriarchy was too big for most people to take on and unlikely to be easily resolvable. The question was how to find a way to advance the broader agenda—one piece at a time. Activists were also concerned with making women's lives better.

Although the ultimate goal was stopping rape, the initial focus was improving the treatment of rape survivors and making it easier for government to prosecute rapists. Both political progress and organizational maintenance required a two-track strategy. On one track, activists sought to provide services that government was failing to provide. Activists established feminist rape crisis centers, which provided a range of services to women, ranging from counseling and victim advocacy to self-defense training—or rape-proofing. The establishment of these centers coincided with a political effort on a second track, mostly at the state and local levels, forging alliances to press for rape law reform, which made it easier to convict rapists, and services that altered the conduct of local police, hospitals, and prosecutors. Within a short period of time, these efforts were remarkably successful.

The provision of services gave volunteers something to do that provided some relief and some satisfaction, such as staffing hotlines. Ultimately, it also provided a source of revenue as local governments contracted out services to the rape crisis centers, which became less overtly political and more professionalized (Gornick and Meyer 1998). On the advocacy front, activists across the states succeeding in achieving rape law reform in forty-six states within about five years, generally in the directions that activists demanded. Of course, this left the larger issues of patriarchy untouched.

The organizations and activists within the movement have periodically revived the movement and their own political prospects by finding new ways to press the larger issues with the edge of a smaller issue. Thus, activists organized against marital rape in the late 1970s, battery in the 1980s, and then date rape. By the end of the 1980s, much of the advocacy shifted to treating victims who remembered incest that occurred years earlier. The point is that each issue, directed toward larger politics, was intended to be a leading edge in a broader movement. At the same time, each issue frontier was attractive to a somewhat different composition of activists and supporters. The point is that organizers work to find a point of political action that has a place on their own list of important issues but also is salable to a larger audience.

This issue is hardly peculiar to the movement against rape and is, in fact, the issue that all groups deal with. Thus, civil rights activists argued about the primacy of voting rights on their political agendas during the early 1960s, and peace activists focused on nuclear testing until the Vietnam War and the Limited Test Ban Treaty mandated a shift. In the abortion battle, although organizations on each side have a broad general mission—restricting abortion or maintaining access to safe, legal abortion—the issues pressed at any time vary, in response to political circumstance (Meyer and Staggenborg 1996). Each side has the dilemma of maintaining a sense of urgency among its committed activists. Thus, when abortion rights seem to be relatively secure, antiabortion activists try to find restrictions that large numbers of people will view as potential viable and worth supporting, for example, parental notification requirements or bans on particular procedures. Abortion rights groups focus on the threats represented by these new restrictions and emphasize the threats to abortion rights represented by their opponents. Groups successful in adapting to the politics of the moment will survive and sometimes matter. Those that don't will fade away from political significance.

STRUGGLING FOR CONTROL

Most commonly, committed members of an organization are responsible for promoting—or avoiding—changes in the organization's agenda or tactics. The establishment of any organization requires a tremendous commitment of resources and/or effort. Frequently one individual or a small group of people has to dedicate itself tirelessly to build an organization; unsurprisingly, it feels a sense of ownership about its creation and has a difficult time adjusting to ceding or sharing governance of that organization with others. Candy Lightner and Cyndi Lamb, for example, worked with a small group of others to found Mothers Against Drunk Drivers (MADD), later renamed "Mothers Against Drunk Driving," in 1980 in the wake of the deaths of their teenage daughters. Lightner's commitment stemmed from her personal tragedy and anger and was essential to make the dream of an organization a reality. It meant working long hours without compensation, repeatedly contacting funders and politicians, even in the face of initial refusals. As the organization grew, however, Lightner's commitment was less important than the professional skills needed to run a large organization, and she and the organization parted ways. MADD now includes more than six-hundred chapters across the United States, and managing relations among the participants in the organization and its supporters is more important than establishing the importance of the cause. Meanwhile, Lightner, still committed to the cause—and others—writes and speaks about her experience in starting the campaign.

Again, Lightner's story is not unique. Helen Caldicott, an Australian physician living in the United States, refounded Physicians for Social Responsibility (PSR) as a vehicle for a campaign against nuclear energy. Caldicott was a powerful and polemical speaker who terrified and mobilized crowds about the dangers of nuclear radiation in the 1970s. She was quick to expand and refocus her efforts on nuclear weapons and gained even more attention. She spoke about exterminism and the end of life on the planet by the end of the decade and called the elections of 1984, then 1986 and 1988 the most important of all time. Ultimately she grew frustrated with PSR—as its members grew frustrated with her—because the polemical line wears out over time, and organizers want to do more than support a charismatic leader.

Caldicott founded a new organization, Women's Action for Nuclear Disarmament, more in line with the political line she was developing, and the process of growing an organization that required more stability than the founder could provide recurred, and she returned to Australia.

Founders are generally not the same people who are the ultimate managers of large bureaucratic organizations. Organizations need to find ways to institutionalize governance so that they are not dependent upon the unusual—extraordinary individual commitment, personal commitment, or critical—and occasional—events. The key is to find a way of institutionalizing so that an organization can continue to grow in the absence of the extraordinary leader and to allow members' input in order to maintain commitments and connections.

Common Cause, a self-described "citizen's lobby," was founded in 1970 by John Gardener, a former secretary of health, education, and welfare, explicitly to represent the public interest in the political battle against "special" interests. With this broad vision—and no obvious or natural constituency—the organization has to be responsive to members' concerns in order to stay alive. The organization dealt with this problem by establishing a relatively large board that provides direction to the professional, and paid, staff, now numbering about fifty. The board members are elected by the membership to staggered three-year terms. In effect, members can influence the direction the organization takes not only by leaving, but also by direct democratic input into its decisions (Rothenberg 1992). Common Cause has become a well-established lobby group on Capitol Hill that takes on a wide variety of issues, but it does not mobilize action, beyond donations, at the grassroots.

We can identify a simple pattern: organizations that maintain a clear and minimally varying agenda tend to survive only as small, often marginal factors. Those that prioritize stability and professionalization will be more flexible on the other dimensions of their politics, particularly issues. Of course, this dilemma is frustrating for members and for organizers.

Sometimes organized groups within political organizations try to force a shift in focus. Take the contemporary example of the Sierra Club. Founded in the 1880s by environmentalist and writer John Muir, the club is the oldest environmental organization and has long been concerned with a broad range of issues that protects the environment. The membership has included backpackers, hunters, canoeists, fishermen, preservationists, and liberal political activists of all sorts. It is governed by a board of fifteen members, elected by the membership, who set a broad agenda and oversee a professional staff that pursues that agenda. Quite apart from politics, however, the Sierra Club spends a considerable part of its budget each year on maintaining an office and professional staff and communicating with members. The immense resources it has amassed, including not only money, but also a visible identity, mean that the organization itself can become not only a vehicle for politics, but also a site for political struggle.

In 2003, a coalition of vegetarian activists and anti-immigration activists mounted an electoral campaign within the club to push the club's agenda along the coalition's preferred lines. Because all members have the right to vote for the board, this campaign included a drive to sign up new voters that scared long-time Sierra Club members.

With an annual budget of nearly $100 million and 750,000 members, the organization provides a rich resource and a broad platform for activists, but perhaps one whose stability could be undermined by dramatic political shifts. Fearful that criticism of immigration to the United States and a platform that decried raising animals for human consumption would alienate long-term members and compromise the organization's political viability, longtime members, including eleven former presidents of the organization, campaigned against the coalition's preferred candidates. They charged political subterfuge, contending that outside activists with no commitments beyond the issue of immigration were plotting to take control of the club.

"It's important to have hunters and fishermen in the Sierra Club," Carl Pope, executive director, said. "We are a big-tent organization. We want the Sierra Club to be a comfortable place for Americans who want clean air, clean water, and to protect America's open spaces" (Bustillo and Weiss 2004).

The battle over the future of the Sierra Club encouraged even other outsiders to consider joining the club and counterorganizing to prevent what looked to them like a hostile takeover. In fact, each side sought to mobilize outsiders to join the club to protect its side of the debate. The tensions about the relative importance of people, animals, and the natural environment have been recurrent in the organization's long history as organizers and activists have disputed the best ways to promote an environmental agenda. Some opposed the organization's stance against the war in Iraq as potentially divisive and distracting, whereas others argued that a broad environmental agenda required an antiwar stance. In effect, the well-established organization provides a place to lodge claims and a place in which activists can argue about what they want to do.

A different Sierra Club might not join with disparate groups to oppose war. The key issue here is the focus on relations among organizations and the internal and external factors that drive cooperation and competition. The challenge, of course, is for any group to maintain its own identity and prominent place within a social movement while supporting the efforts of allied organizations that might grow so strong as to overshadow it. It's not easy or obvious, and it is the stuff of politics. Ultimately the insurgent campaign to add opposition to immigration to the Sierra Club agenda was overwhelmingly defeated.

SOCIAL MOVEMENTS AS COALITIONS

At least in the United States, social movements are coalition affairs, featuring sometimes loosely negotiated alliances among groups and individuals with different agendas. Although it is a grammatical convenience to speak about the peace movement or the antiglobalization movement or the environmental movement, such a label distorts the reality of a social movement, reifying boundaries and movements that are actually much sloppier affairs. As in the example of the antiglobalization demonstrations in Seattle, activists differed on goals and tactics but shared an interest in staging a large protest against the World Trade Organization. Virtually all of the participating groups offered comprehensive, often competing, diagnoses of the evils they were protesting and as well as the alternatives they were promoting, yet those broader agendas were collapsed into a broad—and publicly ill-defined—protest against globalization. Even while they disagreed among themselves about many things, all agreed, at least implicitly, that the most important enemy to challenge at that moment was the people meeting to promote global trade.

Social movements are always about more than their explicitly articulated claims, and the full range of concerns is much broader, more diverse, and more contested than we can see in any single event. Challenging movements are comprised of organized groups and individuals cooperating, to some degree, on a set of common issues. Although scholars in the 1970s (e.g., McCarthy and Zald 1977) recognized that organizations are responsible for stoking and shaping mobilization and maintaining identity during slack periods, scholars have paid relatively little attention to the dynamics of political coalitions.[1]

Early work on social movements identified movements as the province of groups and individuals outside the "polity," that is, the formal institutions of government (e.g., Gamson 1990; Tilly 1978). In reality, however, this oversimplified the reality of social movements in at least two important ways. First, in a contemporary liberal democracy such as the United States, the sharp demarcation between conventional politics and movement politics is hard to find. Elected officials protest, sometimes even engaging in civil disobedience, while activists who protest also vote, lobby, and participate in party politics. Coalitions of successful social movements straddle the boundaries between institutional and extrainstitutional politics.

Second, social movements are not themselves single units, but rather are comprised of organizations with a range of interests. At its height, any social movement in the United States has a range of organizations participating, serving—and soliciting from—distinct constituencies, employing a range of tactics in pursuit of different ultimate goals. Because these groups enter activism with distinct priorities and longer-term goals, a movement's interaction with mainstream politics affects the strength of coordination among its participating groups. The attractions of protest or mainstream politics vary for each group, as will its commitment to the strongest movement of the moment.

Each expression of political demands can be only partial. Activists and organizations generally offer broad analyses of social ills, only a small portion of which can be expressed on a placard or banner or articulated in a demonstration. A given campaign or event can offer the chance to make claims only on the most urgent or promising set of issues. Choosing to speak on something means that something else receives less attention—even if only for the moment.

---

[1] This is a topic that begs more research, and recent research points to a variety of interesting questions and means for answering them. See Gerhards and Rucht 1992; McCammon 2001; McCammon and Campbell 2002; Zald and McCarthy 1987; Staggenborg 1986; Rochon and Meyer 1997; Meyer and Corrigall-Brown 2005; and Van Dyke 2003.

For any organization, the initial decision to join a movement, such as the movement against corporate globalization, immediately necessitates other decisions: first, what, if any, alternative policies to offer; second, what means to use in making claims; third, who, if anyone, to work with in making these claims. Every decision carries with it potential costs and benefits. On the one hand, cooperation among groups increases the visibility of the movement, increasing its chances at political efficacy. Additionally, because organizations have distinct audiences, a broad coalition affords the prospects of mobilizing a wider range of people, tactics, and entry into a greater number of institutional niches. Organizations can specialize in terms of issues or tactics, enhancing not only the profile of the movement as a whole, but also its volatility and flexibility (Staggenborg 1986).

On the other hand, participation carries risks. To illustrate this point, we can look at the movement against the recent war in Iraq, which was animated by hundreds of large and small organizations across the United States, loosely organized in at least five distinct, but sometimes overlapping, coalitions. By cooperating with groups that may appeal to the same funders or members, an organization may obscure its own identity in service of the larger movement, hurting its own visibility and survival. Alliances can compromise identities and can put organizations in league with unreliable or tainted allies. In the case of the antiwar movement, most participants opposed the politics of International ANSWER (Act Now to Stop War and End Racism), which supported Iraq's right to self-determination. The decision to get involved in any issue is more obvious for some organizations than for others. The decision to oppose the war through nonviolent action, including civil disobedience, was simple for, say, the War Resister's League, a small pacifist group nearly hundred years old, whose identity is defined by precisely such actions and whose small organizational profile is supported by loyal donors committed to the absolute nature of the WRL agenda. In contrast, the decision to participate is more difficult for organizations such as the National Association for the Advancement of Colored People or the National Organization for Women because they maintain a profile and base of support largely on other political issues. Undertaking a strict antiwar stance or engaging in particularly contentious tactics or affiliating with marginal groups is rife with risks. At once, it threatens access to a set of political insiders, potentially directs attention away from other issues the group sees as critical, and may alienate supporters, members, and sometime allies. In addition to making a statement on issues of vital concern, participation against the war can afford such a group the opportunity to mobilize, raise its organizational profile and visibility, and perhaps direct more attention to other issues of its concern. That a large portion of the leadership or membership may see the antiwar position as appropriate only sets the stage for a decision, it does not define it.

Coalitions are a key form for structuring dissent and protest in the United States. A coalition includes a range of groups that bring with them different constituencies, analyses, tactical capabilities, and resources to cooperate on some piece of a political agenda. The template flyer at any large demonstration in the United States today is comprised of a laundry list of organizations (cf. Gerhards and Rucht 1992). The cost of joining, immediately, is only the potential risk of association. The broad coalition makes visibility of an issue more likely but may allow an organization's particular profile to be obscured by the movement as a whole or enable groups that compete for resources to overshadow it or obscure its agenda. For the issue, however, coalition politics is generally beneficial. Increased visibility aids in the pedagogic goals of movements; numerous groups, ranging from professional associations to third parties to ethnic associations, give potential members a place to join in and provide additional access points to government. As a movement grows in power, more groups find incentives to join in, to use the bright light of a successful mobilization to bring attention to themselves and their causes. This is what we saw in the extraordinary February 15 and March 15, 2003, marches against the war in Iraq that took place around the world and in the "virtual march" on Washington, which claimed to mobilize more than two million people, attempting to shut down normal politics through a barrage of e-mail.

At the same time, the peak of mobilization is always limited, at least partly because political leaders respond, and responses always change the dynamics of coalitions—even though unambiguous victories and defeats are relatively rare. Changes in policy, political alignments, or even rhetoric alter the constellation of political opportunities for each organization, leading to a reconsideration of previous political choices and alliances (Meyer 2004). Although the dynamics of coming together and growing apart are mediated by personal relationships and political skill, the critical factor is the relationship of the movement as a whole to external political circumstances.

The nuclear freeze movement illustrates this process. Uniting to oppose the Reagan administration's arms control and nuclear weapons policies during the early 1980s, a broad coalition united behind a "nuclear freeze" proposal that participating groups defined differently (Meyer 1990; Rochon and Meyer 1997). At the height of mobilization, the movement comprised groups that opposed nuclear weapons altogether and advocated unilateral action and others that saw the freeze as a vehicle to use in forcing the Reagan administration to return to the previous U.S. policy of bilateral arms control negotiations and moderated technical modernization. As the administration responded to movement pressures, moderating its rhetoric, cutting the growth in military spending, and reestablishing arms control negotiations with the Soviet Union, the freeze coalition dissipated. Differences among the various organizations emerged more prominently as institutionally oriented politics consumed a greater share of activist efforts. Groups that had enlisted in the freeze movement because they faced closed doors on Capitol Hill left the coalition when those doors opened, even as getting into Congress meant accepting a version of the nuclear freeze that allowed nuclear weapons modernization and construction to continue. As the practical limits of this institutional and instrumental orientation became clearer, however, organizational leaders found it increasingly difficult to cooperate. The more institutional wing saw the prospect of progress. The disarmament wing saw a sellout on the horizon. The War Resister's League, for example, emphasized that it was a pacifist organization calling for unilateral action in its fundraising letters, distinguishing itself from the large number of its partners that would compromise with the horrors of nuclear weaponry and war. The middle, that is, those groups that were normally concerned with other issues, saw less to organize around (Meyer 1990, 1993a; see also Sawyers and Meyer 1999).

Coalition dynamics roughly approximate similar decisions about participation for individuals (Meyer and Corrigall-Brown 2005). Groups join coalition efforts when they see a particular set of issues and efforts as urgent and potentially efficacious. When external circumstances change, altering either the perceived urgency or efficacy of mobilization, groups will return to the core activities that sustain them. Whereas paper coalitions may continue, the commitment to coordinated collective action dissipates. More commonly, the coalitions become new organizations on their own, staking out the positions articulated by the coalitions and then competing with member groups for funds and attention.

MANAGING COALITIONS:
SPECIALIZATION AND DIFFERENTIATION

As we've discussed, social movement organizations have mixed incentives for cooperating. On the one hand, cooperation makes the cause stronger; on the other hand, cooperation makes each individual organization less distinct, potentially less visible, and means ceding control of image and politics to something larger. How do groups manage this?

Sometimes through explicit coordination and sometimes through historical development, groups develop ways of managing their own differences and tensions in order to continue. Groups can specialize in terms of tactics, politics, and/or constituencies. In the best of times, this means that the movement as a whole can offer a broader challenge, engaging a more diverse range of people, and can overcome temporary difficulties that any organization has. In other words, it can cooperatively carve out distinct places in a social movement.

Take, for example, the history of the civil rights movement in the United States. The National Association for the Advancement of Colored People, founded in 1909, was the major organization in a small and not very visible movement, employing a range of strategies but focusing on argument and moral suasion. In 1930, Thurgood Marshall helped orchestrate the separation of a legal wing of the organization into a free-standing organization, the NAACP Legal Defense Fund (LDF). The fund was able to raise money for the dedicated purpose of filing lawsuits challenging segregation. By focusing on this strategy, the LDF was able to avoid the constraints of a large membership organization and to focus on a narrow range of strategies and claims. Focusing on this strategy also afforded an expert leadership great autonomy in deciding what to do, how, and when.

Other organizations, with different origins, contributed to the early growth of the movement. The Congress of Racial Equality (CORE), spun off from the pacifist Fellowship of Reconciliation (FOR), would later stage direct action campaigns against segregation. Still, when the new wave of civil rights activism took off in the mid-1950s, partly a response to the successful litigation strategy of the LDF, which had argued *Brown v. Board of Education* before the Supreme Court, new organizations formed. First was the Southern Christian Leadership Council, based around the network of Christian ministers supporting local direct action campaigns. Then, in 1960, when the Greensboro sit-ins started a wave of sit-ins across the South, Ella Baker pressed SCLC leaders to support students in forming a new organization, SNCC, which would provide the most visible direct action wing of the movement.

The four large organizations, NAACP, SNCC, CORE, and SCLC, argued vigorously among themselves. Yet, taken together, they worked in the service of the same general goals. SNCC gave the larger, more mainstream organizations a visibility they could not have achieved on their own, as well as reach into new constituencies. At the same time, SCLC and NAACP leaders could talk with mainstream politicians on behalf of the larger movement. Each organization brought its own tactics, style, and constituents to the movement, and each organization did not bear political responsibility for its allies, nor could it control them.

At a much smaller level, contemporary racist organizations have the same sort of patterned relationship. Kathleen Blee (2002) documents the persistence and organization of four distinct strands of racist organizations: the Ku Klux Klan, neo-Nazis, Christian Identity activists, and skinhead youth gangs. Again, each strand serves a distinct constituency and can benefit or distance itself from the others as circumstances suggest.

Sometimes coordination takes place without explicit discussions. Organizers just target their efforts to open niches and unfilled slots and steer away from tactics and claims they think are already well covered. But coordination can be explicit as well. Will Hathaway and I (Hathaway and Meyer 1997) document the explicit negotiations among peace groups that divided up activities and proposals in weekly meetings. The Monday Lobby Group developed a practice of *cooperative differentiation*. As a whole, this coordination gave the peace movement a broader, more diverse set of tactics and supporters, providing more diverse access points to government.

Once established, political organizations tend to persist (Wilson 1995) but not automatically. Organizers work hard to keep their organizations alive, sometimes at the expense of the movements that created them, trying to ensure not only the survival of their positions, but also the capacity to lodge new challenges when circumstances improve. Even so, new social movement organizations continually form. This is partly the result of new waves of action, partly the result of the process of institutionalization and ossification of organizations leaving political space for new claimants.

Take the case of the modern environmental movement. Frustrated with what he saw as the Sierra Club's moderate stance and political tactics, key staff member David Brower started the Friends of the Earth (FOE), which, he planned, would take a stronger position on behalf of the Earth. Still, over time FOE developed its own network of funders and routinized relationships with politicians, and Dave Foreman broke off a radical wing of that movement to form the direct action-oriented Sea Shepherds and a radical network of activists. Although activists associated with the Wilderness Conservancy, which raises money to buy and protect land, might explicitly distance themselves or even criticize the enviroterrorism of Earth First!, each benefits from the existence of the other—most of the time. We can actually observe a pattern of organizational birth. Established groups seem rarely to initiate new movements, although they may be critical in what happens after the movement has emerged. New campaigns generate new groups, most of which establish themselves firmly as interest associations in American politics. Relationships among those groups are critical in shaping the development of social movements in America.

COALITION POLITICS AND SOCIAL MOVEMENT CYCLES

Recognizing the dynamics that drive independent groups to cooperate and to differentiate, we can trace a cycle of social movement engagement by focusing on coalition dynamics. Initially, and most of the times, individual groups work to service their members and try to keep their issues in front of the public. Because there is little attention to these issues, there is little incentive for close cooperation. Because resources for a set of issues are relatively scarce, all groups carve out reasonably distinct profiles, cooperating only on an ad hoc basis on a particular bill or particular event.

Activists within groups are continually launching projects that they believe will spur others to join them, but initiatives also often come from outside established groups. This process is like prospecting. Generally, even the most clever framing of a salient new issue can't gain political traction unless government helps by opening doors to a new set of actors, by discussing substantial change on a set of political issues, or by shutting out a particular set of actors. Essentially, the start of a serious social movement comes from a possible change in condition that encourages activists to engage an issue aggressively, either by raising the urgency of collective action or by lowering the costs.

After an idea or claim begins to take off, other groups join in, attempting both to benefit from the attention and new people attracted to the cause and to help the effort succeed in affecting policy. The first groups that join in are likely to be those historically concerned with the cause, but endorsers will not be so limited. A cause or movement that has demonstrated appeal will engage a range of groups seeking both influence and attention. As an effort generates increased attention, partly by engaging more groups and endorsers, the incentive for new groups to join in will increase. Thus, growing helps a movement grow.

As the range and number of groups endorsing a movement and as the amount of resources within those groups tops out, groups will find ways to define themselves apart from the larger movement, in other words, to differentiate. Importantly, this is a reflection of interaction with government and mainstream politics. A change in political circumstance, by policy reforms or policy failure, changes the calculus for many challenging groups such that a social movement coalition begins to dissipate.

Just as increased growth increases growth, the beginnings of unraveling also increase unraveling and differentiation within a movement coalition. As differentiation increases, it has the corollary effect of discouraging new people from joining a movement. The small, more differentiated, less visible movement offers both a more limited sense of urgency and more limited prospects for influence.

In summary, coalition dynamics accentuate the dynamics of movement growth and decline, increasing and speeding growth on the upward part of the trajectory and speeding decline and differentiation when a movement starts to falter. Savvy mainstream politicians understand this and calculate a mix of concessions and constraints to limit a social movement's challenge. Savvy activists work to maintain the breadth of a movement coalition for as long as possible.

THE STRATEGY AND TACTICS OF SOCIAL PROTEST

The history of draft resistance in the United States starts with conscription, and it has sometimes been violent. In the Spring of 1863, the Civil War didn't appear to be going well for the North. Facing defeats on the battlefield and horrific casualties, the Union forces were also facing a severe shortage of manpower. In addition to casualties, desertion was widespread, and the three-year commitments that volunteers had signed were about to expire. In March, President Lincoln signed a conscription bill into law. It provided for lottery selection of male citizens from 20–45 throughout the Union. The citizenship qualification meant that only white men would be drafted, for $300, they could buy exemption.

Unsurprisingly, the proposed draft was unpopular in New York, as was the war and President Lincoln. Working men were particularly incensed by the buyout provision that they would be unable to afford, but there were other grievances as well. The war had driven large price inflation that far outstripped any growth in wages, and in the period leading up to the beginning of the draft, antiwar editors published inflammatory editorials that emphasized the costs of a war fought on behalf of black people. Some Democratic politicians decried Federal intervention in local affairs, and warned of the likely competition between black and white workers.[1]

The first lottery in New York, held on Saturday, July 11, 1863, provoked concern and discussion, but little hint of the events that would unfold the following week. On Monday, July 13, working men across the city stayed home from their jobs and met in Central Park, carrying placards protesting the draft. They then marched to 47th Street and 3rd Avenue, where the next round of the draft lottery would be held. On the way, some cut telegraph poles and wires, while a group of Irish women used crowbars to pull up the tracks on the 4th Avenue street car line. Crowds stopped the streetcars on the 2nd and 3rd Avenue lines by surrounding the cars.

By midmorning, when the selection had begun, the Black Joke Engine Company #33 arrived dressed in their firefighting gear to protest the induction of one of their men. Using their equipment, they attacked the lottery selection wheel and set the building on fire. Draft

---

[1] This account draws from Bernstein (1990), Cook (1974), and Harris (2003).

protesters spilled out into the streets of New York, violently attacking prominent Republican politicians, abolitionists, and pro-war Democrats. Some also began to attack black people, including children, on the streets. Beatings quickly turned into hangings on the lamp posts of New York City. Groups of workers surrounded factories involved in the war effort, shutting them down. By midday, local authorities ordered the draft selection to stop, but events had already begun to spin out of control.

Late in the day, some rioters abandoned the anti-draft demonstration to try to keep the public order. Engine Company 33 returned to the Upper West Side to try to stop arson and looting, and other draft opponents began to work against the rioters to protect life and property. By the next day, historians report, most of the rioters were Irish Catholic and shared broader grievances than the draft or the war. From an initial focus on agents of the Federal government or the draft, rioters turned to attack and loot Jewish- and German-owned stores and Chinese peddlers. Particularly, mobs attacked virtually anything that represented the black population in New York City. Rioters at the waterfront gathered to drive blacks out of the area using both threats and violence.

By Wednesday, the Mayor and Governor had mobilized several regiments of the New York National Guard to join the police in keeping the public order, and the Federal government sent troops from Gettysburg, Pennsylvania to assist in putting down the riots. The troops focused on taking back the factories and restoring a semblance of social control. By the end of the week, the city had calmed, but more than one hundred people had been killed, and the property damage was extensive. (In the following years, politicians seeking to make their own political points with the events sometimes quoted casualties in excess of one thousand deaths.) The draft was suspended for more than a month, but the government was able to resume the lottery without incident by the end of August.

The story of the New York City draft riots demonstrates clearly the importance of social movement tactics. Ultimately, opponents of the draft were unsuccessful in doing more than stalling implementation of the draft lottery for a relatively short period. The riots certainly created uncertainty among authorities, who did not know what to expect next and were reasonably scared of what might happen. But the riots also divided opponents of the draft and legitimated harsh repression. Social movement activists need to devise tactics that create uncertainty and express their views, but also provide some kind of foundation for subsequent activism. Activists also have an obvious interest in developing approaches that build support and mobilize allies, rather than drive natural allies away. Finding this balance is always difficult.

Take the case of AIDS activists.

In 1987 a faction of gay and lesbian activists committed to militant action to combat AIDS. Although the first reports of AIDS came at the start of the decade, President Ronald Reagan in particular, and the federal government in general, was slow to recognize and respond to the disease in ways that reached the gay community (Shilts 1988). Even as the disease swept through gay populations in several large cities, and even as local officials struggled to find sensible and effective responses to AIDS, the federal government didn't acknowledge the existence of a problem. Frustration built within the gay community, but political action developed more slowly. At a March meeting, playwright Larry Kramer gave a provocative speech at the Lesbian and Gay Community Services Center of New York, announcing that two-thirds of those present might be dead within five years; he called for direct action (Rimmerman 2002).

ACT-UP (AIDS Coalition to Unleash Power) formed in response to Kramer's provocation. By the next year, chapters had formed in large American cities, including Los Angeles, Boston, Chicago, and San Francisco. ACT-UP was based on direct democracy and direct action. Organizing around the slogan "Silence = Death," ACT-UP staged demonstrations at medical conferences and political meetings. ACT-UP members blocked doors, staged die-ins, and threw condoms and blood. By design, the demonstrations were colorful and confrontational, with slogans and conduct matched to a claim that the struggle really was about life and death. They virtually always ended in arrests and televised coverage of screaming protesters, sometimes identified as "people with AIDS."

Like most movement campaigns, ACT-UP's campaign had multiple goals. At base level, participants called for access to more and better treatments for AIDS and called for the FDA to speed the approval process for new drugs. But this was a tip of an iceberg. In order for this to happen, the AIDS crisis demanded a more generally vigorous response from the government, including more aggressive research on the disease, public education on prevention of its spread, and greater tolerance for gays and lesbians.

ACT-UP's aggressive tactics represented only a segment of the gay and lesbian movements and for only a relatively brief time. In 1983, large cities had witnessed candlelight vigils to draw attention to the disease and to lend support to its sufferers, while gay and lesbian communities around the country created service and information centers that dealt with the whole range of needs of the community. By the end of 1987, a group of activists arranged the first display of the Names Project Quilt, a massive collaborative effort to commemorate people who had died of AIDS. Comprised of three-by-six-foot panels, each marking someone's life, the quilt engaged people across the United States and ultimately around the world. People feeling grief at the loss of a loved one or anger at the responses of the government started sewing. It was displayed across the United States even as it continued to grow, culminating in a 1992 display in front of the Washington Monument. The Quilt grew to include more than eighty-two thousand names and forty-five thousand individual panels, totaling an estimated 51.3 miles of fabric. Laid out on the Mall in Washington, it took up 1,270,350 square feet, the equivalent of forty-seven football fields (http://www.aidsquilt.org/).

The vigils, the protests, and the Quilt were all almost contemporaneous tactics of a large social movement confronting a difficult political environment. Each action generated some opposition within the gay and lesbian community, and each generated a great deal of support. Each action was part of a larger social movement strategy. Although activists talk about strategy all the time, figuring out just what it is and how it develops is difficult. Although strategy constitutes the largest part of debate within social movements, scholars have been slower to come up with usable ways to think about strategy. Here we can think of strategy as comprised of three interrelated elements. *A strategy is a combination of a claim (or demand), a tactic, and a site (or venue).* Because a movement always includes a variety of organizations, in looking at the choice of strategies, it's best to think of one organization at a time and to think of strategy as also containing an organization's relationship to other social movement organizations.

In this chapter, we'll spend the most time on tactics, but note that tactical choice makes sense only in the context of other choices a social movement organization makes. Let's examine strategy by passing through each of these elements in turn. To begin with, we have social movement claims (demands). In this regard, we see political opportunity as particularly salient. In the case of the AIDS movement outlined earlier, gay men had a wide range of grievances with mainstream politics and culture, but external circumstances, particularly the spread of a new disease, forced an AIDS focus upon many activists. As discussed elsewhere, organizers who are interested in mobilizing need to pick demands and issues that seem urgent enough to generate attention from activists, but that also seem sufficiently amenable to human action that people will stay engaged. The same calculus applies to authorities. Demands need to appear actionable enough to avoid being dismissed, yet challenging enough to inspire attention. The activist who demonstrates for good weather, for example, or even for an end to eating meat in the United States, is unlikely to generate much meaningful support. Because social movements are comprised of multiple organizations and associated individuals, different demands will compete for attention within a movement, and the responses of audiences and authorities will bring additional attention to some while obscuring others. In focusing on tactics, we'll see the critical importance of the anticipated responses of various actors, including activists, supporters, authorities, and bystanders. All of these relationships are mediated by the relationship of a group and a tactic to the variety of outlets operating in mass media.

TACTICS: ENGAGING ACTIVISM

Let's now turn to the issue of tactics, which, we'll see, is clearly linked to sites and claims. We need to think about these actions as different sorts of tactical choices for a social movement. When a formal organization, a less formal group of activists, and an individual engage a political issue, each chooses from a large menu of tactics of influence, ranging from political violence to mainstream political participation. Every tactical choice carries different risks and potential benefits. We can start by looking briefly at these three choices and then turn to the larger issue of tactical choice.

The first tactic described, the candlelight vigil, demonstrates the commitment of a group, both to itself and to others. It brooks no confrontation with authorities; at the same time, it can serve the function of building identity and cohesion within a group. By taking this relatively modest action, an individual differentiates himself from most of those around him and sees his action echoed by others. The vigil also signals bystanders of some kind of issue. The target of the action is ambiguous, however, and it's not always clear what those holding the vigil expect others to do—aside from care.

The second tactic, the ACT-UP disruptions, does all of these things—and more; it also demands a response from authorities. The disruptions are impossible to ignore because they interrupt the everyday routine of both targets and bystanders, and they often involve explicit transgressions of the law. Immediately the disruptions up the ante and are far more likely to generate attention and reactions—if not always favorable ones. The choice of site—a medical conference, a Roman Catholic cardinal's speech, an annual shareholders' meeting of a drug company, for example—suggests a vision of who is responsible for the AIDS crisis and simultaneously identifies a clear target—even an enemy. Moreover, the tactic of aggressive action sends a message to the community not only of urgency, but also of power and vigor. Activists viewed the disruptions as dramatic demonstrations of their own strength and resistance (Gamson 1989; Gould 2002).

The Quilt is more like the candlelight vigil, although it gives participants more to do (sew a segment) and artistically demonstrates the depth and scope of the problem of AIDS.

There are no clear enemies identified by the project as a whole—though there is huge variance in the particular segments. In projecting the issue as art as well as politics, it makes for softer politics than ACT-UP. The Quilt invites bystanders to join by walking among the quilt segments and looking at memories of lives lost. It builds solidarity within, perhaps extending it to others, and also provides an opportunity for fundraising at each exhibition.

It's tempting to paint these distinct tactics as part of an evolution, but, in fact, they coincided. Most movements are not only comprised of multiple organizations, but also employ multiple tactics at the same time. Although by the end of the decade many AIDS activists had come to criticize ACT-UP, there is no reason to believe that those at die-ins weren't also sewing quilt segments or standing silently on vigil.

A social movement tactic may be a direct effort both to effect change and to send a message to a broader public. In terms of direct influence, most social movements are severely limited in what they can do. On one end of the political spectrum, participation in elections, including making contributions to political campaigns and offering and supporting referenda, can change the people who make decisions or affect policy directly. Such efforts are, however, a small portion of what social movement activists do in the United States. At the other end of the political spectrum, direct action against an individual, company, or branch of government can also affect policy. In 2003, for example, an environmental activist bombed a car dealership that specializes in selling Hummers, vehicles that use a great deal of gas. Immediately this action took several large cars off the market and cost the car dealer—and/or his insurance company—a lot of money. Similarly, animal rights activists who break into a laboratory and free rats see their efforts as directly achieving a social good. This is, however, also a small portion of the effects of social movement tactics. To return to the three tactics mentioned earlier, only the ACT-UP confrontations could be said to have any direct impact at all, and a modest one at that—the confrontations made it harder for some meetings to take place. And, obviously, that impact is only a small part of the story.

To understand the process of tactical choice and the development and influence of a range of tactics on policy, politics, and social movements in the United States, it makes sense to take a step back from our examples and consider how people think about engaging in social movement activism as both an alternative to—and an addition to—more conventional political activity, such as voting and donating money to campaigns. Think about the famous calls to action, ranging from Martin Luther King's *Why We Can't Wait* to the pseudonymous "Andrew MacDonald"'s *The Turner Diaries* (apparently written by one William L. Pierce), or rabble-rousers from abolitionist orator William Lloyd Garrison to populist nationalist radio broadcaster Father Charles E. Coughlin. The primary task of these texts and people is to convince, energize, and mobilize supporters—but mobilize to do what? Henry Thoreau's essay on civil disobedience seeks to justify his own actions in withholding poll taxes in protest against slavery, but he doesn't call upon others to do what he did—except in the most general way. Most of the text and speech is designed to convince people that something is wrong and that they ought to do something, but just what is generally unclear. Indeed, the business about tactics is usually discussed in smaller, more familiar groups. To mobilize means to induce someone to do *something*—but what? What do people—or organizations—consider after they decide a cause is worth supporting?

In picking a tactic, a means for advancing a claim on a matter of policy, the incipient activist wants to do something that might be effective, that is consonant with whom he thinks he is, and that is not going to take more effort or risk than is necessary. Let me emphasize that all of this isn't necessarily conscious, deliberate, or—in a narrow sense—rational. In thinking about the rational considerations underneath what may seem like a spontaneous decision, we can develop a deeper understanding of social movement tactics. In thinking about tactical choice, we need to consider not only the obvious issues of costs, including risk, and likely impact, but also identity.

Identity: A Sense of Place

The social location of an individual affords him or her *resources* and *constraints*. When George Soros, who has made billions of dollars trading currency internationally, decides to support the development of an "open society," he can establish a foundation, hire a professional staff, publish books, Web sites, and pamphlets, and offer fellowships. This is an attractive set of tactics but not one that is broadly available to most people with causes. Soros's wealth affords him options that most concerned Americans do not have. When Robert McNamara, as secretary of defense in 1967, began to nurse doubts about the wisdom and viability of the American war in Vietnam, he was well positioned to bring attention to his doubts through relatively modest actions—ones he didn't take—but he could call a press conference or write a book. At the same time, as secretary of defense, he was constrained while in office to support the policy he helped design and the president at whose pleasure he served. Similarly, former Attorney General John Ashcroft, a passionate opponent of abortion, was constrained, both in that occupation and in his previous job as a U.S. senator, to obey the law, including Supreme Court decisions with which he may disagree. Holding a position in government, elected or appointed, effectively restricts an individual to using legal tactics to pursue political change, and an appointment in the executive branch of government leaves partisans to work within the constraints of their patron, the president. Still, these constraints are easily overshadowed by the access to power and public attention that these appointees enjoy.

In sharp contrast, when we think about, say, African Americans in the South during the 1950s, obvious constraints loom larger than opportunities. Many supporters of civil rights could not even vote, much less introduce legislation in Congress or a state legislature or call a press conference that might be attended. They were likely to be poorer, less educated, and more distant from any meaningful levels of power than a Soros, a McNamara, or an Ashcroft—to say the least. They also would be far more likely to be arrested or beaten by police officers than those advocates within government—or even the white college students who sometimes joined them in struggles for civil rights. To make the point more generally, the way in which an individual is viewed by the larger society—and the resources she brings to the political cause—influences directly both the availability and the viability of the range of tactics. The press conference is a reasonable strategy for someone who thinks the press is likely to show up; the petition campaign is a reasonable strategy for someone who can coordinate large numbers of volunteers—or pay to staff a campaign. The familiar peaceful demonstration is a bad tactical choice for individuals or groups that can't assemble large numbers. Imagine, for example, a "rich persons' march on Washington." Such a march would be unlikely, first, because rich people have more direct ways to project political influence, and second, because such a tactic squanders the assets rich people have in order to have them compete on terrain (numbers) where they do not enjoy such an advantage.

When a large group of doctors makes a pronouncement about the wisdom of a proposed change in medical policy, it is more likely to be heard than a comparable group of, say, supermarket workers. This is a function of status and perceived expertise.

Groups that lack resources of numbers, wealth, and status are more likely to take on the risks of civil disobedience or violence. One critical component of making a wise tactical choice is making sense of the resources of your group and yourself. Numbers, status, expertise, organization, commitment, and social location all matter in important ways, and the savvy activist tries to match the tactic with the resources of the constituency.

The impact of any collective action is a function of many things, but the match of tactics to resources is critical (Tilly 1978). Large numbers of people engaged in a common action draw attention, and the larger the numbers, the less dramatic the action taken has to be. People with higher status or recognized expertise in an area can command attention without numbers or dramatic action; a former general, for example, criticizing a military posture enjoys more credibility than someone without such a commission—regardless of his training or opinions. A few dozen winners of the Nobel Prize, by issuing a statement, can generate more publicity than tens of thousands of nonprize winners. Importantly, however, there is a great deal of variation in the way in which groups of people are regarded— in other words, there's a lot of range between a general or Nobel Prize winner and an everyday citizen, and status and expertise can be fairly specialized.

Race, occupation, income, and location all influence how a collective action is regarded, and activists often spend a great deal of effort trying to make sure that they are regarded as worthy and appropriate spokespeople for their causes. When veterans of the First World War marched on Washington to demand their service bonuses, they emphasized that they had served the United States and were therefore worthy. Others have to work even harder to establish their legitimacy and worthiness as collective actors. As mentioned earlier, the four young men who started the Greensboro sit-in in 1960 dressed in their best clothes, wearing jackets and ties, to demonstrate both their seriousness and their worthiness. Large numbers can compensate for fewer resources of other kinds. More dramatic action can compensate for smaller numbers. And so on. Like someone considering whether or not to attend a party, a potential activist thinking about, say, attending a demonstration, is likely to think about who else will be there. It's not just about rubbing elbows with friends or celebrities, but also about encountering a supportive vision of self: these people are like me.

Identity: A Sense of Self

Just as there is a set of resources that is inherent to every movement campaign, activists and organizations bring to bear their own beliefs about who they are and what's appropriate for them to do. Physicians may not have to break the law to get attention, but they may also not wish to do so, viewing it as a violation of their professional identity. People are always most likely to embrace tactics that feel comfortable and familiar, that are consonant with their images of themselves. Religious Catholic activists who spill their own blood on missile silos or sit in prayer in the doorways of women's health clinics take on tactics that feel like an expression of their moral and spiritual identities but that would be anathema to others who share their political concerns. They witness for their beliefs and see their actions as being consonant with those beliefs.

People start with images of themselves as moral, pragmatic, idealistic, consistent, disruptive, gentle, or committed that shape what they will consider doing. One who takes pride in a "pragmatic" conception of himself might be loathe not only to throw blood, but also to show up at a street demonstration—whose connections to policy are far more attenuated than those of more conventional political acts, such as voting or donating money. The activist's conception of himself or herself is challenged by any activity beyond the normal day-to-day politics, and in certain contexts, even registering to vote can represent a challenge. Transgressive behavior, including breaking laws or rudely challenging authorities, is a particularly difficult step for most people to take.

Like individuals, groups are also constrained by organizational identities (see Clemens 1993) that make some tactics possible and eliminate others. Here members of the professional staff of an organization are attentive not only to how they see the organization, but also to how a range of outside actors sees the organization. Tax-exempt organizations must be mindful of the Internal Revenue Service, their own board of directors or trustees, and their funders. They must also pay attention to those they seek to influence and to think not only of the battle at hand, but also of the organization's longer-term plans and prospects. An organization's identity constrains actions and issues, and these things are always risky to change. Partly for this reason, new campaigns and efforts often spur the formation of new organizations, which enjoy more flexibility in defining themselves through new actions and issues.

The prospects for political influence are always a consideration in picking tactics, but it's almost always impossible to tell what action is likely to be most effective in changing the actions or minds of those who make policy. Indeed, the safest assumption is always that collective action won't work and that when it does, there will always be plenty of alternative explanations for any change.

PROTEST AS COMMUNICATIVE ACTION

If the direct effects of social movement actions are usually extremely limited, then we need to consider efforts as being bigger than those effects. In the United States, and for that matter in all of the wealthy democracies, government and society serve as not only targets, but also mediators between social movement activists and their targets. In this regard, we need to consider every action by a social movement, every tactic, as both a performance and as a means of *communicating*. Further, every tactic has three broad and distinct audiences, who are themselves composed of different groups. We can gain additional understanding of the role of tactics by considering these audiences separately: *authorities, activists,* and *bystanders.* Communication with these audiences is broadly possible only with the help of *mass media,* which can affect the presentation of the message and activists to others, as we will consider. Ultimately, the media become a fourth audience.

A tactic sends a message to authorities about a group's commitment, size, claims, and potential to disrupt. A tactic also sends a message to *activists* about the same things. And a tactic sends a message to *bystanders* about a group's concerns, intentions, and worthiness. In every case, activists hope and plan for responses: concessions or repression from authorities; intensified commitment from activists; and support from bystanders, either by joining in the struggle directly or by pressuring authorities to respond to activists. The audiences themselves interact and affect one another, such that a social movement's actions push events without much control of what happens in response—for good and bad.

Authorities

But this view is so general that we can take it apart more, category by category. Let's start with authorities. At any given time in the United States, most movements face both sympathetic and antagonistic authorities, often at different levels of government—remember, political variation within government is what James Madison planned. Obviously these people have their own agendas, which include keeping or increasing their own power—as well as any commitments to issues or constituencies. A social movement event becomes a piece of ammunition that can be deployed by either side in a debate. The pressure of disruption, for example, can put an issue on the political agenda but can simultaneously discredit those who are advocating for change and legitimate government repression.

Further, action within different political venues demands different norms and tactics, which operate as constraints on choice of claims and tactics. Achieving influence through the legal system means marshaling legal arguments and avoiding extrainstitutional appearances. Influence within Congress, for example, is more likely if a group or movement can mobilize people to participate in electoral politics, organizing voters and contributing money. Replacing one member of Congress with an ally through elections is more likely to exercise effects by communicating the strength and commitment of a movement than by shifting one of 435 votes on an issue. One targeted defeat may cause some others to moderate their positions by making an explicit threat, to work in elections effectively, credible. Achieving influence is generally about convincing policymakers of unpleasant consequences if they don't respond.

At the same time, whereas the authorities who make decisions about the matters of policy that activists generally protest are often far away from the site of protest, other authorities must deal with the actual protest tactic. Police respond to protesters who threaten even the slightest disruption and to all large groups, regardless of how disruptive their intentions are. Although police officers may have their own political preferences, the responses to protest are not generally about those preferences, but rather about maintaining local control of an event (McCarthy and McPhail 1998). For activists who want to influence more distant audiences, it is essential that whatever takes place between police and activists turn attention to the cause, rather than to the nature of the event itself. Here we can think again of the kind of curve outlined in our discussion of political opportunity. A demonstration that doesn't threaten directly to disrupt can be easily managed by police, and even if it's large, generally ignored by policymakers. A demonstration that threatens destruction of property or violence against people can invite repression, and the tactics of activists can obscure whatever motivated them to act in the first place.

We can see these dynamics, and concern about these dynamics, playing out in the long and public debate about civil rights, jobs, and the 1964 World's Fair, held in New York. The Brooklyn chapter of the Congress of Racial Equality (CORE) had been trying, with limited success, to get attention and action from the city and local businesses on discrimination and to encourage the creation of more jobs. The CORE group saw the World's Fair, held in the neighboring borough of Queens, as an opportunity, openly speculating about the disruption that would occur if just a few dozen cars suddenly ran out of gas on the highways approaching the fair (Purnell 2001). The threat itself generated a great deal of attention, most of it negative. Established civil rights organizations, led by the NAACP, chastised the CORE group, arguing that such a tactic would set the cause of civil rights back years. Pro-civil rights senators criticized the CORE group on the floor of Congress, and a spirited debate took place within activist circles and on the editorial pages of the major newspapers about the justifiability and wisdom of the proposed "stall-in." Supporters argued that desperate times call for desperate measures, that in a world that is unfair, maybe people should not have such an easy time getting to a World's Fair. Opponents argued that the connections were too strained and that the stall-in would alienate potential supporters of the civil rights movement by creating costs for the city and for people just trying to get to work. For nearly a year, the debate raged locally, occasionally spilling into national media. On the day of the proposed action, April 22, 1964, a Wednesday, there was no noticeable disruption in traffic.

Activists

From this intramovement debate, we can now look at the effect of tactical choice on a social movement. We recall that every movement is comprised of activists with a diverse range of commitments and concerns. In order to be effective, a tactic has to speak to their experiences and not suggest actions they find abhorrent. As example, the dramatic action of a Paul Hill, in shooting and killing a physician who performed abortions, or a Timothy McVeigh, in blowing up a federal building, has a polarizing—and ultimately demobilizing—effect within the social movement each thought he supported. A successful tactic will embolden or energize more activists, without pushing away other sympathizers. It will communicate to other activists the possibilities of change and enhance the feeling of political agency, that is, that people like them can make a difference.

Bystanders

Finally, and probably most importantly, are the bystanders. As we've stressed, most people are not only not activists, but also not active politically most of the time. Recalling E. E. Schattschneider's (1960) advice about watching the crowd in a fight, we will do well to focus on the public responses to social movement tactics. A tactic takes on meaning as it generates attention and response from authorities, both proximate, such as police, and more distant, such as policymakers. The performance of an act of social protest etches an image of all the players involved into a broader public view and takes on political meaning as it affects the activities of all those involved—and those watching—afterward.

We can use the efforts of the AIDS movement in the 1980s as a means for exploring these issues. In a shorthand reading of the three sorts of events mentioned earlier, those at the candlelight vigil represented concern about an issue. They could safely be ignored by authorities, yet they could pique the conscience of those who saw them, encouraging others to pay attention to AIDS. The ACT-UP protesters who spat at physicians or clerics at conferences were acting out defiantly; they meant to bring attention not only to the issue, but also to themselves as potentially powerful and disruptive collective actors who would force authorities to respond—if not to the issues, at least to their efforts. Meanwhile, those who made and displayed the AIDS Names Project Quilt publicly shared their feelings of human loss. In the quilt, the participants could try to forge empathetic ties with their audience: feel what I feel. A dramatic ACT-UP confrontation takes on meaning as an audience chooses sides, seeing the activists as desperate crusaders or deranged deviants and seeing the beleaguered doctors as innocent victims or insensitive bureaucrats. To the extent that an activity has the potential of engaging the crowd on behalf of the activists, it becomes powerful, demanding a response from authorities seeking to prevent that power from developing.

Obviously, actors within these three broad categories of audiences interact with each other in ways that aren't always predictable. The successful mobilization of bystanders, for example, can leverage additional pressure on policymakers—or cause the resistance to dig in; in a related way, police repression of protesters can heighten the fear of potential activists, turning people away from a campaign, or it can demonstrate injustice and mobilize additional participation.

Take, for example, the recent case of a self-described peace and environmental activist who identifies the large consumption of oil as a major cause of American foreign policies he finds abhorrent, the most urgent of which is the war against Iraq. According to the FBI, this young man visited a car dealership early one morning before it opened and planted ten bombs underneath some of the cars. He was responsible for destroying 125 sport utility vehicles and the dealership office, doing an estimated $3.5 million in damage (Krikorian and Chong 2004). The number of people who shared his cause is surely much larger than the number of people who endorsed his conduct. His conduct could bring attention to his cause but not necessarily welcome attention. If people who share his beliefs are widely seen as those who use bombs to make their points, the issues probably lose more support than they gain. Still, the issues are there.

The Unabomber

The case of Ted Kaczynski's struggle over eighteen years to stop environmental and human degradation raises the same issues of public support. Kaczynski mailed camouflaged bombs to twenty-three people whom he believed were at the roots of this degradation by technology: computer programmers, engineering professors, technology advocates, advertisers, airline officials, and so forth. He killed three of them and wounded sixteen, some severely. FBI investigators, followed by the mass media, called the unnamed killer the "Unabomber." Tiring of this tack, he also must have realized that murder and mail terror—at least by themselves—would not achieve his political goals. He said, in a letter to editors of *The New York Times,* that his organization, FC, would stop the attacks if the *Times* published his manifesto, decrying technological modernization and its effects on the environment and human life.

In consultation with the FBI, the *Washington Post* published the manifesto, "Industrial Society and Its Future," which was nearly thirty thousand words long, as a small-type, eight-page supplement to the paper, splitting the costs of publication with *The New York Times.* Kaczynski and the government shared an interest in getting his words out and widely circulated. For the Unabomber, it was a more direct way than letter bombs to promote his ideas—on his own conditions, complete and unedited. For the government, it presented the opportunity to get out more information on the bomber, perhaps to someone who knew him, who might then come to the FBI with information about how to track him down.

The FBI's bet paid off better than Kaczynski's did—or at least sooner. Reading through the manifesto, David Kaczynski recognized his brother's ideas and his language. Deeply worried about his brother and horrified by the letter bombs, David negotiated through a lawyer with authorities to turn in the Unabomber, with the understanding that his brother would not be subject to the death penalty. Roughly six months after the manifesto appeared in print, in April 1996, the FBI arrested Theodore Kaczynski in his remote and austere Montana cabin.

The ensuing trial played out as a tragedy over more than two years, with Theodore Kaczynski ultimately alienated not only from the American justice system, but also from his brother and his attorneys. His troubled and unusual background, which included an undergraduate degree at Harvard University, a Ph.D. in math at the University of Michigan, and an appointment to the faculty of the University of California, Berkeley, was followed by life as a recluse in Montana, borrowing small sums of money from his family, riding an old bicycle to town, trapping rabbits and growing vegetables for food, and complaining about technology. Ultimately, he was sentenced to life in prison.

Although Kaczynski's text is widely available on the Internet, the story of the Unabomber is not generally one of ideas, but rather one of psychological torment. Indeed, there really isn't anything in the manifesto that wasn't widely available beforehand. Despite publication by major newspapers and the big promotion given it by years of drama, it has vanished in the clutter of polemics that fills bookshelves and virtual space on the Internet. Activists within the environmental movement don't claim him as an ally or an activist. Indeed, Kaczynski's personal story, surely to his ongoing torment, is all that remains of decades of what he saw as a fundamentally moral and political struggle. In our terms, it was a clear example of failed communication. Could it have been otherwise?

In focusing on the issue of communication, it's critical to recognize that the efforts of activists are rarely about direct communication with authorities (they don't have the access) or audiences (they don't have the resources). Rather, their efforts reach broader audiences only as mediated by others. We now turn to the role of mass media in the projection and framing of protest.

MEDIA AS AUDIENCE AND INTERPRETER: MARKETS AND AUDIENCES

The *Washington Post* printed Theodore Kaczynski's own words, but it used far more newsprint, over a much longer period of time, to describe his actions and his background. To a large degree, social movement activists are dependent upon the mass media to project their ideas and actions to a broader audience. Indeed, upon returning home from a demonstration, it's common for activists to switch on the television and radio, to see whether their actions and ideas were covered at all and then to examine how much and how. Given the size and scope of the United States, mediated communication is a necessary component of any movement strategy (Ryan 1991; Rohlinger 2002). Activists must consider the mass media as an audience for their efforts and also as a medium of transmission of information to reach others. Understanding the nature of media in the United States will help us understand how the dynamics associated with movement media relations play out.

First, *media* is a plural noun (*medium* is the singular form). The mass media in the United States are comprised of numerous outlets, including newspapers, magazines, television stations and networks, radio stations and networks, and Web sites. To speak about the political bias of "the media" simplifies to the point of distortion, even though we hear advocates on both ends of the political spectrum doing so constantly. There is, instead, considerable variety within the media, even considering outlets that aspire to reach relatively large audiences. Although particular outlets have explicit political commitments or orientations, to be sure, the media include a range of such commitments. It's more helpful to consider this range in order to see the operating of the media and their relation to social movements in America.

Second, unlike in most other rich countries, almost all media outlets in the United States are not owned and operated by the government, and most operate as businesses. The dominant business model is one in which advertisers pay for most of the operations and profits of a media outlet. Take, for example, the newspaper model. Although the major newspapers in the United States charge for subscriptions or single copies, the money they collect in this way covers only a small part of production costs. Most revenue comes from advertisers. Pick up a newspaper today and flip through the pages, and you'll see that most of the space isn't devoted to news, but rather to advertising. Because publishers and businesses can arrange advertisements in advance, they are laid out first, with space left aside for news and features yet to be written; this is called a "news hole," which papers must fill each day. In contrast to the famous *New York Times* slogan, it's less "all the news that's fit to print" than all the news that fits.

Advertisers pay newspapers to run their ads in hopes that people will see them: In other words, they pay for access to an audience that includes people who might buy their products. The larger and more attractive the audience, the more advertisers are willing to pay. All audiences, of course, are not equal. Although advertisers are generally willing to pay larger fees for larger audiences, they are also interested in targeting their efforts to the readers or viewers most relevant to their products. Manufacturers of, say, skateboarding gear are understandably reluctant to pay to reach senior citizens, and insurance companies are less interested in reaching teenagers than people old enough to be likely to think about buying insurance. Advertisers want to reach people they think will be interested in what they have to offer.[2] Take a look at who advertises in the papers and magazines you read or on the television shows you watch, and you'll get some sense of who advertisers think you are.

The content in a paper is designed explicitly to deliver audiences to advertisers. Indeed, take a look at the distinct sections in a daily paper, and you'll get a sense of how targeted advertisers are—and how responsive papers can be. The business section, for example, is generally filled with ads touting computer products and wireless communication, whereas the sports section features ads for sporting goods, tires, and hair restoration products; the arts section hosts large ads about new movies, the real estate section features listings of available properties, and the automotive section features car advertisements. This is all a function of who advertisers think reads each of these sections—and newspapers do

---

[2] In fact, advertisers will work to make sure the places they advertise provide content they think will interest their target demographic. Gloria Steinem (1990), formerly editor of *Ms. Magazine,* an organ of the feminist movement, explained that the magazine's dependence on advertisers could actually affect its content. Advertisers with deep pockets often demanded "complementary content," that is, features that would support their advertising: recipes for food companies, beauty features for cosmetics companies, and so forth. Rather than continue to solicit such ads and negotiate—or refuse to negotiate— such compromises, *Ms.* adopted a new business model that rejected advertising altogether.

extensive self-studies and surveys to provide information about their readers, broken down by section. To at least some extent, the need to please advertisers drives content. The typical automotive section is more than 90 percent ads, but papers will assign a reporter to write a piece in each issue describing a new car. It's doubtful that the automobile industry generates enough *news* in most media markets to justify a full section, absent the willingness of dealers and manufacturers to buy ad space all the time.

Although newspapers may have political biases, the business bias is almost always stronger. A publisher's prime concern is printing news that will attract readers. This does generate a bias, but one that is directed to attractive stories, those that feature conflict, celebrities, and drama generally. A successful editor, whatever her professional commitments, will keep an eye on the readers' interests. This does generate a bias in news coverage, but not one that can be neatly defined as liberal or conservative. Rather, editors are biased in favor of stories and presentation of stories that they see as attractive. This means that the bulk of any newspaper will be stories that an editor thinks people will want to read, that readers will find *interesting*. Being interesting is not the same as being *important*. The quality of the air or the state of technological education in the United States is clearly important, but it is likely to be less intrinsically interesting to most readers than a movie star's latest relationship woes. Further, newspapers are heavily biased toward covering *news,* thought of as something that is different today than yesterday. "Nuclear weapons still exist" or "Americans don't like to pay taxes" are headlines we're unlikely to see because they don't represent news.

Successful newspapers print all kinds of material every day that are designed explicitly to generate an audience, and it's hard to think of it all as news. Take a look at your local paper, and you're almost certain to find television and movie listings, a comics page, and a horoscope. The health and business sections will feature a large share of news the reader can use: a report on how to start an individual retirement account or an evaluation of a new diet. There will be a sports section, in which the most recent games, matches, or meets are covered as news, although the long-term importance of such events is almost always limited to life inside a sport. Printing such features is all about generating an audience.

A large part of the newspaper is laid out and determined by factors far outside the control of activists, reporters, or even editors. Amid the advertising and features, activists compete for attention in the news. Here it helps to think about the world of the reporter, who needs to generate publishable copy, often on short deadlines. When an editor makes decisions about what news to cover each day, the reporter has to decide what to put in a story. The pressures of deadlines and the conventions of journalism guide much of what happens next. The reporter will attend an event—if she knows in advance when it will happen, where, and how to get there. She'll phone call people for reactions, developing a clear bias in favor of people and organizations that return phone calls by her deadlines, and speak to the issues she's reporting on—in other words, for groups that understand what she needs to do her job. This gives an advantage to groups that have phones and people who will be sitting by them. This means that those who have listed phone numbers, sit in permanent offices, and employ paid staff are more likely to appear in the news than are others. The greatest advantage, of course, goes to elected officials and government offices; they routinely employ press officers whose primary responsibility is to provide the mass media with information they can use. Activists for any cause start with a disadvantage, but one they can manage if they attend to the workings of the media and focus their efforts accordingly (Ryan 1991).

The reporter, typically a general assignment reporter, who covers a protest action is unlikely to develop deep expertise in the issues being contested because she will be covering a wide variety of issues on a day-to-day basis. Simply, she doesn't have the time. The time pressures, in conjunction with the generalist training of journalists and the focus on events, rather than issues, that defines most journalism, explain most of what appears in mainstream news. Understanding the constraints, we can see why journalists rely on institutional sources for news, cover novelty, and use familiar scripts and forms for doing so.

Now we need to situate that newspaper in a larger universe of media outlets. The same pressures that face the journalist working for a newspaper are multiplied and intensified when we turn to television stations. The costs of production and the scarcity of time and space mean that social movement activists face a steep uphill struggle in trying to get coverage on the television news. And again, networks feature all kinds of stories that are picked because of their capacity to generate audiences, rather than their intrinsic importance.

Television stations, radio stations, daily newspapers, and general interest and specialized journals all play distinct roles in a larger prism of the mass media. Each cultivates a distinct, but not exclusive, audience. Moreover, as cable television, blogs, and the Internet generally have proliferated, even large audiences are smaller than ever before. Thus, whereas we think about television news and large daily papers as targeting a "mass" audience, other media outlets succeed by delivering specific, targeted audiences to advertisers. The audiences can be sorted by interest, geographic region, age, gender, job, or even politics. It's a mistake to treat all media outlets as the same, in terms of getting an activist message in, or in terms of reaching and influencing the public debate in a dramatic way. Deana Rohlinger (2004) suggests that in thinking about the mass media and movements, it makes sense to conceive media as a prism. Whereas specialized media at the edges of the political spectrum may be easiest for like-minded activists to reach and present their information to, they don't reach a broad new audience. In contrast, the mainstream mass media, which are targeted to a broad audience, offer a higher payoff for getting in but also the prospects of greater distortion—and of course, a greater challenge for getting in to begin with. The increased prevalence of Internet blogs and Web sites make it easier and easier for individuals to engage only viewpoints they already share and to avoid unwelcome information at the same time. In essence, people are able to find information that serves and reinforces what they already believe. The good news for social movement activists is that this growing supply of dedicated media, in effect, online movement organs, allows activists to reach many of their faithful without ever engaging mass media. At the same time, in order to engage and mobilize a broader audience, mass media remain essential.

The mass media are critical for getting movement messages and movement activities to a larger audience; they are also critical for defining a challenging group and a political issue to allies, opponents, and authorities. For these reasons, we need to view the mass media as both a target for activist efforts and a conduit of activist messages to authorities, allies, opponents, and bystanders. Media coverage identifies issues as salient, as potentially amenable to action, and also projects an image of who is acting and how. Social movement organizations have an interest in getting out to a broader audience nothing their issues, but also information about their activities and in having their elements *framed* in a favorable way. This means having the issues presented in a way that suggests the necessity of citizen action and the potential of political influence. Further, because there are always multiple organizations working on each side of the political issue, groups have an interest in being identified as the relevant—and responsible—actor in a dispute. In other words, although it's great to have your argument made in the mass media, it's also important to have your organization credited with making it.

WINNING ATTENTION

In terms of getting coverage in the mass media, the first fact for activists to keep in mind is that their issues generally aren't making news. To observe, for example, that there is tremendous economic inequality in the United States and that poor people have a hard time managing describes a *condition,* not an *event*—or even a broadly recognized problem. The mass media are ill disposed to cover conditions or issues. At some points, however, issues become events when something else is tied to them. If Congress is considering a bill, for example, or the Supreme Court is about to issue a decision, then the issue is tied to an event, which affords an opportunity for media coverage. Journalists call the event a "news peg," on which they can hang a story. By their actions, institutional actors can create what scholars call "critical discourse movements," that is, times when a set of issues is salient and likely to receive coverage. Some events are predictable or even recurrent. Budgets need to be passed, and governors and presidents have deadlines for making their presentations for legislative proposals. The presentation of budgets, for example, gives activists a chance to talk about their issues if they are funded by government—or could be.

Anniversaries and some holidays are also predictable times for getting issues out. Crusaders against hunger or poverty know that journalists use the Thanksgiving holiday for covering these issues. August 6 and 9 are the anniversaries of the dropping of atomic bombs on Hiroshima and Nagasaki, respectively, and afford antinuclear activists the opportunity to talk about nuclear weapons issues. Both abortion rights activists and antiabortion activists, as another example, use the January anniversary of the 1973 *Roe v. Wade* decision on abortion rights to stage commemorations, figuring that journalists will use the occasion to discuss the issue.

Accidents, crimes, and international events can also create critical discourse moments. When the nuclear power plant at Three Mile Island, Pennsylvania, shut down with a malfunction in March of 1979, antinuclear power activists around the United States had a new opportunity to make arguments they'd been honing for years and to bring those arguments to a much broader audience. High-profile crimes also afford activists an opening in the mass media, if they can attach their demands to them—and it doesn't always take a crime. Feminists enjoyed an opportunity to frame the issue of sexual harassment when, unexpectedly, the confirmation hearings of a man nominated to serve on the Supreme Court, Clarence Thomas, produced one witness accusing him of inappropriate behavior in the workplace. The nomination hearings provided an unanticipated occasion for social movement activists to discuss the broader issues as well as the specific case. The August 1955 murder of Emmitt Till, a fourteen-year-old boy from Chicago who was visiting family in Mississippi, gave advocates of civil rights a chance to get their perspective into the mass media by providing a window into segregation and discrimination in the South. Similarly, high-profile rape trials have always allowed antirape and feminist activists to offer their analyses of the larger problem and to make their recommendations about social and legal change. Social movements can take advantage of the event when organizers work to position themselves to comment on it.

Activists can also create events. During World War II, Bayard Rustin, a peace and civil rights activist, floated the idea of a mass march on Washington, DC, in which activists would argue for government action for civil rights. Racial segregation in the military during the war provided an impetus for Rustin to make civil rights claims, but the idea of a march on Washington went far beyond that narrow issue. For years, this idea circulated around activist circles, and in 1963, Rustin finally organized the event in conjunction with the leaders of the major civil rights organizations of the day. The occasion of more than a quarter-million activists converging on the Mall in front of the Lincoln Memorial created a news peg for journalists to use in writing about civil rights and the civil rights movement. Papers across the nation were filled with stories and pictures of the march, with particular attention given to Martin Luther King's "I Have a Dream" speech.

The large demonstration is a staple tactic for social movement organizations seeking attention, and if well timed and well attended, it can afford the media the chance to write about the issues. Of course, such an event can overshadow the issues, or conduct at the demonstration can undermine coverage of the issues. As Todd Gitlin (1980) notes in his account of media coverage of Students for a Democratic Society, daily newspapers and television news covered demonstrations in ways that ultimately undermined the organization in particular and hurt the antiwar movement in general. Counterdemonstrators, for example, who supported the war were given equivalent coverage in most stories, even though their numbers were much smaller. In this way, organizing a demonstration created an opportunity for the opposition. Journalists generally focused on the most colorful, that is, disruptive or bizarre, elements at a demonstration, thus discrediting the movement as a whole. Further, partly because of SDS's internal problems, activists themselves got most of their information on the movement and SDS from mainstream media. In effect, CBS News and *The New York Times* appointed leaders for the movement, identifying people who would produce good stories for them. Unable to control its own message, SDS was particularly vulnerable to being defined by outsiders—and not to its advantage.

In order to be newsworthy, demonstrations generally have to be large (McCarthy, McPhail, and Smith 1996), but the larger the demonstration is, the harder it is to control. What's more, organizing a demonstration is extremely time-consuming and expensive, in terms of both money and other organizational resources. Some elements of coverage are inherent in the nature of an event. Events that are large, dramatic, new, and filled with conflict and at least the potential of disruption are always more likely to get coverage. But timing also matters a great deal. Events that reflect issues that journalists view as significant or politically ripe are more likely to be covered than others, thus turning us back to our focus on the political context. To create news pegs, social movement organizations can do other things that offer different benefits and risks.

Drama and Coverage

We can start with the most disruptive sorts of actions, including violence against self and others. In the United States, resorting to violence for a social movement is always a risk; because of the relative openness of the political system, groups that use violence are easy to brand as criminals. Even opponents of the draft turned against the rioters. When activists in the antiabortion movement kill doctors or threaten to kill doctors, the story of the crime obscures much discussion of the cause. The news stories are more frequently about the event than the cause, which doesn't serve the movement well. Violence against one's self sometimes works a little better. In 1965, as the movement against the Vietnam War was growing, activists started a lobbying effort to curtail growing military involvement in Vietnam, but activists felt they hit roadblocks almost immediately. On March 16, following the model of a few Buddhist monks in Vietnam, Alice Herz, eighty-two years old, a Quaker, and a member of Women's International League for Peace and Freedom, doused herself with gasoline and set herself on fire on a street in Detroit. This act brought attention to the seriousness of some people's opposition to the war (DeBenedetti and Chatfield 1990: 107). Herz also inspired others to follow her example. In November, another Quaker, thirty-two-year-old Norman Morrison, committed self-immolation in front of the Pentagon. The event and the cause were widely reported, so much so that hundreds of counterdemonstrators in New York responded to the organized burning of draft cards—another protest against the war— with the chant, "Burn yourselves, not your cards!" (DeBenedetti and Chatfield 1990: 129). Obviously, this attention comes at great cost.

Transgressing the law in some way can also generate a news peg for the mass media, and flames are photogenic. Beyond burning draft cards, activists within the antiwar movement also burned draft files. In a dramatic act of civil disobedience, on May 17, 1969, Catholic priests Daniel and Philip Berrigan, along with seven others, entered a draft board near Catonsville, Maryland, seized as many files as they could carry, and covered them with a homemade napalm. This burning also drew a great deal of attention to the cause—and to the Berrigans, who would employ similar tactics in the service of their causes over the next thirty-five years. Here, too, however, the disruption and violence of the act, although generating attention, can overshadow the cause that inspires it. This was certainly the case as others—and the Berrigans themselves—repeated their act of witness.

Although such dramatic action can sometimes draw attention to the issues activists care about, it also carries the inherent risk of deflecting attention away from those very issues. Further, what comprises news changes over time, and an act if repeated often enough, it is no longer newsworthy. Thus, the first civil disobedience actions by antiabortion activists in front of women's health clinics received good play in the media but soon became routine for journalists. In order to make something newsworthy, activists need to escalate—by increasing the numbers who turn out or changing the tactic to something more attention-getting. In looking at the media coverage of the new left, Todd Gitlin noted (1980: 182), "Where a picket line might have been news in 1965, it took tear gas and bloodied heads to make headlines in 1968." Of course, when the solemnity of a picket or a vigil or a disciplined civil disobedience action is no longer newsworthy, what might be newsworthy is often so because it is easily dismissible.

Activist organizations can also create their own news in ways that may be harder to dismiss—if easier to ignore. Calling a press conference and announcing the results of a study are other ways to get media attention. So, when a group announces a new effort to get involved in an electoral campaign or to target its efforts toward a particular issue, a press release can generate attention—if other circumstances are in alignment (slow news day; editors or public concerned with the issue). Similarly, a report of information from a study about an issue of concern—the rate of taxation, the numbers of abortions, the rise or decline in poverty—can generate attention, particularly if it comes with convenient and interesting facts. Of course, the organization promoting the issue is there to control the frame and some aspects of the coverage.

Celebrities and Regular People

Famous participants not normally known for politics can also generate attention for a movement or movement organization. In the mass media, celebrities are people who are well known, to use Daniel Boorstin's (1973) clever turn of phrase, "for being well-known" (Meyer and Gamson 1995). Because journalists know that photos of famous actors or musicians can help sell papers and magazines, the presence of celebrity is one way to break through the clutter of the mass media to gain attention. However, at the same time, the political story itself is changed into a celebrity story and can often be discredited as a result.

The campaign to preserve Walden Pond offers an instructive example. Although notable for its role in Henry Thoreau's life and writing, Walden Pond, as Thoreau himself acknowledged, is much like hundreds of other ponds in New England. Because of Thoreau's status in American literature, however, the state of Massachusetts created a small park around Walden Pond, offering swimming and nature trails. In Concord, Massachusetts, a local real estate developer proposed the construction of townhouses directly abutting the pond, generating intense opposition. Local activists succeeded in convincing numerous celebrities, including a group of southern California musicians, most visibly Don Henley of the Eagles, to join their efforts to resist development. Local media were quick to report on the efforts of the celebrities—and to ridicule their lack of knowledge about the area, local politics, and even the environment. Development supporters were effective in injecting countervailing issues, particularly the issue of low-income housing, for which the celebrities were unprepared. Although development stalled, it stalled at a price for all involved. Now it has become almost formulaic to dismiss activist celebrities as embracing the cause of the moment—without any necessary understanding of the cause.

Indeed, during the long lead-up to the 2003 war on Iraq, one notable and persistent opponent of the war was Janeane Garofalo, an actress-comedienne. Garofalo reports that she was often picked to represent the antiwar case by reporters and television hosts hostile to the antiwar movement, who would counterpose her arguments against those of a professor or military expert who supported the war. "They have actors on so they can marginalize the movement," she said. "It's much easier to toss it off as some bizarre, unintelligent special-interest group. If you're an actor who is pro-war, you're a hero. If you're an actor who's against the war, you're suspect. You must have a weird angle or you just hate George Bush" (quoted in Kurtz 2003). In effect, Garofalo argues, she was used to trivialize the causes she cared about (DeNovella 2003). Although an individual organization can choose to certify who speaks for it, a multiheaded movement can't exercise the same kind of control. Indeed, spokespeople identified by the mass media may have little to do with the organizational infrastructure of a movement. Whether or not Garofalo is correct in claiming that producers picked her because she was less schooled in the relevant issues than those people she debated, it is certainly true that her celebrity would be more attractive to television producers than a less famous person who might know more about foreign policy or Iraq.

So, the first challenge in dealing with the mass media is getting your issues addressed and your events covered. Beyond that, however, you want them covered in a way that legitimates your concerns and your identity, even encouraging others to do the same. In an odd way, such coverage, smooths rough edges off identities and off political analysis. The coverage of the activists supporting the nuclear freeze in the early 1980s, for example, was overwhelmingly positive (Rojecki 1999). Activists were consistently portrayed as normal people, "housewives, professionals, normal every day people . . ." But in the process of legitimating the activists, the mass media generally focused on a definition of their claim that was quite different from what freeze leaders actually wanted. Although the freeze was conceptualized by Randall Forsberg, who had written the proposal as the first modest step in a larger campaign to remake world politics, in the mass media it became an unfocused call for a return to the old arms control process and a demand for some restraint on the military build-up then in progress.

Focusing on the everyday people, the people who will seem familiar and comfortable to an imagined audience, often means ignoring or hiding the rough edges of a movement. Thus, when gay activists organizing for the right to same-sex marriage seek to portray themselves as normal, like everyone else, they may push drag queens to the edges of the parade. Animal rights activists focus on abuse of pets and don't emphasize the radical vegans in their midst, and peace activists speak in the language of pragmatism rather than pacifism. Managing the media is thus a difficult chore and a source for conflict within social movements, not the least because journalists are resistant to being managed.

Organizers

Finally, because organizations compete within a movement for attention and funding, activists want to get credit for what they do. The group that gets to speak for a large and diverse movement, such as the campaign against the war in Iraq, gets to define the profile of the movement as a whole: Is it pacifist? Anti-interventionist in general? Isolationist or internationalist? Does it condone civil disobedience or violence? Obviously, the profile of the movement affects its success with bystander publics and authorities, and the organization that gets the lion's share of attention will have advantages in getting new members and financial contributions as well. Thus, in her study of the abortion conflict in the United States, Deana Rohlinger (2004) found that Planned Parenthood, the National Abortion and Reproductive Rights Action League (NARAL), and NOW got most of the attention for the abortion rights side and that the National Right to Life Committee (NRLC) got most of the attention on the antiabortion side. Whereas a number of local groups followed the big three on the abortion rights side, there was no organization close to the NRLC on the antiabortion side. Indeed, disruptive and sometimes violent organizations that appeared for relatively short periods in a decades-long conflict, staging demonstrations or even killing doctors, dominated the profile of the movement for years at a time, much to the frustration of the majority of antiabortion activists because such organizations made it difficult for politicians to make concessions to the larger movement and made many people reluctant to join the larger movement.

Further, Rohlinger found that the media prism she identified worked in surprising ways. Although activist messages were far more likely to appear in targeted media outlets, such as political weekly magazines, the organizations themselves were unlikely to be profiled. Reporters, columnists, and editors told Rohlinger that they did not see a necessity for contacting organizations to get their views of the conflict because they shared their views. Thus, movement ideas got exposure with a friendly audience, but the organizations carrying them politically often didn't.

The most mainstream actions that movements embrace, such as lobbying, fundraising, or working in electoral campaigns, rarely generate much attention. They lack the drama of the protest or demonstration and also feature institutional actors prepared to explain what is going on and take credit for it. Being more common, they also are inherently less newsworthy. In some ways, for a movement to choreograph a strategy focused on public attention means emphasizing actions that are less clearly tied to mainstream politics and picking tactics that are more attractive to media than to policymakers.

SOCIAL MOVEMENT TACTICS

The point for activists is to pick tactics that promote a cause without obscuring or overshadowing it. In doing so, they can consider issues of resources, efficacy, audience, and identity. But there are always many unknowns. Those scheduling a demonstration can never reliably predict how many people will show up on the given day. Given all of this uncertainty, we need to consider why the patterns of social movement tactics have been remarkably constant over time. New ideas, such as the "stall-in" or the AIDS Names Project Quilt described earlier, are relatively rare and don't tend to stay on the menu for long. Indeed, given the range of possibilities, it is worthwhile to consider why the actual range of tactics that social movements in America have embraced remains relatively narrow (Tilly 1993). Even when we cross the ideological spectrum, we see activist groups on the left and right choosing mostly from a familiar menu of rallies, demonstrations, marches, and even civil disobedience tactics. The targets, issues, and claims change much more frequently than do the actual actions. Is it a failure of the imagination?

In fact, executing a social movement tactic means trying to activate responses from authorities, bystanders, and supporters, and therefore, resorting to a familiar form makes sense. Organizations, including those of authorities and challengers, seek to reduce risks, and employing a familiar tactic is an effective way to do this and to minimize the costs of taking a new action. Let's not be glib about what the nature of these risks can be. At the most mundane level, few people may turn out, and a great deal of planning can produce no visible mobilization or political effect. But it can be much worse: activists can fight, perhaps violently, among themselves, or factions can attack passersby or targets; authorities can react with violence such that activists are hurt or killed. The extent of risks means that, paradoxically, organizers tend to be strategically and tactically conservative. By this, I don't mean that they necessarily shy away from confrontation or from comprehensive claims, but rather that they are likely to try to re-create, rather than create, a new way to make their claims.

An activist coalition that opts to stage a demonstration can rely not only on the experience of the organizers within its midst, but also on its supporters, who have been to demonstrations before. They recognize a limited number of potential sites, depending upon their anticipated size and the layout of the city. They know where to rent sound equipment, where to set up in a public park that is proximate to bathrooms and electricity and offers easy access for attendees. They know printers or copy shops that can handle the volume of leaflets to be printed, how to make signs, whom to call for making speeches, and what time a demonstration can start. They also know how to make arrangements to clean up the area after the demonstration is over.

Beyond this, they also know the relevant authorities. Increasingly, activists negotiate with police in advance of a demonstration to ensure predictable outcomes—even if those outcomes include token violation of laws and arrests. The constraints of civil liberties mean that activists enjoy the constitutionally protected right to present their grievances, although local authorities are entitled to make restrictions for reasonable time and place. By negotiating with police in advance, demonstrators can work to ensure that their event will take place and that everyone involved will be able to get home safely. Police can determine a reasonable expectation of their staffing needs; if there is to be civil disobedience, they can make arrangements for stretchers and buses to transport protesters without hurting them and make sure there is space in arraignment courts so that protesters can be processed efficiently. Moreover, they can keep the rest of the city relatively protected from the effects of the activists.

Much of this is explicit. John McCarthy and Clark McPhail (1998) have detailed the development of "public order management systems," (POMS), that is, procedures to minimize violence, surprise, and ultimately disruption. Negotiated protests offer the advantages of both safety and predictability for all concerned. At the same time, however, they undermine one of the key resources that social movements can deploy, that is, disruption of the conduct of daily life. Oddly, the reliance on familiar tactics lends a kind of ritualized quality to a demonstration or picket. Because it's something that almost everyone has seen before, it is easier to dismiss or to categorize as another one of those events that enthrall or offend you. Because it is something that authorities have managed before, they can, with reasonably reliable expectations, count on managing it the next time out without overreacting.

Members of the mass media also play into this ritualization of protest. Organizers, having not only experience, but also maybe even explicit study of the media (e.g., Ryan 1991), can figure out how to capture the attention of journalists. They can figure out what sorts of images will be attractive to those with cameras, and they can prepare not only press releases, but also sound bites for interviewers. They often cultivate reporters and thus know whom to call well in advance of the event—and journalists know where to stand to get a good view yet avoid the action. Everything can happen smoothly, such that the ritualized conduct of a demonstration can itself be a kind of institutionalization of dissent.

In this chapter, we've explored the determinants and effects of activist choices about strategy and tactics. Activists make choices cognizant of the likely responses of supporters, authorities, and bystanders and pay particular attention to how their actions will be portrayed to those audiences. Taking any action changes the circumstances of all those who follow, such that the boundaries of the stage and the positioning of actors within it change over time. Activists are further bound by their sense of themselves, undertaking actions they see as consonant with who they are, and this filters out a whole range of potential actions for most people.

Importantly, we've seen that although the potential range of actions is wide, what actually takes place is rather narrow and strikingly familiar. Social movements march on Washington, D.C., regardless of the time, the issue, and the constituencies involved. After a tactic is safely established, it is picked up by a broader range of political actors and becomes another staple in the repertoire of collective action. We'll next turn to see what impact this has.

In the preceding discussions, we've outlined the dilemmas inherent in decisions about strategy and tactics. By looking at one common category of action, civil disobedience, we can see how the dilemmas play out in action.

CHAPTER 6

CIVIL DISOBEDIENCE

John LaForge and Barbara Katt were convicted of breaking into the Sperry Corporation's offices in Minnesota on October 11, 1984. Two months earlier they had poured their own blood onto two prototype computers for the Trident submarine guidance system and then smashed the keyboards with hammers, attempting to pacify in biblical style the swords of the modern era. They appealed their conviction on the grounds that they broke criminal trespass laws only to prevent the greater harm that would result from a nuclear war; they found a sympathetic response in the court. U.S. District Judge Miles Lord upheld the convictions but praised the activists, suspending their six-month sentences. He claimed his decision was an attempt "to force the government to remove the halo with which it seems to embrace any device which can kill and to place, instead, thereon a shroud—a shroud of death, destruction, mutilation, disease and debilitation . . . Can it be that those of us who build weapons to kill are engaged in a more sanctified endeavor than those who would by their acts attempt to counsel moderation and mediation as an alternative method of settling international disputes? What is so sacred about a bomb, so romantic about a missile? Why do we condemn and hang individual killers while extolling the virtues of the warmongers?" (quoted in Meyer 1990: 204).

Elizabeth Ann Tilson stood in front of a Wichita family planning clinic in August of 1992, trying to stop women who might want abortions from entering, as part of a larger campaign against abortion. She was convicted of criminal trespass, fined $1,000, and sentenced to six months in jail. She appealed her initial conviction, arguing, as Katt and LaForge did, that she broke trespass laws in order to prevent the violation of higher laws, specifically, the murder of unborn children; she found a similarly sympathetic judge. Sedwick County District Judge Paul W. Clark ruled in Tilson's favor on July 21, 1992, overturning her conviction, endorsing her defense, and stating from the bench that "The scientific community is of the opinion that life in homo sapiens begins at conception and harm is the result of termination of life under most circumstances" (*Ithaca Journal* 1992: 21).

Some observers would surely applaud both judges for fealty to higher laws—or condemn them both for ignoring state laws. I guess that most of us, however, would want to pick and choose among which higher laws to respect, urging judicial discretion and leniency for civil disobedients whom we find sympathetic. We need to think about civil disobedience as part of a larger social movement campaign's repertoire of action and understand it in the context of the larger dynamic of a social movement.

Civil disobedience has become a routine part of the repertoire of contention for challenging movements in the United States. Its movement across the political spectrum often confuses people who formerly defended the practice and endorsed the movements of the moment that used it. As civil disobedience has become more widespread, however, facile justifications and analyses are far more difficult; alliances and opponents have shifted, and definitions and qualifications have stretched or ossified along with the political sympathies of the analyst. Indeed, even Lt. Colonel Oliver North, then working in the National Security Council, cloaked himself in Henry Thoreau's mantle as a civil disobedient when he defended before Congress his decision to lie to Congress and conceal information about various illegal campaigns the Reagan administration conducted. Without endorsing the substance of his claims, much less its own definition as civil disobedience, the American Civil Liberties Union defended North, forging an odd alliance.

In looking at how activists actually employ civil disobedience in a variety of social movements, it's clear that its meaning changes depending upon context. Legal and political theorists define *civil disobedience* broadly as an open and public defiance of accepted law or norm, undertaken purposefully with the intent of altering state policy. Within this broad definition, there is considerable debate as to whether civil disobedience necessarily entails acceptance of state authority, recognized lack of other means of political influence, acceptance of criminal punishment, or avoidance of some degree of violence (Zashin 1970).

For civil disobedients, the symbols associated with standing against the government in the service of high moral purpose remain attractive, but the context associated with particular campaigns brings new meanings to the tactic. The preceding examples illustrate the inherent problems. In Tilson's case, the defendant's arrest was one of more than 2,700 (involving some 1,700 people) during forty-six days of antiabortion demonstrations in Wichita, part of Operation Rescue's Summer of Mercy campaign.[1] The antiabortion movement has powerful allies, including three of the previous four presidents, and civil disobedience and direct action are only a small part of its efforts, which include public education and electoral politics. Whereas some within the movement endorsed Operation Rescue and applauded Judge Clark's ruling, others feared the fallout of polarizing abortion politics.

Clark's decision allowed Tilson to go free, but it doesn't directly do much more than that. It doesn't change abortion policy in any way. Although it may encourage other antiabortion activists to emulate her example, Clark's decision does not ensure that any other antiabortion activist, or even Tilson herself, would receive similar dispensation from any other judge—or even from Clark on another day. By allowing Tilson to tell her story, explaining the place of civil disobedience in a larger moral and political narrative and amplifying that story, Clark's decision may spur additional civil disobedience, but this is hardly assured. By itself, this court, or even the Supreme Court, is extremely limited in what it can do to promote social and political change.

Similarly, Judge Miles Lord lamented that the most he could do from the bench was to free the Sperry disobedients and offer rhetorical endorsement. Like Tilson, LaForge and Katt were part of a much larger social protest movement, this one concerned with peace and nuclear weapons, a movement that as a whole maintained an ambivalent relationship to civil disobedience even as it staged a variety of challenges within the legal system and

---

[1] The antiabortion movement's use of the symbols and some of the tactics of the civil rights movement follow here, too, as the Summer of Mercy was clearly intended to evoke the romanticism and appeal of the Student Non-Violent Coordinating Committee's Freedom Summer (1964), which later appeared in Vietnam Summer (1968), Survival Summer (1977), Peace and Justice Summer (1984), and Union Summer, which started in 1996 and became a permanent training program for the AFL-CIO.

elsewhere in American politics (Levin 1992; Meyer 1990). Unlike the antiabortion movement, the antinuclear weapons movement of the 1980s lacked a powerful ally in the Oval Office, but it claimed greater public support, at least as expressed through public opinion polls. Even as Lord proclaimed the justice of the disobedients' cause, however, the movement in the streets was fading, and mainstream activists were increasingly comfortable distancing themselves and the movement from dramatic civil disobedience efforts (Epstein 1991; Meyer 1993a).

Clearly, in order to understand civil disobedience and its relationship to politics and policy, we need to understand its place in diverse and diversified social movement campaigns. Here we will review a brief history of civil disobedience and writing on civil disobedience in the United States, identifying two distinct forms, one collective and at least partly instrumental, the other individualistic and justified by claims to some kind of "higher laws." Analysts generally, and mistakenly, focus on only the individualistic form. In thinking about social movements, however, it is more important to consider a second, collectivist mode of civil disobedience in which civil disobedience actions are part of a larger social and political campaign and justified by claims to community norms in addition to any "higher laws." We are particularly concerned with how the practice and its meaning change across different contexts. There are two aspects of this issue: first, the transportability, or what Tarrow (1998) calls "modularity" of civil disobedience as a tactic from one movement to another; second, the relationship of civil disobedience to larger social movements, particularly in its changing visibility and role at different times in a protest cycle.

CIVIL DISOBEDIENCE AND/AS COLLECTIVE ACTION

Open, principled, and often political, defiance of law has a long history, and it is tempting to term in retrospect all cases of such activity "civil disobedience." Americans are familiar with two examples from Greek theater that offer distinct models, each carrying with it different political implications. In the first, Sophocles's *Antigone,* the heroine defies her uncle in seeking to bury her brother in accord with religious practice. The action is individual, ultimately futile, and tragic. The play ends with Antigone and her fiancé (the king's son) dead and the king himself living on to suffer. The second model comes from a Greek comedy by Aristophanes. In *Lysistrata,* the heroine and title character, exhausted by the ongoing wars around her, organizes women in Athens and in other warring states to stop sleeping with their husbands and taking care of their children until the men stop making war. The women also seize the treasuries in their homelands and do everything possible to make the ongoing conduct of war impossible. Frustrated, the men acquiesce to the women's wishes, and the play ends with peace and sex. In fact, *Lysistrata's* example, of civil disobedience as a practical political strategy carried out by communities, rather than a moral witness, is a more applicable model to most American instances of civil disobedience, but *Antigone's* model is far more familiar to most activists in the United States and certainly to most analysts.

We can compare these plays as archetypes of different models of civil disobedience. In both cases, the protagonists were women, people historically without much in the way of means, standing, or access for participation in conventional institutional politics. Lacking institutional routes for influence, and lacking the physical force to overturn or reshape the system, these activists attempted to exercise influence by ceasing to provide expected obedience and compliance and thereby to support tacitly the policies they challenged. Confrontation with the state was direct, but on terms other than those the state chose. Civil disobedience was politics by other means, a politics that is most attractive to those who perceive little prospect of meaningful political influence within institutional politics.

The differences between these models of civil disobedience are equally important. Antigone justified her act by reference to higher laws, in this case, the laws of the gods, finding moral authority in personal relationships with the divine and her dead brother. She defied precisely the law she found unjust, and the act in itself, burying her brother, completed her political campaign. She acted alone, asking no support or excuse from those around her. In contrast, Lysistrata and her allies acted collectively and, indeed, transnationally in concert with women in other warring states. Authority and justification for their claims and their action came from their relationships with each other and their created community. They broke no specific law in abstaining from sex with their husbands and lovers, but this particular noncooperation was a forceful confrontation with the war-making states at their most direct contact with them.

Further, collective abstention itself was part of a larger political campaign. The women also refused to care for their children and seized a temple and the treasury. Their actions carried no inherent rationalization or justification because the women proclaimed that abstinence from domestic duties of all sorts was difficult and unpleasant. Rather, sexual noncooperation, along with the other political activities the women chose, won its justification in bringing about larger social and political change, not in itself. Defiance took meaning only in the context of a larger set of goals, specifically the end of war. In this regard, the women appealed to no higher laws, but rather to their collective values and to their shared experiences bearing the costs of war.

We thus have two distinct models or ideal types of civil disobedience. In one, the act is individual, expressive, moralist, and political only in the most minimal sense. In the second, civil disobedience is one tactic in a larger campaign featuring numerous other tactics; it is collective and instrumental, and it may involve violation of laws and practices not inherently offensive. Both models have coexisted and continue to coexist, but Antigone's heirs win the lion's share of attention from analysts and from activists seeking to justify their acts. Antigone's tragedy illustrates the sobriety and commitment of civil disobedients in much of the literature (e.g., Bedau 1969; Carter 1973; Perry 1988; Walzer 1970; Wofford 1969), whereas Lysistrata's far more effective campaign, conveyed in comedy, generally escapes attention.

As a result, the large body of literature on civil disobedience that has emerged provides insight into understanding moral justifications of disobedience and the conflict of civil disobedients and the state but little insight into the relationship of civil disobedience to the larger social and political movements of which it is frequently a part. The tragic vision represented in Antigone, in which moral action is a thing apart from politics, bringing with it severe costs for all involved, looms heavily over contemporary interpretations of civil disobedience, even though most contemporary actions are much closer to the Lysistratan model. We have an individualistic model of civil disobedience that essentially leaves no space for political efficacy as a relevant criterion for evaluation. It is also a model that resonates well with American individualism.

Disobedience and Dissociation: Thoreau as Model

Henry Thoreau is part of the problem. Perhaps the most articulate exponent of civil disobedience—and surely among the most influential—Thoreau is also likely its least typical. Living at Walden Pond, Thoreau did not pay poll taxes in 1842, refusing to support a national government that allowed slavery and conducted an illegal war in Mexico. Among abolitionists, even in Concord, he was not alone in taking such an action. Bronson Alcott, Louisa May Alcott's father, author, and utopian community builder, had earlier encouraged opponents of slavery to dissociate themselves from the federal government through tax resistance. Thoreau spent a single, but much-celebrated, night in jail in July 1846 before a relative paid his outstanding tax—and continued to pay the tax in subsequent years. The author meanwhile returned to his life of contemplation. Two years later Thoreau gave a lecture at the Concord Lyceum entitled, "On the Relation of the Individual to the State." It is this lecture, later published as "Civil Disobedience," rather than the tax resistance itself—which he claimed to give little consideration later in life—upon which Thoreau's place in the repertoire of collective action rests. It is an ambiguous legacy.

Like Antigone, Thoreau acted alone and quite apart from the organized abolitionist and antiwar campaigns of which he was surely aware. Indeed, he made no connection between his own resistance and even that of other abolitionists in Concord, transcendentalist and otherwise, where he was neither the first nor the most persistent disobedient. There is, however, an appealing romantic bombast in Thoreau's bold rhetorical stance against the government. He proclaims himself as ultimate authority for all actions, publicly severing all ties with outside organizations he has not explicitly made, including, of course, the federal government. (He claims to be proud of paying local taxes in order to be a good neighbor.) And he treats the government's codified tolerance of slavery and conduct of the war in Mexico as self-evident instances of injustice. Thoreau explicitly calls for a source of moral and political authority higher than the law, the Constitution, or the Bible—the individual conscience. Thoreau frames resistance to American government as characteristically American. This is bold and appealing, as long as you agree with him.

Thoreau was far less concerned with changing government policy, however, than with dissociating himself from it. "It is not a man's duty," he explains, "as a matter of course, to devote himself to the eradication of any, even the most enormous wrong; he may still properly have other concerns to engage him; but it is his duty, at least, to wash his hands of it, and, if he give it no thought longer, not to give it practically his support" (1969: 33). Thus, the political efficacy of tax resistance as a topic was of far less interest to Thoreau than the moral inconvenience of compliance. Thoreau bears his short prison record proudly, asserting his moral and spiritual freedom even while incarcerated, announcing that "(u)nder a government which imprisons any unjustly, the true place for a just man is also a prison" (p. 37). But what are we to make of the years following Thoreau's night in jail? That the federal government no longer imprisoned men unjustly? That slavery had come to an end? That the author sought more efficacious means of political action? Thoreau's disappointing response was that he had other things to worry about. Although he suggested that collective action by hundreds or thousands might actually end slavery, he was clear that he wasn't going to expend effort on anything beyond his own efforts.

I have treated Thoreau's essay at length here, partly because of its influence and partly because virtually all of the appealing and troubling aspects of civil disobedience as collective action are addressed in it. Thoreau at once proclaims individual responsibility for government actions, draws broadly the boundaries of complicity, and announces the potential efficacy of unilateral action in the service of conscience. He is not, however, a political tactician or activist in any sense, and he leaves the real problems of politics and policy for others to ponder. Indignation may be the start of meaningful politics; it is not, however, a substitute.

Civil Disobedience beyond Concord

Thoreau's essay far outlived his action and found its way around the globe and into the hands of, among others, Mohandas Gandhi, who encountered the essay as a student in England (Shridharani 1962). Gandhi saw civil disobedience as both a political tactic and a moral instrument, and he attempted to use it for political ends, first in a campaign against racial discrimination in South Africa, then with substantially more success in the service of a national independence campaign in India. Although Gandhi used Thoreau's language of moral action, he was also an organizer who virtually always engaged thousands of others in his efforts. He spoke of convincing his opponents, rather than coercing them, but he was certainly willing to fill the jails with protesters, offering more than a small element of coercion. Via reports of Gandhi's campaigns, civil disobedience returned to the United States through religiously inspired peace and civil rights activists, carried initially by a transnational pacifist group, the Fellowship of Reconciliation.

Like Gandhi, whose writings he encountered in graduate school, Martin Luther King spoke and wrote of the moral necessity of civil disobedience; he, too, used the tactic as part of a larger legal, social, and political strategy for change. As a young minister in Montgomery, Alabama, King brought, along with his rhetorical and organizational skills, a knowledge of collective action to an emerging bus boycott. Success in Montgomery, however, came not only through the boycott, but also through vindication by the U.S. Supreme Court, which ruled Alabama's bus segregation laws unconstitutional (Piven and Cloward 1977: 211). Although King wrote appealingly about "higher laws," this meant not simply divine laws of God or nature but also federal laws and the constitution. The alliance between activists and federal authorities proved to be a powerful combination for the early civil rights movement and was critical for mobilizing outside support.

Note how King makes use of both national law and Christian symbolism in his famed "Letter from Birmingham City Jail": "Since we so diligently urge people to obey the Supreme Court's decision of 1954 outlawing segregation in the public schools, it is rather strange and paradoxical to find us consciously breaking laws . . . there are two types of laws: There are *just* and *unjust* laws. I would agree with Saint Augustine that 'An unjust law is no law at all.' . . . A just law is a man-made code that squares with the moral law or the law of God. An unjust law is a code that is out of harmony with the moral law" (King 1969: 77). Thus, even while appealing to the federal government and the Constitution, King makes it clear that he views government authority as contingent rather than absolute.[2] Importantly,

---

[2] The degree to which this duality was intentional, a self-conscious political framing of acts and claims, is an important question for historians of the civil rights movement. It seems most likely that King, an extremely deliberate political tactician and writer, consciously sought to build a broad constituency of support by using every justification and moral appeal available.

for King and the civil rights movement, civil disobedience was never more than one tactic in a broad and integrated campaign for civil rights and social justice.

The early civil rights movement appropriated symbols of liberal justice and mainstream political culture, invigorating or redefining them by juxtaposition of context. Integrated groups of activists asked to see the Declaration of Independence in segregated libraries; men wore coats and ties, and women wore church attire when conducting civil disobedience; demonstrators carried American flags in civil rights marches; disobedients prayed, sang spirituals, or recited the Pledge of Allegiance when awaiting arrest, quoting the Gospels or the founding fathers whenever possible. No doubt this aided the movement in gaining some element of public sympathy and winning important support from "bystander publics" (Lipsky 1968) by defining integration as a self-evident consensual value, endorsed by both God and the U.S. Constitution.

This approach effectively skirted difficult questions of political/moral authority for disobedience. The civil rights movement of the early 1960s conjoined individual conscience and divine and constitutional authorities in justifying and supporting its efforts against local governments, setting the stage for virtually inevitable conflict when those sources of legitimation would not line up so neatly.

It was the civil rights movement's apparent successes with civil disobedience, however, that firmly established this form of collective action for challenging movements in contemporary American politics. Activists for diverse causes used a variety of forms of action under the rubric of civil disobedience, to some degree expecting some elements of the state responsiveness and popular sympathy that Martin Luther King and the civil rights movement won, albeit mostly well after the events themselves. King's rhetorical and legal strategy of dual legitimation, however, to both "higher" absolutes *and* to more earthly federal laws, has escaped serious scrutiny. King's approach has encouraged subsequent claimants without comparable allies in the federal government to frame their claims in exactly the same way as civil rights activists did.

In looking at King's writing, later dissenters can find no clue as to why the responses that antiwar, antitax, antinuclear, antiabortion, and antipollution activists win from the courts, the media, or the general public pale in comparison with those of the earlier movement, or even, for that matter, why later civil rights movement activists have failed to re-create the political momentum of their forebears. The civil rights movement sent analysts to search for justifications of disobedience buried deep within the law. At the same time it encouraged activists to make claims based on "self-evident" propositions grounded in subjective moral conscience without exploring the potential conflicts between these.

WHERE AND WHY LEGAL THEORY FAILS: COMPETING AUTHORITIES

Civil disobedience in the civil rights and antiwar movements of the 1960s provoked a spate of legal theory on disobedience and political obligation in the United States, virtually always ignoring the difficulty in bridging the gulf between conscience and the law and virtually never addressing the relationship between civil disobedience and social movements.

Supporters of the "rule of law" either rejected outright civil disobedience as a threat to law or sketched out extremely narrow circumstances under which civil disobedience could justifiably be used to "test" local laws against the Constitution (Fortas 1968). Partisans of the antiwar and civil rights movements allowed that civil disobedience might indeed breed disrespect for the law, but that this was probably a good thing (e.g., Zinn 1968). Legal and political theorists engaged in complicated pyrotechnics to delineate the boundaries of justifiable civil disobedience to protect only movements with which they agreed. Justifications grounded in an individualistic, liberal politics and emphasizing individual morality effectively factored out the complex social movement politics in which civil disobedience is generally nested.

When activists engage the government through civil disobedience, they fight a battle about authority. The government's position is the simplest: it makes laws, and in a democracy, these laws reflect majority will, albeit with constitutional constraints; the government has the responsibility for enforcing those laws. In deliberately breaking laws, activists assert alternative sources of authority: international law, individual conscience, divine guidance, and/or the Constitution. Activists who claim the legitimacy of their positions, be they against war, discrimination, or abortion, feel no compunction to recognize the government's authority, only its power.

When a civil disobedient violates laws or challenges policy, she is not simply challenging the court, the government, or even some moral community to recognize the essential justice of her claims. The disobedient may choose to act in accord with a competing authority with no necessary hope of finding vindication beyond moral witness. Individuals do not derive their moral values or political preferences from some abstract relationship with the divine; rather, their choices are embedded in social relationships with varying degrees of autonomy from the government and mainstream politics. Thus, civil disobedients often describe their actions as examples of true obedience (e.g., Muste 1969), suggesting that the commitments to community values take precedence over those to the state. As Jean Gump, then in Alderson federal prison for beating on a missile silo with a hammer, explained, "I'm a law-and-order nut . . . When the speed limit says 25, that's what I go, not 26, not 30. My children don't even like to ride with me, because I obey the signs, even if it's 3:00 AM in the morning and there's not a car around . . . [but] These laws that protect weapons are immoral, against international law, and simply must be broken. These are not laws that will contribute to life, but are protecting the end of our species, the destruction of our planet, because all of these laws are in place to protect nuclear weapons. Our laws are designed, written, and enforced to protect the war industries. So they just have to be broken, and you may do what you have to do. I've already done what my conscience told me to" (quoted in Wilcox 1991: 52–53).

Sister Ann Montgomery, one of the original Plowshares Eight (a small group of civil disobedients against nuclear weapons), explains her attack on a General Electric plant in King of Prussia, Pennsylvania, in terms no less absolute. She finds her inspiration in "neither international laws, nor history, but the word of God. It is this call of the prophets and Jesus to beat swords into plowshares which is real . . . I'm afraid right now. I'm afraid in jail. And I'm afraid when I do one of these actions. But the word of God explains why I'm here. I'm literally convicted by this word of God to beat swords into plowshares" (quoted in Wilcox 1991: 197). Montgomery goes on to explain to the sentencing judge that she will continue to conduct civil disobedience and direct action against nuclear weapons when she is allowed to leave prison: "I *have* been upholding the law." Secular authority will always be secondary to this sort of belief.

Citizens confront the demands of competing authorities or moral communities in choosing their actions. American policymakers and citizens generally belong to more than one moral community, defined by a shared tradition, potentially making conflicting claims upon their preferences and conduct in the political arena (see Perry 1988). It's hard to negotiate working agreements on basic values within the United States because communities, religious or geographic, can exercise independent authority on their terrain. We see in debates on abortion or the definition of marriage conflicts about values that the government can't decisively resolve. In one commonly articulated justification of civil disobedience, following the rhetoric of Gandhi, the act is an appeal for dialogue and understanding.

This is an appealing notion, but one that actually describes little of the realities of civil disobedience. It is hard to imagine that the decision to defy the law openly is ever undertaken lightly, especially in light of potentially severe costs. One may vote, or even send a check, based on a reasonable supposition about a policy issue; it's far less likely that someone will risk beatings or imprisonment or sit on railroad tracks in front of a moving train with the intent of starting a dialogue. In order to escalate dissent to collective action, organizers work to ensure activists' certainty in their cause and their colleagues. Thus, the American civil rights movement, the antiabortion movement, the antinuclear power movement, and the movement against corporate globalization all required extensive training sessions for participants in civil disobedience, sessions that emphasized not only the character and tactics of a particular action, but also importantly the justice of their cause (e.g., Dwyer 1983; Epstein 1991).

Rather than an appeal for judicial reinterpretation, policy reform, or democratic dialogue, more commonly civil disobedience is an *assertion* of an alternate source of authority, with an eye toward engaging outside audiences. The American civil rights movement, for example, sought to interpose national government authority on areas of social and political life previously ruled by state and local governments. Antiwar activists appeal to a variety of authority sources to justify and motivate their actions, among them international law (via the Nuremberg precedents, which allowed the international community to punish Nazi war criminals); they ask that the government be subject to external standards in making foreign policy and claim a responsibility as citizens to impose the authority of this higher law. Similarly, a large segment of antiabortion protesters tries to impose the authority of the church on areas normally seen to be part of secular life.

The juxtaposition of different authorities occurs at a civil disobedience action and is offered again within the legal system. Sometimes the confrontation in court is the intended target of the disobedients, sometimes just a necessary aftereffect. The resonance of various alternate authorities within the courts or a larger public varies according to constituency and context. Constitutional appeals, for example, win more serious attention and sympathy in the legal system than do appeals to church. The appeal to church authority, however, may ultimately provide access to a deeper reservoir of symbols and support within a broader community, mobilizing activism and support that could be more powerful than any court in achieving policy changes.

Local action groups opposing nuclear power and nuclear weapons, Barbara Epstein (1991) reports, use civil disobedience not only as a political tactic, but also as away to assert and build new community values. Although the activists certainly hope to influence government policy, this is a long-term and indirect objective. More immediately, they work to create a new culture, including ways to organize society. They aim to create, in micro-cosm, the world they want to see by making decisions in the way they imagine the larger government should, emphasizing democracy, nonviolence, and compassion. Using such "prefigurative politics" (see Breines 1982), groups such as the Clamshell Alliance and the Livermore Action Group resolutely emphasize the connection between their goals and the means they use to achieve them. In other words, their politics is based on directly creat-ing the kind of society in which they want to live, establishing in effect a "community of protest" and juxtaposing it with the larger political world. Tactical victories on particular issues, Epstein (1991: 269) argues, are far less important than the ongoing process of build-ing the protest community. She concludes that in contemporary America "protest politics must be utopian, in the sense that it must hold out a vision of a nonviolent and egalitarian society, and that it must build the new society within the shell of the old by creating a space within which these values can be realized as far as possible."

Clearly the same sort of political tactic, civil disobedience, serves different purposes for different activists at different times in a protest cycle. We'll next consider how trans-portable, or modular, civil disobedience is across movements and across time.

CIVIL DISOBEDIENCE AND SHIFTING CONTEXTS

Civil disobedience has appeared in a wide range of movements in a number of countries, often with the same basic set of legitimating texts; everybody likes to quote Thoreau, Gandhi, and Martin Luther King. Sometimes activists on both sides of a political conflict employ civil disobedience in their efforts. Whereas once civil disobedience was seen as the domain of relatively powerless groups, now numerous challengers claim powerlessness and alienation from the political system as their necessity for, and justification of, civil disobe-dience, even if their own marginality, say, as students or fundamentalist Christians in the United States, is less than immediately obvious.

Changes in context and constituencies can be both shocking and confusing, as re-cent movements underscore. In the late 1970s in Boston, members of the same local groups that had violently resisted busing to integrate the public schools chained themselves to the doors of fire and police stations to protest harsh cuts in the state's budget and services, cuts mandated by referendum-driven tax reductions. In the mid-1980s, antiabortion activists appropriated not only the tactics, but also the moral language and symbols of the civil rights movement to organize illegal and harassing demonstrations outside medical offices and health centers that performed abortions. In some of these demonstrations, both pro-ponents and opponents of abortion rights broke federal and state laws while claiming ad-herence to higher laws.

Civil disobedience has become a staple tactic in the repertoire of American social movements. The transportability of a tactic from one set of issues and constituencies to an-other raises important questions about the nature of this repertoire. Do the politics and gov-ernment of the United States encourage the development of certain kinds of strategies for social movements? Do the dominant strategies change over time? Are there certain kinds of constituencies who will choose to use civil disobedience, or are there certain issue areas for which the tactic is most relevant? We will discuss the notion of civil disobedience as one tactic in a repertoire of contention available to challengers in the United States, then examine what sorts of groups are likely to find civil disobedience most useful and attractive and when they are most likely to choose it and suggest ways in which the tactic may change in the context of different movements.

Modularity across Movements

As tactics become well established, and as everyone involved develops a good idea of what to expect in the course of a political conflict, Sidney Tarrow (1998) argues that tactics become "modular," that is, applicable to a range of different issues, constituencies, and contexts. The modern repertoire of social movements, he contends, is built around flexible tactics that can better sustain challenges in indirect forms and over a longer period of time than can the more direct, issue- and region-specific tactics of the older repertoire.

Tactics, claims, and organizational forms that appear successful can diffuse across national boundaries, social movements, and constituencies. Social movement influence "spills over" the loose boundaries of one movement to another through shared activists, through coalition work between groups across both issues and national boundaries, through mass communications, and through broad cultural changes that a movement may help create (Meyer and Whittier 1994). Mass media coverage of the civil rights actions of the 1950s and 1960s particularly reached an audience well beyond the protesters and authorities engaged in this struggle. It is not surprising then that when people who witnessed the civil rights campaigns, even if mediated through television, become activists on behalf of their own concerns, they see the tactic of civil disobedience as available and viable. It is familiar, carries powerful associations, and implies claims deeply rooted in moral conviction. In this regard, it makes sense that community activists in Boston who lost their fight to preserve "neighborhood schools" would adopt some of the tactics that appeared to work for their opponents pursuing racial desegregation (Useem 1980). The diffusion of civil disobedience as a tactic is not bounded by the ideological boundaries of a community, but rather can move across the political spectrum.

We need to begin to think about who is likely to use civil disobedience, under what circumstances, and importantly, toward what ends. Civil disobedience generally involves immediate instrumental objectives, but the gains of direct action are modest in the context of broader movement goals. Civil rights activists, for example, used direct action to desegregate buses and libraries but surely hoped that successful efforts in one locality would obviate the need for freedom rides or sit-ins elsewhere. Similarly, Plowshares activists propose to begin unilateral disarmament by damaging U.S. nuclear weapons; antiabortion activists claim to take dramatic action to save a single unborn life but clearly hope to influence policy beyond the scope of a single clinic. Activists attempt to influence the policy process by symbolicly interfering with policy implementation.

The increased use of civil disobedience by a wide variety of groups indicates its secure place in the contemporary repertoire of American social movements. Partly, this fact reflects changes in the structure of political opportunity in the United States such that extrainstitutional tactics appear more available and attractive to challengers. In this regard, the growth of bureaucracy, government's increased scope and simultaneously weakened capacity for implementation or innovation, and the diminishing strength of political parties may all contribute to making institutional politics less attractive to numerous constituencies (Meyer and Tarrow 1998). At the same time, the active role of the federal judiciary in the 1950s and 1960s, especially on civil rights and civil liberties issues, may encourage challengers to develop strategic trajectories that pass through the legal system. The decentralized and divided legal system, much as the larger federal state that contains it, encourages challenging movements to divide their own efforts in the same way.

Concurrent with the development of a more activist Supreme Court, television grew as a mass medium, permeating deeply into American politics and culture. The drama of civil disobedience reproduces nicely on television: there are action and conflict with readily identifiable sides. As a result, civil disobedience appears as a particularly effective way for activists, particularly smaller groups of activists, to project a message to a broader public. Also of critical importance, the increased use of civil disobedience by numerous groups in itself encourages new groups to adopt the tactic. Protesters, politicians, and police all know what to expect from the use of civil disobedience, effectively reducing the risks for all involved. Police, for example, commonly ask protesters to designate who among them wants to be arrested (McCarthy and McPhail 1998). Supporters who don't want to be arrested can take on defined support roles, ranging from conducting legal observation to carrying messages to picking up protesters after their arraignments. Subsequent iterations of civil disobedience, along with occasional modifications, ritualize its conduct, making it an increasingly legitimate and available form of pressing political claims. Paradoxically, increased legitimacy and predictability diminish the pressure that civil disobedients can exercise directly, such that collective action becomes more expressive than instrumental.

WHO USES CIVIL DISOBEDIENCE? CONTEXT, CLAIMS, AND CONSTITUENCIES

As we've discussed, activists make strategic calculations about both claims and tactics, mindful of their available resources and the most likely responses from government, supporters, opponents, and bystanders. In looking at the increased frequency of civil disobedience, we'll consider what this tells us about more institutional politics in the United States, paying particular attention to the sorts of movements likely to employ civil disobedience and for what ends.

As we discussed in the first chapter, American political institutions are designed to invite, but also to frustrate, social movements. By providing reasonably available access to mainstream politics, Madison and the other founders hoped to stop the development of divisive and potentially disruptive political conflict between the government and challengers. But civil disobedience suggests exactly that. We need to separate out how open the United States is to particular constituencies and how open it is to particular claims.

Government responds to protesters' efforts directly through police action and subsequent processing through the legal system; options range from heavy sanctions to general tolerance. Government also responds to the claims of dissidents, with options ranging from substantial policy reform to complete neglect. Both dimensions affect how attractive civil disobedience is as a strategy for social movement activists.

Severe repression can preclude the widespread use of civil disobedience because it raises both the costs and risks of the action. If police are likely to beat protesters, or courts likely sentence them to long terms in jail, it stands to reason that fewer people will break the law for political purposes. Although some are willing to face the most dire consequences in order to press their claims, most of the time this will be a small number of people. If non-violent direct action invariably leads to harsh punishment, fewer people will engage in it. The proliferation of large-scale civil disobedience campaigns is predicated on a large degree of government tolerance. In the United States today, peaceful civil disobedients are generally arrested peacefully, with a minimum of force, and processed through arraignment quickly. Heavy jail sentences and fines are the exception rather than the rule. Of course, it hasn't always been this way. Increased ease in processing civil disobedients reduces the costs for all involved, making civil disobedience both more attractive and less disruptive.

Policy responsiveness also bounds the likelihood of civil disobedience and collective action more generally. Activists will choose the kinds of conduct that seem most likely to be effective and least risky. Dissidents are unlikely to march outside the White House if they believe they can have a meaningful audience inside. When the government is responsive to a movement's appeals for policy reform, activists are unlikely to take on the risks of breaking the law. In effect, the extent of government tolerance bounds the possibilities of civil disobedience as a tactic; the extent of government responsiveness determines how necessary it appears as a political strategy for influence. Both dimensions vary over time and across constituencies. Tactical choice reflects leaders' perceptions of their group's claims; resources, particularly numbers and commitment; trust in authorities; and trust in their own communities.

First, majorities are unlikely to stage civil disobedience campaigns because it wouldn't appear necessary; ostensibly, they can win with conventional political strategies.

Second, given the nature of the tactic—bold, open, and nonviolent confrontation with the government—civil disobedience is most likely to be employed by groups that can frame their policy differences with government policy in stark and moralistic terms. It is hard to envision staging sit-ins to promote a more active Nuclear Regulatory Commission, for example, whereas calling for shutting down a particular plant is precisely the kind of absolute and nonnegotiable demand that can create the impetus for individuals to take personal risk in extrainstitutional action. Similarly, antiabortion activists don't block clinic entrances to call for parental notification laws, but rather to stop abortion. Of course, their efforts may aid allies working within institutional politics and pressing for increased regulation of abortion. Similarly, peace activists may commit civil disobedience for nuclear disarmament, while more moderate allies lobby for arms control.

Third, as civil disobedients seek out confrontation with opponents who have an acknowledged and overwhelming advantage in physical force, the tactic presupposes a relationship of some minimal amount of trust between the activists and authorities. To be sure, civil rights activists in the United States in the early 1960s faced severe repression, frequent beatings, and occasionally death. Nonetheless, there was generally a supposition that by mobilizing outside support, including the federal government, local governments would show some restraint in handling the disobedient disturbances. In other words, although there was a great deal of talk about faith in God and justice, activists also had to have some faith in their government—at least at the federal level. Since that campaign, as the costs of police overreaction have become clear, many police departments, especially those in cities frequently visited by civil disobedience actions, developed routinized ways of clearing demonstrators quickly and with minimal visible violence (McCarthy and McPhail 1998).

As a result, today antinuclear and antiabortion activists do not expect to be beaten if they do not resist arrest. Constituencies that have some sizable potential base of support either in government or in the general public are therefore more likely to choose civil disobedience as a tactic than are groups without comparable support that might be understandably wary about turning themselves over to police.

Fourth, because civil disobedience as a tactic entails strong personal commitment and some element of physical risk, it is most likely to be used by groups in which the members have some strong personal connections to each other, so that the perception of risk is somewhat moderated by feelings of solidarity. The civil rights movement built itself first upon preexisting indigenous social networks, primarily within local churches, as did much of the antiabortion movement. People engaged in civil disobedience alongside friends and allies whom they knew well (Morris 1984). Alternatively, movements can create new synthetic communities built around a political campaign. In the case of the antinuclear power movement, activists organized into affinity groups of ten to twenty friends to stage protests. United by the issues and a shared political culture, antinuclear activists used the affinity group structure as a means both to build solidarity and to internally control movement tactics (Dwyer 1983). This affinity group structure was replicated in more recent campaigns against corporate globalization (Smith and Johnston 2002; Thomas 2000).

Finally, it is critical to remember, as we've stressed here, that social movements in the United States are always composed of a variety of groups, cooperating on some issues while competing on others, in a larger campaign including a broad range of both tactics and demands. Civil disobedience *may* mean that a group of activists within a movement eschews either violent direct action or conventional politics, but no group can make those decisions for an entire movement. The presence of even ideologically distant allies pursuing other strategies shapes the political opportunities available to those who commit civil disobedience. Institutional allies can work to protect and build tolerance for their own radical flank. Alternatively, they can disavow connections with civil disobedients, making marginalization and repression more likely.

TACTICAL ADOPTION AND ADAPTATION

Of course, even as new constituencies *adopt* tactics innovated by other groups, they *adapt* them to their own purposes. The practice of civil disobedience changes as new groups use, refine, and redefine it, as does its role for a particular group. For blacks in the American South in the late 1950s and early 1960s, civil disobedience was a way to be assertive while trying to make certain that any repression by government authorities would be visible to outsiders. Movement leaders portrayed nonviolent civil disobedience as a show of strength, rather than as essentially the only proactive tactic available to southern blacks. Activists used civil disobedience to escalate political participation and to draw outside support into the movement by use of the media.

In his study of civil rights activism and its relation to the Voting Rights Act of 1965, David Garrow emphasizes that civil disobedience, contrary to movement leadership's public claims, was not an effective tactic for the movement to promote dialogue with the opposition or to convince state governments of the justice of the movement's goals. Rather, it was effective because it was a way to broaden the scope of the political conflict. Garrow focuses on the political benefits resulting from provoking local authorities into violent reaction. Martin Luther King, Garrow (1978) argues, deliberately sought out sites to protest where he was reasonably sure local authorities would react violently, thus generating media attention and public sympathy for the protesters from outside parties. King counted on disciplined and ostensibly moderate civil disobedience in the context of local police overreaction, forging links between his constituents and more moderate allies while straining relations between segregationists and their passive allies in government.

In Birmingham, Alabama, Commissioner of Public Safety Bull Connor proved to be the perfect target for King. Connor ordered his police officers to use fire hoses and dogs to disperse the demonstrators. The attacks on nonviolent marchers, including children, made graphic visuals on national television news, putting pressure on the federal government to intervene to protect the marchers. In contrast, in Albany, Georgia, where the movement staged a year-long campaign of civil disobedience, Police Chief Laurie Pritchett managed to arrest quickly and nonviolently all of the numerous groups of protesters he encountered. The campaign drew little outside attention and changed few minds.

Learning from these examples, King chose to cap the campaign for voting rights with a demonstration at Selma, where he was reasonably certain County Sheriff Jim Clark would react as Bull Connor had. Local police and Alabama National Guard, equipped with riot gear, broke up the first civil rights march in Selma, beating the demonstrators with nightsticks and using tear gas. The movement failed in a sometimes-articulated goal of persuading local opponents but quite clearly was successful in mobilizing the federal government and sympathetic publics in the North, over the long term winning a strategic victory. What's important here, as well as in other cases, is that the tactical choice of civil disobedience was part of a larger political strategy, based on predicted responses of both local and national audiences. Disobedience was a way to escalate the conflict, polarizing supporters and opponents and, critically, engaging bystanders in the larger conflict.

In contrast, for the antiabortion movement civil disobedience was a way to deescalate tactically while involving and unifying new activists in the campaign. Abortion opponents saw Ronald Reagan's victory in 1980 as a hopeful watershed event. Reagan spoke openly against abortion and promised to appoint judges who would respect his vision of the sanctity of human life (Craig and O'Brien 1993). He had used the issue to raise money and mobilize voters for years before running for president and made it a key issue in the primary campaign for the Republican nomination. In office, partly because of the nature of the presidency and the checks and balances Madison built in, and partly because he didn't want to risk alienating a majority of voters, Reagan delivered much less than the antiabortion movement wanted.

In 1983, the antiabortion movement suffered two serious setbacks: in June, the Supreme Court ruled in several cases that localities could not unduly restrict women's access to abortion. Shortly afterward, the U.S. Senate defeated a proposed constitutional amendment explicitly stating that the right to abortion is not guaranteed. In reaction, a substantial portion of the antiabortion movement began to emphasize extrainstitutional means of participation (Ginsburg 1989: 49). These means included prayer vigils, marches, pickets, and large demonstrations; in 1985, President Reagan spoke to demonstrators in Washington, explicitly supporting their cause and their efforts. The tactical diversity in the mid-1980s also featured more problematic tactics, including abortion clinic bombings, arson, parcel bombs, and shots fired at the home of Supreme Court Justice Harry Blackmun, author of the original abortion decision. As site-based violence increased, so did rifts within the movement; partisans of direct action aggressively criticized their purported allies in government for "snubbing" them. Pressure on governmental abortion opponents to condemn the violence of the movement also increased.

Operation Rescue emerged in a way that, oddly, healed splits in the antiabortion movement, offering aggressive site-based opposition to abortion, but without the negative and polarizing effects of violence. It provided abortion opponents a route to more aggressive action than conventional politics without insulating them totally from mainstream politics. It also promised a direct means for stopping—or at least delaying—some abortions.

The brief treatments of the civil rights and antiabortion movements focus on the effects of civil disobedience on a movement's dealings with allies, adversaries, and bystander publics; it's also important to recognize that tactical choice influences the social movements themselves. In her study of the movement against nuclear power in the 1970s, Dwyer (1983) argues that staging civil disobedience campaigns became the organizing focus used to mobilize opponents of nuclear power in site-based campaigns. At the movement's height, the civil disobedience campaigns at various construction sites mobilized thousands of people.

Barbara Epstein (1991) suggests that opposition to nuclear power, and later to nuclear weapons, was only a piece of a comprehensive cultural revolution. The "nonviolent direct action" movement, she contends, used these issues to build community through "prefigurative politics." Civil disobedience, for the campaigns of the 1970s, entailed an affinity group structure run by direct democracy and consensus, with rapidly rotating leadership. Civil disobedience, in this case, was the motivation and source for a variety of campaigns and a unifying force for the movement. All of the site-based campaigns, however, were short-lived because the movement was unable to innovate new tactics to continue mobilizing people. Protest at operating and proposed nuclear power plants, direct and visible targets, to stop their operation became the dominant tactic and claim in a rigid and inflexible repertoire, far removed from the actual locations in which important decisions about nuclear power were made. The point is that the choice of tactics affects organization within a movement as well as its relations with authorities and audiences.

CIVIL DISOBEDIENCE AND PROTEST CYCLES

Tactics change as they move across different movements; they also change in relation to when they appear in a movement's trajectory. Civil disobedience may indeed be present before, throughout, and after the sweep of a cycle of protest, but the number of people participating and their relationship to a larger political campaign will change over time. Whereas some groups in a social movement campaign will use civil disobedience, others will use conventional political strategies throughout its trajectory, with one or the other set of actions predominant depending upon perceived political opportunities and the strength of one faction or another within the movement.

Activists make their own decisions about tactics, paying attention to the relative size and strength of a larger social movement campaign and their perceptions of available opportunities for political influence. Government shapes these opportunities—as well as activist perceptions of them—encouraging some forms of political action and claims while discouraging others through neglect or repression. Both activist choices and government responses are likely to change over time in response to each other and to other changing circumstances. In order to make sense of civil disobedience as a tactical choice, we need to place it in the context of a particular campaign.

Groups without the power to win by working conventionally within the political system, those likely to choose civil disobedience, derive their greatest potential influence by demonstrating their capacity to disrupt the practice of politics as usual. It is not necessarily the disruptiveness of an action itself that is powerful and threatening; it is challenging opponents in unexpected ways, creating uncertainty about what challengers might do in the future (Tarrow 1998), and calling into question ruling coalitions. Such surprise and uncertainty are necessarily limited in time because the repetition of an action over time invariably creates some degree of routinization and predictability. Certainty allows authorities to manage their responses and thereby the challenge more easily. *State tolerance is then a double-edged sword, making it safer for activists to engage in civil disobedience but also limiting the efficacy of the tactic.* In order to maximize their influence, movements need to be able to diversify and innovate tactically.

Conflicting pressures create dilemmas for activists. Effective influence on policy is contingent on unpredictability and disruptive potential, but government is most likely to tolerate actions that are predictable and nonthreatening, that is, those that won't be disruptive. Media coverage of movement events and ideas is contingent upon colorful, confrontational, and, above all, *new* kinds of events, with a continual pressure on a movement to escalate. At the same time, continued escalation makes both repression and media portrayals of a movement as radical or marginal all the more likely. At once, civil disobedience appears to be a way to balance these conflicting pressures. It is confrontational but nonviolent, somewhat disruptive but legitimate. It also may be escalated in terms of sites and numbers without necessarily inviting repression.

The tactical choice of civil disobedience activity certainly does not guarantee that a movement can walk this line. Indeed, within the broad rubric of civil disobedience, movements must innovate new approaches and tactics in order to continue to mobilize, grow, and challenge. Perhaps the primary example of successful innovation of this sort is the early civil rights movement. Doug McAdam (1983) traces tactical innovation within the movement from 1955 to 1971, sorting movement efforts into five types of actions: bus boycotts, sit-ins, freedom rides, community campaigns, and riots. He observes that the introduction of a new tactic spurred an uptick in all sorts of movement activity. As he tells the story, by persistently introducing new forms of action when authorities developed ways to deal with the old forms, the civil rights movement was able to continue to grow and to exercise political influence.

Managing this kind of innovation, however, is no easy matter. One aid was the presence of several different groups using civil disobedience and innovating new forms of action. Innovation increases as groups apply familiar tactics to new venues, in the case of the civil rights movement, desegregation of buses, then lunch counters, then libraries. Further, tactical innovations are not wholly independent of the sorts of claims challengers make. Charles Tilly (1992: 17) postulates that tactical innovations increase along with new claims, whereas tactical repertoires rigidify as activity and new claims diminish. The rate of tactical innovation then follows the same general curve as a protest cycle. As protest escalates, new groups stake their claims, adapting appropriate tactics and shifting their efforts from venue to venue. As government responds, repressing, preempting, or more generally institutionalizing dissent, innovation declines with protest more generally.

Such was the case with the antinuclear power movement in the 1970s. The movement was comprised of coalitions that were dominant within particular geographic regions. The Clamshell Alliance, for example, coordinated virtually all protest against the construction of the nuclear power station at Seabrook, New Hampshire. Organized around civil disobedience, however, and governed by consensus, the Clam faced debilitating internal debate about how it might escalate. Ultimately the coalition fragmented over questions such as whether cutting fences unduly compromised the integrity of the movement's claims to nonviolence. Unable to develop new claims or tactics, the movement soon faded (Epstein 1991: ch. 2). Thus, the Clam's civil disobedience efforts, although effective in inspiring a series of regional antinuclear campaigns, soon became routine: unthreatening to local authorities, uninteresting to the mass media, and uninspiring to would-be activists.

Within this extremely self-conscious movement, the Clam's failure provoked a great deal of debate about the utility of civil disobedience in social movements. At the height of the coalition's activity, activist Marty Jezer warned about what he saw as the tactic's inevitable limits. Writing in *WIN,* the War Resister's League's monthly magazine, which reached a relatively small circle of committed activists, Jezer (1977) argued that "(h)istorically, moral witness has proven itself an effective way of starting a movement, but inadequate in sustaining or building a movement already in existence . . . But once people are mobilized to act in a political way, individual witness loses its effect" (quoted in Epstein 1991: 91).

This is what happened to Operation Rescue's efforts against abortion. Developing an aggressive civil disobedience campaign surely helped the movement in 1988 and 1989, simultaneously allowing the campaign to escalate its activity and control its adherents. The movement received more extensive coverage from the mass media and generally without the negative frames that were inevitable in describing arson or parcel bombings. The site-based campaigns created tactical dilemmas both for abortion rights activists and for local governments, who expended large sums of money for extra police details. Devising responses has often divided advocates of abortion rights on questions of whether to use court injunctions, counterdemonstrations, and controversial antiracketeering statutes to counter Operation Rescue.

Partly as a result of the changing political climate, Operation Rescue was unable to escalate from small local campaigns to larger national efforts or even to sustain the local campaigns. The Supreme Court's willingness to allow states to regulate many aspects of abortion activated abortion rights advocates in a variety of political venues and threatened the Republican Party's electoral coalition. It has also encouraged institutional allies of the antiabortion movement to keep their distance from Operation Rescue, whose efforts could be a political liability in electoral campaigns. At the same time, the continued availability of abortion and the relative ease with which local governments have dealt with Operation Rescue have discouraged potential civil disobedients from participating in site-based actions. In efforts in Buffalo, New York, for example, Operation Rescue members were outnumbered on the streets by abortion rights demonstrators (Manegold 1992). The organization's inability to innovate preceded a period of fragmentation and diversification in the movement. As tolerance for antiabortion protests declined along with the prospects for institutional influence for antiabortion activists, only a few were willing to take great risks to escalate their efforts through dramatic political violence, including the assassinations of doctors, while the bulk of the antiabortion movement turned its focus to incremental goals pursued through conventional politics, for example, a congressional ban on certain types of late-term abortions. The example raises key questions about the place of civil disobedience in a protest cycle.

The peace movement of the 1980s suggests that civil disobedience efforts may work differently at certain times in a movement's development. In September 1980, for example, preceding the emergence of the nuclear freeze, a group of Catholic activists attacked a General Electric plant in King of Prussia, Pennsylvania, to bear witness against U.S. militarism. Criticizing General Electric for making guidance systems for Minuteman III nuclear warheads, the protesters hammered on missile nose cones and poured their own blood about the premises before they were arrested. The Plowshares Eight action drew surprisingly extensive, and often sympathetic, attention in both mainstream and movement media, serving to draw critical attention to U.S. nuclear weapon policies and to suggest the need for movement activism (Meyer 1990: 198). Within the context of the ensuing trial, the defendants (including experienced civil disobedients Daniel and Philip Berrigan) tried to appeal to "higher laws" of both morality and international law. Their trial and appeals also drew unusual attention, offering activists the space to put forward new claims about nuclear weapons and national security.

As more moderate political action grew in the following years, however, civil disobedience actions garnered less attention not only from the mainstream, but also from movement organs. Over eighty subsequent Plowshares actions followed, most in the United States, along with a handful in other countries; few of the subsequent actions drew much attention from mainstream media.[3] At the movement's peak, more moderate antinuclear forces actively disavowed the civil disobedients, seeking to maintain a less threatening profile within mainstream political institutions.[4] This suggests that dramatic actions, including civil disobedience, may be most visible and important at certain points in a protest cycle, perhaps when institutional activity appears least promising.

As mainstream activity increases, civil disobedients are likely to be attracted to less colorful and less confrontational means of pursuing their goals. When disobedients are visible, and when more moderate actors see no prospect of institutional political influence, they may have common cause in protecting each other. As institutionally oriented actors appear to make inroads in influencing state policy, they may distance themselves more and more from their own radical wing, hastening the fragmentation and institutionalization of the larger political movement (Boles 1991; Meyer 1993a).

Importantly, this is a strategic choice that both individual activists and organized groups make: to emphasize potential ties between institutional and extrainstitutional wings of a movement or to denigrate and cut those ties. In the early 1960s, even the most moderate civil rights movement organizations recognized their common cause with the civil disobedience

---

[3] An inventory and update of Plowshares actions can be found at http://www.plowsharesactions.org For an analysis of longterm activism see Nepstad (2004).

[4] The Plowshares actions were not the only civil disobedience actions staged in the United States. The pattern of attention to early actions in a campaign, however, with diminishing public and movement attention over time, holds true for other civil disobedience efforts. This is true even of attempts to stage ongoing civil disobedience campaigns, such as the Women's Peace Encampment at Seneca Falls, New York. Originally conceived of as a staging ground for continual protest actions, the camp eventually developed a means of coexistence with local authorities that necessarily entailed it becoming less visible over time (see Krasniewicz 1992).

campaigns. The result of this strategy was that these groups had a "left" to use in bargaining with political authorities and that activists had the opportunity to escalate their own personal commitments through a variety of different campaigns. In contrast, the nuclear freeze movement of the 1980s chose to appear as a "responsible" opposition, actively distancing itself from radical civil disobedience campaigns.

CIVIL DISOBEDIENCE THROUGHOUT A PROTEST CYCLE

Randy Kehler's story serves as both an illustration and a suggestion for further research. A longtime antiwar activist, Kehler had served twenty-two months in federal prisons after refusing to accept conscientious objector status during the Vietnam War. Afterward he continued to work against war and militarism in a variety of campaigns, mostly locally based. He and his wife, Betsy Corner, stopped paying federal taxes in 1977 to protest military spending. Although they filed accurate Internal Revenue Service returns, they sent the taxes they calculated they owed the government to the World Peace Tax Fund instead, trying to withdraw their support (and money) from militaristic aspects of government policy and to fund activities they preferred. Acknowledging the importance of institutional political activity at the same time, Kehler (1992) writes, "Many of us can also chose not to hand over to the federal government some part of our tax money and instead redistribute it to those in need—until such time as those in need become our government's first priority" (see *Peacework* 1992).

Kehler's explicit priority on individual conscience evokes Thoreau's memory, but unlike Thoreau, Kehler did not abandon institutional strategies for political influence. In 1980, Kehler organized the first nuclear freeze referendum campaign, placing a nonbinding resolution on the ballot in three state senate districts; shortly afterward he was named first national coordinator for the freeze effort. As a national leader, he spoke before community groups, lobbied legislators, and testified before Congress. In 1983, at the height of the movement's mobilization, activists seeking to escalate the movement's tactics and claims proposed to incorporate tax resistance into the freeze campaign's strategies. Freeze leadership, including Kehler, worked to make sure the proposal never reached the general convention floor.

In 1989, well after the peak of the nuclear freeze movement, the IRS began prosecution of Kehler and Corner, seizing their bank accounts and eventually their home. Although it may be possible that the IRS was unaware of their tax resistance in years prior, this seems unlikely, especially given Kehler's high public profile in the early 1980s. More likely, prosecuting Kehler and Corner earlier in the decade was politically risky, drawing attention to their efforts and possibly encouraging other antinuclear activists to emulate their resistance. In 1989, however, with the Cold War at an end and peace groups struggling to survive, prosecution was far less visible or risky.

Nonetheless, Kehler and Corner's struggle to keep their home became a rallying point for peace activists throughout New England. In western Massachusetts, local activists foiled the IRS's first attempt to auction the home by working in the community to ensure that no one bid for the house and demonstrated at the auction; the IRS itself bought the house for a minimum bid of $5,100. Later, when the IRS finally found an outside buyer, affinity groups "occupied" the home to try to prevent the new owners from moving in. At the same time, in eastern Massachusetts, tax resisters used the occasion of Kehler's forcible eviction and arrest to engage in public education on tax resistance. The ultimate effects of these efforts on the movement, much less on government policy, are hardly visible. It's difficult to imagine the eviction serving as a spark for a new peace movement given the larger political context, most notably the end of the Cold War. At the same time, it's not at all hard to imagine that the tax resistance, in conjunction with all of the organizing efforts around it, would nourish some mobilizable base of activists that will be available to a new campaign when political opportunities change. If the tax resistance is not a spark, perhaps it can be a "pilot light" for future movements.[5]

The increased use of civil disobedience raises important questions about the changing nature of American political development. As more diverse constituencies, and more constituencies altogether, lose faith in conventional means of political participation alone as a way to protect their interests, protest, including civil disobedience, will continue to increase. The history of social protest in American politics is cumulative, and the safe and successful employment of civil disobedience will encourage new challengers to adopt and adapt the tactic, making effective governance and policy reform more difficult. Paradoxically, even as increased tolerance and ritualization of civil disobedience practices make protest safer, easier, and more prevalent, they also make it less effective. Dissidents concerned with political efficacy will seek new ways to innovate tactically.

The use and meaning of civil disobedience, like those of any social movement tactic, can change dramatically over the life of a social movement, playing different roles at different points in a protest cycle. At the outset of a cycle, civil disobedience may serve to draw mainstream political attention to activists and their concerns. At a movement's peak mobilization, civil disobedience can be a way to unify (or divide) a campaign and a way to allow a movement to escalate and innovate tactically. In a period of retrenchment, civil disobedience can be a way to maintain movement values and to sustain social networks that can be the basis of future mobilization. Although civil disobedience represents the dramatic punctuation marks of a social movement campaign, it is not one of the enduring effects of a successful movement. In the next chapter, we will consider the broader process of political institutionalization.

---

[5] Their story of tax resistance has been recounted in a documentary film, *An Act of Conscience,* which has been distributed in left and pacifist networks.

THE STATE AND PROTESTS

Institutionalization

Julia "Butterfly" Hill spent two years of her mid-twenties living in a redwood tree in Northern California she called "Luna." Hill, and others, camped on platforms in the old-growth forest to make it harder for the Pacific Lumber company to cut down the trees. Essentially, they used their bodies to raise the costs and risks of logging old-growth forests. More than this, however, they used the drama of tree-sitting to project their concerns to a broader audience. Hill's encampment was particularly dramatic, as she remained in the tree through winter storms, braving winds, snow, and freezing rain. She was the most successful in garnering media attention, conducting hundreds of interviews, holding news conferences, and entertaining celebrities in her tree, as simultaneously her relationship with established environmental organizations and even other tree-sitters was often conflicted.[1]

Pacific Lumber had an obvious interest in getting the photogenic Hill to climb out of the tree. In addition to the immediate issue of logging the forest, company executives wanted to stop the bad publicity and the broad attention to the old-growth trees. The glare of the media got worse for Pacific Lumber as another tree-sitter was killed when loggers cut down the tree he was sitting in; the loggers said they were unaware of his presence. At the same time, the death came amidst increasing conflict and accusations between the protesters and the timber company. Pacific Lumber negotiated with Hill's representatives, other environmental groups, and state and federal authorities to end the standoff. On December 18, 1999, Hill climbed down from the tree, honoring a deal she'd negotiated with the company.

In essence, Julia Hill agreed to stay out of the trees and the lumber company agreed not to log in a three-acre area of old-growth forest surrounding Luna. She wrote a book (2000) about her experiences, founded the Circle of Life Foundation to promote environmental and social policies that respected her values, and went on several speaking tours. Pacific Lumber continued logging around the buffer area and continued its business. They had reached an accommodation that allowed each to return to a less visible, more normal, state of affairs, in which both logging of old-growth forests and the environmental movement against such

---

[1] This account draws from Hill (2000), http://www.peaceheroes.com/JuliaButterflyHill/juliabutterflyhill2.htm, and http://www.ecotopia.org/ehof/hill/bio.html.

logging could continue. What happened in this small part of Humboldt County is a small example of the kind of *institutionalization* that characterizes social movements in America.

We can see the process on a larger scale by looking at the movement against nuclear power.

More than sixty five thousand people demonstrated in Washington, D.C., on May 6, 1979, protesting the development of nuclear power. In fact, activists had been organizing against nuclear power almost since its onset, but the Washington demonstration represented a watershed level of mobilization. The previous campaigns had been directed at the sites of actual and planned nuclear reactors. In targeting a march on Washington, activists were intentionally taking the local battles and making them a matter of national concern, laying them at the feet of Congress and President Jimmy Carter, who had proudly announced that he was a nuclear (which he pronounced "nuculah") engineer.

There were numerous reasons for activists to oppose nuclear power. The American government had used the promise of nuclear power, which would be safe, cheap, clean, and reliable, in the 1950s to try to ameliorate public fear about nuclear weapons. Unsurprisingly, peace activists saw opposition to nuclear power as part of the same battle. With the growth of the environmental movement in the 1960s and 1970s, activists increasingly saw the development of nuclear power as an environmental threat, questioning safety, expense, nuclear waste, and reliability. In 1977, a demonstration linking nuclear weapons and nuclear power gathered fifteen thousand people in New York City.

It's not clear that the Washington demonstration would have drawn many more people had not events completely out of the movement's control aided its efforts. On March 28, 1979, six weeks before the planned antinuclear demonstration, Reactor Number Two at the Three Mile Island nuclear plant in Harrisburg, Pennsylvania, displayed a malfunction in its cooling system and was immediately shut down. During the following days, national attention focused on the plant, the efforts of the operators to assess and contain the damage, and the statements of the federal Nuclear Regulatory Commission in communicating risk and reality to the public. As it turned out, the plant's operators had a difficult time diagnosing the malfunction, partly as a result of instrument failures, and were unable to respond appropriately. Within a few days, radioactivity was released into the environment from the cooling tower.

News coverage of the reactor accident, including political responses, factual reports, and satirical sketches on television all drew attention to both the activists' claims and their efforts. Meanwhile, activists were engaged on other fronts. Actor-producer Michael Douglas was immersed in producing (and acting in) a film, *The China Syndrome,* starring Jack Lemmon and Jane Fonda, that told the fictional tale of an accident at a nuclear power plant and reflected a cynical view of both the commercial power industry and the government. It was released shortly after the demonstration. Activists also worked to organize popular musicians of the day, including Jackson Browne, Crosby Stills, Nash, and Young, John Hall, Joni Mitchell, and Bruce Springsteen, to play a series of benefit concerts for the movement in Madison Square Garden. MUSE (Musicians United for Safe Energy) generated positive reviews and a quickly produced live collection album, which raised funds for the movement's key organizations and, perhaps even more importantly, its public profile.

President Carter responded to both the accident and the movement by convening a special advisory commission on nuclear power. Comprised almost exclusively of scientists and executives who supported nuclear power, it made strong recommendations about how to ensure plant safety with the intent of preserving the nuclear power option in the United States. Stricter licensing and safety requirements, in conjunction with greater opportunities for citizen involvement in the licensing process, were not enough to satisfy antinuclear activists. They were, however, enough to stop applications for new nuclear plants. Licensing new plants became more difficult, and building and operating a new plant became much more expensive. Although a few previously ordered plants went into operation after the Three Mile Island accident, no new plants have been ordered since 1979. And the movement against nuclear power faded, even as dozens of nuclear power plants remain in operation.[2]

The story of nuclear power development, protest, and policy response is one that is fairly typical in American politics. Protest emerged in response to a policy problem. Long-term efforts of activists seemed suddenly to come together and reach political relevance in an apparently instant response to changes in political opportunity far beyond the capabilities or intent of activist organizations. Activist organizations, which differed among themselves on not only tactics, but also their rationale for opposing nuclear power and their preferred alternatives, were able to reach a much broader public when the accident at Three Mile Island underscored their concerns. Without necessarily acknowledging the longtime core antinuclear movement or all of its concerns, institutional politics responded. Even as President Carter spoke about the need to continue developing nuclear power, he accepted one critical concern of the antinuclear movement—that of safety. It wasn't only the increased costs of nuclear power that drove the industry into retreat, although those costs were significant. And, although antinuclear activists continued their efforts at existing plants and at plants under construction, the end of new nuclear plants undermined activists' capacity to build a larger and more comprehensive movement. In effect, opposition to nuclear power was incorporated into the licensing process such that the movement had weak grounds on which to mobilize support. And other issues beckoned.

In this chapter, we will look at the larger pattern of political institutionalization exemplified by the antinuclear movement of the 1970s. We will then explore two much longer-term cases of political institutionalization of movements, focusing on the mobilization and incorporation of farmers and organized labor.

PATTERNS OF INSTITUTIONALIZATION

This pattern of movements gaining response without getting credit, making institutional inroads, and actually affecting some portion of the policy process is one endemic to American politics, one that James Madison built into the constitutional design, albeit with more pathways than he imagined possible. For our purposes, we can think of the process of incorporation of some elements of a dissident movement, be it ideas, concerns, or personnel, as *institutionalization*. Importantly, on the one hand, we can't say that the antinuclear movement *lost*. In reality, the new strictures on nuclear licensing represented a substantial impact. On the other hand, we certainly can't say the movement *won*. Although new fuel conservation measures were adopted, a response to both government initiatives and market

---

[2] For comparative treatments of nuclear policy and antinuclear movements, see Jasper (1990) and Joppke (1993).

pressures, America remained—and remains—dependent upon nonrenewable fuels that pollute. Large corporations that operate for profit control America's energy supply, and our economy is tainted by conspicuous consumption of dirty coal and foreign oil.

Rather than seeing the movement as winning or losing, it's more helpful to see the legacy of the movement against nuclear power in the incorporation of some of its concerns, particularly for safety, in the economy and governance of nuclear power. As we said, this process is endemic to American politics. The system that James Madison designed provides numerous access points in government for a broad range of constituencies. In addition to those access points, in the modern era we see the multiplication of places within the bureaucracy for citizens to intervene in political decisions. Responses meant to palliate opponents, in the case of nuclear power, for example, the requirement of crisis relocation plans for all new sites, don't work completely, but they can make it harder for activists to mobilize broader public concern, even as new options for activism open. In effect, government creates the political stalemate on policy that satisfies no one but makes forceful movement politics extremely difficult. In this chapter, we'll consider this broader process of institutionalization and pay particular attention to the long trajectory of the labor movement in the United States.

Institutionalization is the creation of a stable set of relationships and procedures such that the politics of an issue becomes routine, that is, repeatable for all concerned with minimal uncertainty or risk. The conduct of advocacy and issue management takes place without the potential disruption of the basic rules and structures of American politics. The boundaries of possible reforms are reasonably clear to all concerned and are limited. And the relevant actors involved in making policy are identifiable and also limited. It does not mean that the issue becomes resolved, that change no longer takes place or that advocates from a social movement cease to exercise influence.

We'll first review, in general, what institutionalization means and the mechanisms of institutionalization for social movements and government, then we'll look at a few key examples of social movements that have negotiated a kind of accommodation with mainstream American political institutions. Importantly, we will see that the institutional accommodation that makes sense at one point may be problematic years later and that social movements can try to resurrect a more unpredictable and disruptive element of the movement. The story of the labor movement in the United States underscores both the benefits and the potential costs of institutionalization.

MECHANISMS OF INSTITUTIONALIZATION

The American political system was designed to afford challengers the prospects of influence within the political system so that they are less likely to try to topple the system as a whole. In looking at the process of institutionalization, we can see how the access points built into the system prove to be attractive options for activists, even if those points are not necessarily the most effective means available to pursue interests. We can identify several distinct mechanisms of institutionalization afforded by government, and we will then consider the impact that one segment of a movement taking on those mechanisms has on the larger movement.

First, policymakers can incorporate movement concerns by offering consultation, formal or informal, with representatives of a movement. In the lead-up to the 1963 march on Washington, for example, President Kennedy frequently spoke with leaders of the more mainstream organizations, including the NAACP and the SCLC, consulting about strategy and tactics for the movements. By all accounts, he tried to channel movement efforts into voter registration, seeing a set of issues more tractable than economic inequality and more potentially beneficial to his administration and the Democratic Party. President Reagan routinely consulted with self-identified members of the conservative movement, and even as he sometimes disappointed movement leaders, the direct consultation made it more difficult for activists to challenge Reagan in an unfriendly way. Members of Congress and elected officials at the local level are even more accessible to social movement activists. Offering a meeting, or even relatively easy access to an elected official's good offices, is an obvious way to try to harness a movement's energy or even to take the steam out of a movement.

Obviously, the support of a social movement can help a politician's career, and candidates for office are generally even more willing to consult with movement leaders. Social movements are animated by people with commitment, energy, and social and political connections to others like them. These are the sorts of people who might not only vote, but also work in political campaigns and are therefore attractive to political candidates. Of course, aspirants for public office are, minimally, *not yet* well positioned to deliver anything to activists for their support, save for a voice. The routine elections of the United States, as well as the self-nomination process for political candidates, offer innumerable options for social movements, which we will discuss further later.

Second, beyond personal consultation, elected officials can offer social movement activists a platform or a venue for making their claims. In Congress, representatives invite activists to testify at subcommittee hearings. The well-established congressional hearing process offers activists the chance to make their pitch for alternatives and allows elected officials to offer something other than policy reforms to activists in exchange for their support. The hearings themselves allow organizations to portray themselves to their supporters as visible, well connected, and effective, which is an aid for recruiting and for raising funds. Because both minority and majority factions on subcommittees get to invite guests to testify, representatives of groups favored by someone can get access of a sort without much influence.

Third, government can set up more permanent venues for consultation, formally adopting the concerns, and even sometimes the personnel, of a challenging movement. We have seen the development of cabinet offices and executive agencies in direct response to the mobilized efforts of organized interests. The Department of Labor, established in 1913, was a Democratic president's way of paying attention to the labor movement, and this attention continued in 1935, at the height of the New Deal, when Franklin Roosevelt established the National Labor Relations Board, explicitly institutionalizing labor conflict within government. Upon taking office in 1961, President Kennedy established the Arms Control and Disarmament Agency within the State Department, partly as a response to the antinuclear weapons movement. President Johnson, in response to the civil rights movement in 1965, established both the Department of Housing and Urban Development and the Equal Employment Opportunity Commission (EEOC), both explicitly considering the issues that animated the movement. As an effort to incorporate the growing environmental movement, President Nixon established the Environmental Protection Agency. President Carter established the Department of Education in 1979 in direct response to the efforts of public school teachers' unions, and President George H. W. Bush established the cabinet-level Department of Veteran's Affairs in 1989 in a bid to cultivate the support of veteran's organizations.

To be sure, these bodies don't always pursue the same aims as the movements that pressed for their creation, nor do these bodies always welcome their participation. Further, an agency that starts with one mandate can turn toward very different definitions of its mandate in response to changing circumstances. Indeed, presidents who often opposed the creation of new cabinet agencies for someone else's favorite constituencies generally take advantage of the positions to fill when they have the chance. President Reagan, for example, no friend of the teachers' unions, campaigned on a promise to abolish the Department of Education but instead appointed a secretary of education who spent his efforts explaining why there would not be additional monies for education from the federal government (Bell 1988). The same president appointed a head of the Arms Control and Disarmament Agency who vigorously opposed all previous arms control agreements and used his position to do so more effectively than before. Nonetheless, the creation of a formal body concerned with a movement provides a potential resource for activists.

Fourth, government can institute procedures that give an actor or claimant formal inclusion in a deliberative process. Frank Weed (1995), for example, documents the development of a victim's rights movement and its efforts to ensure the consideration of victims in the sentencing politics of those convicted of crimes. Because of the movement's efforts, many states now explicitly provide for the victim's impact testimony prior to sentencing, affording an institutional venue for a movement and the people it represents. Similarly, one response to the environmental movement has been the establishment of more open, and much more complicated, processes attending licensing of new construction of all kinds. Developers must file environmental impact statements, which must be publicly available, and activists have the right to speak at public hearings.

In both of these cases, it's far from clear that activists always win or get what they want from this kind of institutionalization. Judges and juries still enjoy some degree of discretion in what they consider before passing sentences, developers can file misleading statements, and zoning boards can ignore environmentalist testimony. But the process now includes a formal and routine place for activist considerations to be heard, and this can matter for policy—and for activist movements.

Fifth, policy reform can afford activist concerns a place in the process and resources attendant to that place. The case of the feminist movement against rape puts this matter in high relief. When activists against rape mobilized in the 1970s, they sought reform in rape laws to make conviction of rapists easier, including shield laws protecting accusers and staircase sentencing to afford prosecutors discretion in making charges they could prove. They also sought better treatment of survivors of rape from police, hospitals, and prosecutors. In response to this, many feminist rape crisis centers received funding (Gornick and Meyer 1998) to provide victim advocacy and counseling services. In effect, the movement won government support for a fraction of its activities. Of course, this fraction was service oriented rather than oriented toward mobilization or advocacy. Some aspects of this story have also occurred for environmentalists, veterans, social welfare advocates, and advocates of victims of other crimes.

Sixth, and critically, institutionalization includes norms and values, not only in government, but also in the broader culture. Often well before any policy reform, elected officials appropriate the rhetoric of social movements, endorsing their version of movement values, sometimes redefining them in the process. "We shall overcome," the refrain of a civil rights movement anthem, appeared in a speech endorsing voting rights made by President

Lyndon Johnson. Gerald Ford, Jimmy Carter, and Ronald Reagan all endorsed the goal of equal rights for women, an obvious response to the women's movement of the 1960s and 1970s, even as they explained the limits on what their administrations could—or would—do to ensure that outcome; in fact, Reagan was the first Republican presidential candidate since before World War II to oppose adoption of an equal rights amendment, arguing that the goal could be achieved without amending the Constitution. Reagan, the prime target of the nuclear freeze movement, also endorsed his definition of its goals, calling his landslide reelection a mandate for arms control. All contemporary presidents pay lip service to the environmental movement in endorsing the concept of environmental protection. President Clinton, in a statement keyed to ameliorate the conservative antitax movement, declared the "era of big government" to be over, outraging some of his supporters in the process. And in contemporary debate, virtually all national politicians have endorsed some version of equal rights or, minimally, tolerance for gays and lesbians, something that was almost unthinkable just a few years earlier.

These presidential pronouncements both reflect and affect broader changes in the culture, setting cues for the rest of America. In effect, presidential attention legitimates a perspective and provides a foundation for subsequent attention by others, both inside and outside of government. It is almost unthinkable in both the Oval Office and polite company to deny the necessity of environmental protection, concern for peace and arms control, fair compensation for veterans, or equal rights for all sorts of people represented by social movements. These rhetorical achievements and influences represent the institutionalization of social movements.

The relatively available institutionalization of social movements by government fundamentally alters the character of government over time. In effect, by institutionalizing additional concerns and constituencies, the American government gets bigger, more unwieldy, and more internally conflictual. The process of making policy slows, and the difficulties of building governing coalitions becomes more complicated. We will recall, however, that this is just what Madison intended, and if government becomes less generally responsive, it may also become more stable.

The process of institutionalization also presents social movement activists and organizations with difficult choices about whether to continue their efforts and, if so, how. When the door to policymaking deliberations opens, it is hard for an advocate not to go in, even though she knows it means compromises on what she can say if she wants to be effective. The positioning of government to accept and address movement concerns makes it more difficult for social movement organizations to mobilize support. After all, if the president, Congress, or some element of the bureaucracy is directly addressing your concerns, why should you spend the time and effort to march in the streets? People with more expertise, better connections, and more stable bases of politics will do it for you.

In thinking about the institutionalization of social movements, we need to remember that movements are comprised of multiple groups acting in coalitions. Because groups bring with them different, albeit often overlapping, sets of concerns and constituencies and different sets of resources and expertise, the path of institutionalization varies from group to group. At the same time, the path is generally similar across movements. Institutionalization means the process of developing a relatively routine way of dealing with institutional politics such that all concerned can have a reasonable certainty of being able to continue doing what they've been doing.

We think about social movements during their heyday as being comprised of links across a political spectrum, ranging from groups that are often located at the margins of mainstream politics to those that normally operate within the confines—and possibilities—of mainstream institutional politics. When a social movement is at its height, these links create a great deal of uncertainty for authorities, who will be guessing about how far a social movement will go and how much leverage those within government will suddenly enjoy. At the same time, these links also create a great deal of uncertainty for activists; most understand quite well that the time of peak mobilization is limited, but it is hard to know exactly what those limits are when you're in the middle of an active campaign. Will a movement continue to grow and engage new activists and institutional allies? How will authorities respond? How stable will alliances be? What demands will emerge from the broad mass that comprises a social movement? Who will gain leverage to speak for the movement? Institutionalization reflects activists and organizations trying to find workable answers to these questions, if not for the movement as a whole, at least for their own group and individual career.

Institutionalization and Coalition Fragmentation

To set out an ideal type, we can see institutionalization as comprised of three complementary processes, each affecting a different faction of a broad social movement. One faction usually gains some kind of routine access to mainstream politics and culture while limiting the scope of claims that it makes. Another essentially abandons the prospects of making effective politics within mainstream political institutions, turning instead to its base, cultivating its ideas and politics clearly, albeit in settings far less visible to mainstream political actors. The third and largest faction drops or downplays the issues of concern for the movement, with organizations focusing on other issues, and individuals often focusing on their own lives. We'll describe each process in general, then turn to two characteristic examples of social movement institutionalization.

We can think of the move into institutional politics as *cooptation*. By *coopt* I mean to change political location from the outside or borders of mainstream politics to the inside of the political arena. It does not necessarily mean that an individual or group abandons its concerns on sells out, but rather that it adopts a new location for making claims about matters of policy. Cooptation means the process of adapting mainstream political institutions and tactics for your own purposes (see Selznick 1953). At the same time, the move into institutional politics requires an accommodation to the rules, routines, procedures, and norms of mainstream politics. Broad claims and demands take a back seat to narrower, more incremental reforms. The rhetoric of ultimate goals gives way to one of shorter-term possibilities, and the tactics of defiance and disruption are overshadowed by those of persuasion and alliance building. Cooptation doesn't mean that social movement groups become less effective, but it does mean that they see their prospective achievements playing out in a series of smaller steps.

We can think about groups forced outside mainstream politics and culture as being *marginalized*. For authorities, marginalization can be achieved by repression and forcible exclusion. Although this has certainly happened in American history, more commonly, absent a broad social movement, authorities can generally ignore groups on the margins. For those on the margins, not worrying about access to large audiences or decision makers means that they can hold to a pure stance on their issues of concern, nourish internal relationships and identities, and speak their truths as clearly as possible, albeit to smaller audiences (Taylor 1989).

In thinking about marginalization, we need to remember that the American government has occasionally used forcible repression, surveillance, and harassment to drive groups out of the public eye and political relevance and individuals out of political activism altogether. Anarchists and labor leaders from the 1880s onward were attacked by police and private security companies and prevented from speaking to interested audiences or organizing workers. Pacifists who urged the United States to stay out of World War I were arrested, sometimes serving long jail sentences for using their constitutionally guaranteed right of free speech. Communists faced similar social, political, economic, and legal sanctions episodically in American history, as did nationalist organizers for African Americans, Latinos, and American Indians. Far-right organizers, including patriot militia, neo-Nazis, and racists, have been subject to harassment and surveillance by government, making it far more difficult for them to recruit new members or get their ideas out to a larger public.

All this acknowledged, active repression is a far less frequent tactic than simple neglect, or what political theorists in the 1960s and 1970s called "repressive tolerance" (Wolff, Moore, and Marcuse 1969). It is far easier and less costly to ignore the lone speaker carting his own soapbox around than to arrest and prosecute him. The street-corner recruiters are usually ignored by most who pass by, and active engagement with government just makes it easier for them to get attention. Indeed, in the crowded, cluttered marketplace of ideas, it's easier for virtually everyone to ignore most of them, particularly those promoted by small, less powerful groups.

Finally, when the issues pass from broad political attention, large factions of movements turn their concerns elsewhere. At the individual level, this turn could be to the mundanities of making a reasonable life, pursuing a career, taking care of family, enjoying friends or leisure. High-intensity activism at the height of mobilization is not sustainable over the long haul for those who have to make a living doing something else. Too many meetings, too much uncertainty, too much attention make the exciting time of mobilization limited. Individuals *demobilize*. This does not mean that they abandon their political commitments and concerns, as we discussed in Chapter 3. Instead, activists find ways of pursuing their political goals, but ways that are less visible, less time consuming, and less like participation in a movement. We can say they become depoliticized, at least in terms of their daily attention.

Other organizations, and many individuals, turn their attention to other issues that now seem more pressing, more promising, or more in line with their core mission. The nuclear freeze movement, for example, at its height included ethnic identity organizations, women's groups, and groups committed to ending U.S. intervention abroad. When the freeze movement faded, these groups didn't abandon politics or even social movement activism, but rather they focused on something other than the movement that had held them together.

These processes play off each other. When some groups gain access to mainstream political institutions and try to make use of it, their one-time allies who abhor the compromises they see have little incentive to make an accommodation to old allies they see as having abandoned them. From the other side of this process, groups that adapt to a more pragmatic pursuit of their goals see those groups that are more extreme as unnecessary baggage, perhaps too naive or extreme to be effective and potentially as a liability. Summarily, both sides develop a willingness to let the bridge that held them together collapse, and this collapse makes it more possible for authorities to accept a smaller, more manageable version of a social movement inside while simultaneously policing the boundaries to keep the larger, sloppier, more extreme version out. Institutionalization is based on a kind of channeling (Jenkins and Eckert 1986), some factions in, and some factions out.

Of course, when this starts to happen, the largest group of activists, which has a range of other concerns, sees less to hold onto in the way of a social movement. The institutional wing, working through lobbying or electoral politics or lawsuits on more incremental versions of its demands, gets less attention, and issues seem less urgent. The marginalized wing seems less relevant. And the same bandwagon effect that operates when a movement is growing operates in the same way in reverse when a movement fades. As one group opts out, others have less interest in staying. When fewer people appear likely to attend a demonstration or public meeting, the attractiveness and urgency of turning out at that meeting also diminish. Meanwhile, through institutionalization, some portion of a movement's goals receives some attention, and maybe the claims that motivated broad activism in the first place seem less urgent or, alternatively, less amenable to change.

POPULISM AND AGRICULTURAL MOVEMENTS

The story of Populism in America clearly demonstrates the process of institutionalization. To understand what happened, we can return to the problems that farmers have encountered since the founding of the United States, most notably, the cost of borrowing money. Like the farmers whom Daniel Shays organized in western Massachusetts, farmers in the South and West of the United States after the Civil War had difficulty paying back money that was worth more than what they had borrowed. For creditors, that is, people who lend money, inflation is the worst evil imaginable; it means that repayments on loans they receive will be worth less than the money they lent. But farmers aren't creditors; rather, they routinely borrow money to cover the costs of planting and harvesting a crop, to be repaid when the crop is sold. Inflation is hardly the same worry to them; instead, at least a little inflation makes it easier for them to repay loans. When the supply of money is loose, that is, easily expandable, this creates inflation because each dollar is worth a little less. In contrast, when the supply of money is tight, or limited, inflation is limited and can even operate in reverse, creating "deflation," that is, the increasing value of each dollar. Because farmers secured their loans with the only collateral they had, their farms, hard economic times brought on by bad weather or a bad economy led to foreclosures and to farmers being forced off their land.

At least since Shays's day farmers have pressed for a more flexible monetary policy and tolerance or debt forgiveness in hard times. After the Civil War, farmers, mostly in the South and West, faced hard economic times. Payments on the war debt had the effect of keeping the cost of borrowing money high. Over time, individual farmers discovered that their predicaments were, in fact, widely shared and largely beyond their control. Working harder or planting more didn't ameliorate the economic difficulties of crippling debt. The initial efforts involved self-help cooperatives, in which farmers would band together to share information, to try to secure fair prices for their produce, and to manage their debts. Ultimately they began to turn to politics when these self-help efforts proved largely ineffectual. They pressed for softer money, easier credit, and, in effect, more inflation. Farmers established local and regional organizations, including the Grange and the Greenbacks, to represent their interests. They contested elections, offered cooperative credit arrangements, organized meetings, and generally engaged in the sort of movement politics we've come to associate with more recent American history. The Greenbacks went so far as to demand paper money, whose supply would be controlled by the government, rather than by something that seemed arbitrary, that is, the supply of gold. (When the U.S. Treasury guaranteed the value of any note in gold, the supply of paper notes was strictly limited and the value of currency protected, to the detriment of debtors.)

These regional campaigns faced opposition from a well-established core of both the Democratic and the Republican parties, which represented both local and national interests of merchants, bankers, and creditors most generally. The Republicans' strength was based in the North and in the small pockets of freed slaves and abolitionists in the South. They were built upon the solid support of commercial interests and banks. The Democrats, strongest in the South, based their electoral appeal on anti-northern and anti-Republican feelings that held over long after the Civil War had passed. "Waving the bloody shirt" was shorthand for referring to the experience of the war and Reconstruction and was a reliable way to get Democratic votes in the South from the 1870s until at least the 1960s. At the same time, statewide Democratic parties in the South were most responsive to the same sort of commercial interests the Republicans supported in the North. In short, neither party was very responsive to the concerns of farmers or the question of credit.

In order to find a political space to represent the interests of farmers and others, the movements grew over time into a series of political campaigns, culminating in a more or less unified political party, the People's Party, or Populists, formally established to compete in the presidential election in 1892. From the mid-1880s, farmers' alliances accelerated their efforts to protect farmers by advocating the strict regulation of interest rates and limits on foreclosures while attempting to extend their leverage by mobilizing more farmers. The organizing effort, in a time well before radio or television, was based on traveling recruiters and small meetings in churches, schools, and farms. Activists tried to develop what were, in effect, cooperative banks that would issue their own notes with limited interest. They also tried to offer usable benefits to farmers, including cooperatives that bought and sold commodities and farm tools and provided such new products as crop insurance. Ultimately, however, they faced the difficulties of the political system because they could not issue their own currency, nor without political influence could they achieve the protectionist tariffs that the farmers needed.

Farmers were reluctant to turn to politics, both because of the difficulties of doing so and because they were enmeshed in an essentially conservative political culture. As Farmers' Alliance leader Charles Macune said, "The people we seek to relieve from the oppression of unjust conditions are the largest and most conservative class of citizens in this country" (Goodwyn 1978: 90).

The political response was to organize around the bases of American political culture, emphasizing nativism, democracy, and self-reliance. At its most radical, this response translated into a demand for the democratic control of currency, by which states would issue currency based on their local needs, and inflation would serve the majority—at the expense of their creditors. The demand for democracy and the entry into electoral politics required alliances among disparate groups that were difficult to sustain. Specifically, in order to build effective electoral majorities, the farmers had to forge partnerships with factory workers, who were by and large ethnic immigrants, mostly Catholic, in the cities. They also needed to forge partnerships with former slaves and their children trying to work as farmers in the South. In one fantastic image of possibility, L. Frank Baum's *Wizard of Oz* can be read as a political allegory. In order to get to the Emerald City (paper currency), Dorothy—from Kansas—must enlist the help of the scarecrow (farmers) and the tin man (industrial workers), aided by the lion (courage). But the legacies of nativism, racism, and particularly the Civil War proved daunting challenges to overcome.

The agrarian movement enjoyed dramatic growth, connecting previously disparate regional and local campaigns, but also tremendous internal diversity, based on the history and concerns of those regional and local campaigns. The Farmers' Alliance held a national convention in August 1890 in an effort to consolidate a broad alliance and to turn its members from a focus on self-help to a national political effort. This meant a direct attack on the two-party system and on each of the parties. But mainstream politicians would not stand still while the movement targeted them. Instead they repositioned themselves to capture some elements of the agrarian movement's constituency. In Nebraska, for example, agrarian interests supported "fusion" electoral slates, linking the Democrats with the Populists. This fusion produced Congressman William Jennings Bryan, who embraced *some* of the Populists' demands, for example, protective tariffs. The permeability of the Democratic Party, in welcoming both Populist voters and some portion of Populist ideas, particularly at state and local levels, proved to be both an opportunity for the Populists and their ultimate undoing. The dilemma is an obvious one: alliance with a major party promises the prospect of winning elections, something that is essentially impossible for independent third parties, given the nature of the American electoral system. At the same time, coalition comes with compromise, and the task of winning an electoral majority means softening and broadening ideas to include others with interests that may be quite different or even contradictory. As the Populist movement grew, it wrestled with this dilemma, coming up with different solutions in 1892 and 1896, neither of which was ultimately satisfying.

The Populists and National Electoral Politics

In July of 1892, the Populists met in Omaha, Nebraska, to nominate a ticket for the fall's presidential election. For president, the convention nominated James Weaver, a former Union general, and, to balance the ticket James Field, formerly a Confederate, from Virginia. Weaver and Field ran on a strong and provocative platform that spared nothing in the way of polemical rhetoric. In its preamble, the Populists announced that

> [w]e meet in the midst of a nation brought to the verge of moral, political, and material ruin. Corruption dominates the ballot-box, the Legislatures, the Congress, and touches even the ermine of the bench [judiciary].
>
> The people are demoralized; most of the States have been compelled to isolate the voters at the polling places to prevent universal intimidation and bribery. The newspapers are largely subsidized or muzzled, public opinion silenced, business prostrated, homes covered with mortgages, labor impoverished, and the land concentrating in the hands of capitalists. The urban workmen are denied the right to organize for self-protection, imported pauperized labor beats down their wages, a hireling standing army, unrecognized by our

laws, is established to shoot them down, and they are rapidly degenerating into European conditions. The fruits of the toil of millions are badly stolen to build up colossal fortunes for a few, unprecedented in the history of mankind; and the possessors of these, in turn, despise the Republic and endanger liberty. From the same prolific womb of governmental injustice we breed the two great classes—tramps and millionaires. The national power to create money is appropriated to enrich bond-holders; a vast public debt payable in legal-tender currency has been funded into gold-bearing bonds, thereby adding millions to the burdens of the people.[3]

The platform called for a dramatic increase in the supply of money through free coinage of gold and silver; a graduated national income tax; government ownership of railroads, post offices, and telegraph services; an eight-hour workday; government seizure of land from the railroads, speculators, and foreigners; the direct election of presidents and senators by the voters; the institution of referenda and initiative petitions; and the end to the strike-breaking private army, the Pinkertons. The platform also expressed explicit support for the Knights of Labor, then engaged in a volatile organizing campaign.

With this radical agenda, the Populists received more than one million votes, nearly 9 percent of votes cast, an impressive achievement for the first effort at a national campaign. Given the nature of the electoral system, however, that 9 percent translated to just 22 of 444 electoral votes (the party carried four states and parts of two others), less than 5 percent of the total. Moreover, Weaver's background proved to be a distinct liability to voters in the South. The Democratic candidate—and previous president, Grover Cleveland—who was an avowed "gold bug" (supporter of hard money) and overtly loyal to commercial interests in his home state of New York, carried all the southern states and won the election with 46 percent of the vote and 277 electoral votes (62 percent of the electoral votes).

The results of the 1892 election show clearly the obstacle course of American electoral politics that social movements must navigate. First, although the Populists performed very well for a new political party, 9 percent of the vote generates no institutional access to power. It doesn't generate even a proportionate share of the electoral vote, which is designed to overstate majorities. The electoral system reinforces the two-party system and encourages voters to choose the party that is closest to their view, even if not a perfect representative— or even if it's not very close. Second, given the calculus of the Electoral College, sectional loyalties are critical in any election, which means that any effective national coalition will be very broad. Third, winners take all, and in pursuing the best instead of the possible, you can actually cost your cause the possibility of influence altogether.

The Populists learned these lessons, and what they learned conditioned the outcomes of the next election. More than that, Democrats across the United States also learned about the power of the Populists, or at least their agenda. Now we can see in retrospect the dilemma as clearly as all of the activists in both parties did. How could the Populists maximize their political influence? One option was to continue to propound a radical agenda, one that played best in southern states. Over time, and with a great deal of organizing effort, the People's Party might broaden its support and deepen its analysis. At the same time, it was highly unlikely to win a national election. It might, in fact, help the party *least* sympathetic to its claims win the White House by pulling off significant blocs of voters in key states. For

---

[3] http://www.wwnorton.com/eamerica/media/ch22/resources/documents/populist.htm

the Democrats, the last part of this scenario was the most salient as a threat. More than that, however, the Populist vision held sway over a group of people that would extend its efforts to politics, a group that could be gathered up by some other challenge.

The growth of what Lawrence Goodwyn (1978) called a "shadow movement" took off after the election of 1892, although its roots dated back to the origins of the movement, as entrepreneurial politicians in both the Democratic and the Republican parties tried to peel off part of the Populist platform to cultivate voters for their own purposes. After the election, even as Populist lecturers worked the hustings, trying to build the cooperative movement, parts of the agenda showed up with increasing frequency in the speeches of non-Populist politicians. In each state, the coalition of possible Populists with more modest reformers in the Democratic or Republican Party took slightly different forms, but the process of institutionalization played out through these coalitions, sometimes gaining the People's Party little more than rhetorical endorsements.

Most notably, a young Nebraska congressman, William Jennings Bryan, took the theme of silver-based currency and ran with it—literally. In 1892, Bryan had confessed that he knew nothing about the issue but resolved to take it up because it was popular in Nebraska. In fact, the silver issue served some of the farmers' needs but also carried appeal beyond. With no interest in promoting easier currency or credit, many in the western states where mining was a major industry supported free silver simply to increase the demand for what they brought out of the ground. It wasn't an issue of democratic currency, but rather of jobs for miners.

Silver had appeal beyond the Populists and offered the promise of victory to flexible Democrats. At the Democratic national convention in Chicago in 1896, Bryan seized the nomination with a still-famous speech leading up to the critical line, "Thou shalt not crucify mankind upon a cross of gold." Bryan was a passionate advocate of free silver, but this was the only issue from the Populist platform that he had picked up.

When Bryan took the Democratic nomination, turning it into a crusade for free silver, Populists, whose convention was scheduled for St. Louis two weeks later, were faced with an obvious dilemma. They could nominate their own candidate, most likely fiery orator Tom Watson of Georgia, get their full agenda an airing, and lose the election, helping to defeat Bryan in the process. Their movement would probably disappear as a result. Alternatively, they could endorse Bryan, reach a much broader public, albeit with a smaller piece of their agenda, maybe gain access to the White House, establish a foundation for building inroads in government, and make the lives of farmers in the United States better. A hotly divided convention fished for alternatives, with one faction pressing for the nomination of Socialist leader and labor organizer Eugene Debs, but Debs refused to allow his name to be placed in nomination, supporting Bryan instead. The Populists arrived at an odd compromise, handing Bryan the Populist Party's nomination for the presidency but adopting a far more radical platform than the Democrats, one that called for the direct election of senators, nationalization of the railroads, a graduated income tax, and women's suffrage. They also nominated their own candidate, Tom Watson, for vice president, even though Watson himself did not attend the convention.

Watson was left to his own devices to come up with a campaign, and initially he pressed the Democrats to remove their vice presidential candidate, who was a banker. The Democrats did not respond, although late in the campaign they offered some money to help Watson campaign. Bryan kept more than arm's distance from the Populist effort. Although he recognized and accepted the nomination, Bryan would not coordinate his efforts with the Populists, nor would he campaign with Watson. He campaigned on the silver issue but could not engage his Republican opponent in active campaigning, much less active debate.

Indeed, in what might be seen as a foreshadowing of modern campaign politics, the Republican candidate, William McKinley, campaigned largely through surrogates while spending a great deal of money promoting his candidacy. His campaign manager, Mark Hanna, virtually assessed large business interests fees as campaign contributions and developed expensive professional campaign organizations that could operate without McKinley. McKinley took just over 50 percent of the popular vote, which translated into 271 of 447 electoral votes (more than 60 percent). Bryan, running on both the Democratic and Populist tickets, won nearly 48 percent of the vote, but almost all of it on the Democratic line.

After Populism

Bryan would run as a Democrat for president again in 1900 against Theodore Roosevelt and in 1908 against William Howard Taft, but he never again won as many popular votes, as large a share of the vote, or as many electoral votes as he did in 1896. His agenda became even murkier as well; although Bryan had a real commitment to represent "the People," his policy commitments beyond this were exceptionally vague, and he was associated with nativist causes later in life. Beyond his "Cross of Gold" speech, Bryan is today best known for arguing on behalf of the prosecution in the Scopes monkey trial against the teaching of evolution in public schools.

Indeed, the aftermath of the Populist challenge and the trajectories of its most visible partisans give us some insight into the larger process of institutionalization. Populist elected officials and candidates for office found homes in the Democratic or Republican Party, depending upon the region. Some became effective advocates for various reform movements, including women's suffrage. More disturbing was the pronounced movement of some prominent Populists to nativist and racist movements. Tom Watson, activist and orator, represented the people's interest by fighting for white supremacy, against ethnic immigrants, particularly Catholics and Jews, and against African Americans in all walks of life. He was eventually elected to the U.S. Senate as a Democrat from Georgia.

McKinley's election represented a watershed moment in American politics and the foreclosure of some kinds of possibilities for a long time. At the most basic level, never has the degree of political participation in elections been as high as it was in the election of 1896. American elections remained—and remain—governed by sectional loyalties, with one party or the other dominant in most states. The democratic control of credit and currency essentially disappeared as an issue in American politics, ultimately completely blocked by the establishment in 1913 of the Federal Reserve System, which controls the money supply and the cost of credit with the goal of protecting the interests of creditors (Greider 1987).

The fate of the farmers who supported the People's Party was, perhaps, even worse than what they had expected. Squeezed by the pressures of credit, fewer and fewer farmers were able to retain their own land; the rate of land tenancy increased, the number of farmers and agricultural workers declined and does to this day. Meanwhile, the large farmers who survived cultivated not only crops, but also ties with the elected officials they had been unable to replace and a place in the system they had been unable to alter. After World War I, organizations of farmers worked within Congress to secure their interests through a kind of clientelistic politics. Offering electoral support to members of Congress who took care of them, farmers pressed for price supports, credit, and other sorts of subsidies. Rather than contesting elections nationally, farmers supported candidates for office, both Democrats and Republicans, who supported their programs, and in key parts of the country, their support was critical to any candidate for office. Because the programs they supported did not call for a restructuring of either American government or the economy, their supporters in Congress were able to deliver the concentrated benefits the large organizations deemed critical (Hansen 1991).

In 1933, as an early part of the New Deal, President Franklin Roosevelt signed the Agricultural Adjustment Act, which was a direct response to the farm lobby. The act directed the secretary of agriculture (a cabinet position created by the Populists' enemy, Grover Cleveland) to raise agricultural prices so that farmers could pay their bills. Roosevelt and subsequent presidents have allowed the Agriculture Department reasonably broad discretion to manage the supply of basic commodities in order to keep farmers in business. In effect, this has meant support for the growth of the largest producers, and the number of farmers in the United States has declined steadily over the past hundred years, now comprising less than 2 percent of the American public.

On occasion, the plight of the "family farmer" returns to public attention, usually buttressed by protest, such as a tractorcade drive-in on Washington, D.C, in the late 1970s, or charitable events, such as the series of Farm Aid concerts led by singer-songwriter Willie Nelson. But the long decline of agricultural employment and farm land ownership has continued unabated. And although large farmers have survived, even thrived, with the help of the federal government, the pattern the Populists fought against is now well established. Most significantly for our purposes, the institutional accommodation with large agriculture was possible because the farmers abandoned their larger claims about people's democracy, democratic control of currency, and power in the United States. This is a common American story.

And what of the Populists' political demands? It's hard to make the case for a complete defeat because many of the reforms of the People's Party were taken up by others. It's also hard to show that the Populists themselves were solely responsible for these reforms. Although the subtreasury is an idea whose time passed with the Populist challenge, the United States embraced Keynesian economics during the Great Depression of the 1930s, adopting deficit spending and a more flexible monetary policy. It was 1971 before the United States finally abandoned the gold standard.

Other Populist demands were taken up more quickly, as the record of constitutional amendments demonstrates. The federal government turned to an income tax in 1913, enabled by ratification of the sixteenth Amendment to the Constitution, which gave Congress the authority to tax incomes. The initial implementation of the tax was extremely progressive because it applied only to the wealthiest Americans. Over time, the degree of progressivity has fluctuated, but the People's Party got some of what it asked for—even though it wasn't around long enough to claim influence. Also in 1913, ratification of the seventeenth Amendment provided women's suffrage, enacted first by several states and ultimately enshrined in the Constitution by the twentieth Amendment in 1920 (Banaszak 1996). The United States did not nationalize the railroads in response to Populist demands, and the railway industry, particularly passenger travel, declined in response to federal subsidies for highway construction and the growth of air transport. In 1970, President Nixon called for the creation of a national passenger railway, Amtrak, which has faltered largely because of stingy public investment and limited ridership. To see some of the Populist demands taken up by both other social movements and ultimately the government illustrates the complicated process of achieving political influence and the institutionalization of social movements.

LABOR MOVEMENTS AND AMERICAN POLITICS

We can see that the same sorts of processes developed over the longer history of the labor movement in the United States. Like the farmers' movement, expressed through the People's Party, the labor movement at times called for the wholesale restructuring of the American governmental structure and economy. The first inklings of a labor movement in the United States date back to 1830, when industrial workers were still a small portion of the American workforce. The basic idea has always been to afford workers greater leverage in dealing with employers, particularly about the price and conditions of labor. Union advocates have argued, more or less persuasively to American workers, that absent collective organization and bargaining, individual workers will be unable to do anything but make wealthy capitalists wealthier. The basic strategies and debates of the labor movement were all evident relatively early in its history and have recirculated over the movement's long history. First, activists differed in their emphasis on bringing in government action to protect their rights and to represent their interests. Second, organizers disagreed about how to organize, specifically, whether to organize labor unions around skilled labor and particular crafts or, instead, to organize all workers in an industry—or indeed all workers—to bargain collectively. In general, supporters of industrial unionism were much more inclined to embrace explicitly political strategies, whereas craft union supporters gave broader politics a lower priority.

There were winners and losers with each approach. Government action and industrial unionism would be more helpful to less skilled workers, for example, than would be negotiated contracts and craft unionism. At the same time, the latter approach promised to deliver better benefits more easily to more skilled workers. The two approaches coexisted and competed within the labor movement throughout most of its history. The most powerful exponent of the primarily political approach was the Knights of Labor, which dated its origin to the founding of a secret society on Thanksgiving in 1869 and ultimately organized and represented at least 750,000 workers but was crushed by the countermobilization of employers, who made use of state and national government resources to repress the union (Voss 1993). Organizing skilled and unskilled workers together, the Knights inspired capital to counterorganize, establishing Employers' Associations, which employed a variety of tactics to combat labor. The associations would afford employers cooperation in hiring both strike-breakers and private police and also provided intelligence on the best ways to deal with labor militancy. Anticipating a strike, for example, manufacturers might lock out the unionized workers, guarding the factory with hired police and continuing operations with workers often imported from elsewhere who would cross picket lines. By the 1890s, the period of the peak and decline of the People's Party, the Knights had begun to fragment and falter in the face of a national depression.

The American Federation of Labor (AFL), founded in the 1880s, defined itself in opposition to the Knights, whom its organizers described as socialistic. It explicitly rejected founding a political party, emphasizing instead organization by craft. The more skilled workers were able to negotiate better deals with employers by promising labor peace and successfully negotiated the eight-hour workday and workmen's compensation while simultaneously encouraging government to regulate the labor market by banning child labor. Although labor leader Samuel Gompers himself claimed an early affiliation with Marx and Marxism, the history of the AFL in the United States has been to accommodate organized labor with the political structures of the United States and to prioritize the well-being of the workers it organized over the larger working class. The AFL has consistently generated challengers on its left, both from within the affiliated unions and from outside (Kimmeldorf and Stepan-Norris 1992).

The IWW was the best known of the leftist competitors for organizing labor prior to the 1930s. In the context of the Great Depression, John Lewis, leader of the mineworkers, led several unions within the AFL to adopt industry-wide organizing strategies, including a major organizing initiative within major industry sectors, including steel and automobiles. Lewis established the Committee (later Congress) of Industrial Organizations as a faction within the AFL. The AFL revoked the charter of ten of these dissident unions, but the CIO continued to organize throughout the 1930s.

New Deal Responses to Labor

At the same time, the Roosevelt administration responded to labor unrest, including an unprecedented wave of strikes in 1933 and 1934, by offering a secure path toward institutionalization, setting rules for organizers and employers. In 1935, the administration supported the Wagner Act, which included the National Labor Relations Act (NLRA). The NLRA governed and protected the activities of labor organizers and limited what employers could do in response. Activists were allowed to try to organize workers, and employers were specifically prohibited from disciplining workers engaged in union activity. Further, employers were prohibited from establishing company unions, spying on workers, or generally coercing workers from joining a union.

The NLRA also established the National Labor Relations Board (NLRB), which serves as a regulator of labor relations. The NLRB is charged with ensuring fair elections when workers vote on whether to establish a union at a site and with preventing employers from breaking the law to stack the deck in their favor. It can fine employers for unfair labor practices, and it is responsible for monitoring organizing elections, certifying or decertifying unions as the legitimate voice of workers for collective bargaining with employers.

The rate of union organization increased after passage of the NLRA, as did the rate of strikes in support of new unions. In essence, the NLRA is a key event in a longer classic case of institutionalization. It set a clear path for organizers and established rules that regulated an ongoing battle about organizing labor. It also tied the political wing of organized labor to the Democratic Party, a link that continued for the next seventy years. By downplaying larger political claims and negotiating (and honoring) contracts with employers, labor activists provided benefits for their members and stability for their employers. The NLRA effectively established a way in which organized labor could exist and sustain itself without fundamentally altering the nature of American politics or the economy. World War II marked a temporary end to dramatically increased union organizing, partly because the war demanded unity, and partly because millions of young men were mobilized into the military.

Coupled with the industrial mobilization to supply the war effort, employment increased across the United States as African Americans and women entered the industrial workforce.

When the troops returned from World War II, there was a period of intense labor militancy, with strikes across the United States in major industries as workers called for increased wages and benefits and returning soldiers fought to regain their jobs from the women and blacks who had filled them during the war. In 1946 and 1947, President Truman set about quelling labor unrest and establishing the United States as a world power. Endorsed by the largest unions, Truman saw himself as sympathetic to the goals of organized labor but was determined not to let strikes and organizing interfere with industrial production in the United States. He called for wage, price, and rent controls, which, according to organized labor, limited wages more than anything else. At the same time, Truman used executive orders and court injunctions to prevent strikes, leading to fines and arrests for militant labor leaders.

Still, Truman saw himself as ultimately sympathetic to labor's interests; this was not the case for Congress, which was more aggressive in seeking to curb labor unrest. Over Truman's veto Congress in 1947 passed the Taft-Hartley Act, which dealt a critical blow to organized labor. The act guaranteed the rights of workers not to join unions as a condition of their employment and prohibited "secondary strikes" and boycotts, that is, sympathy strikes by workers not involved in a particular contract dispute. The act required union leaders to show they were not members of the Communist Party, allowed the attorney general to execute an injunction against strikes if he deemed the security of the United States to be threatened, and prohibited federal workers from striking altogether.

The stance of the federal government toward organized labor affected the strategies, tactics, and claims embraced by organizers. After passage of the NLRA, America experienced an increase in the number of strikes as well as increased efforts to organize new unions. After Taft-Hartley, however, there was not only a long, steady decline in the number of strikes, but also a declining share of strikes focused on organizing new workplaces, with the greater share of strikes being devoted to wages and hours (Wallace, Rubin, and Smith 1988). Whereas NLRA provided a entry to organizing, Taft-Hartley made new organizing much more difficult—and ultimately less militant in terms of claims and tactics.

At the same time, the United States established itself as a global actor and under Truman's National Security Act of 1948, engaged in the beginnings of a long Cold War with the Soviet Union, which included domestic repression of people with potential connections with Communist ideas or organizations. Responding to this domestic threat, both labor federations purged from their midst perceived Communists, who included some of the most committed and talented political organizers. The more difficult political environment for labor ultimately encouraged leaders of the American Federation of Labor and the Congress of Industrial Organizations to manage their own differences and negotiate a merger, achieved in 1955. This merger represented a substantial change for the CIO unions, which had been more militant, in terms of both tactics and demands, and more generally aggressive politically (Stepan-Norris and Zeitlin 2003), and marked the general moderation of the labor movement as a whole. In conjunction with the restructuring of the American economy, the institutionalization of the labor movement, although providing predictability to both employers and unionized labor, has produced a long, steady decline in the percentage of American workers represented by unions. From 1973 to 2003, the number of unionized workers declined slowly from over eighteen million people to just over fifteen million even as the workforce expanded. Thus, the percentage of unionized workers over the same period declined by about half, from 24 percent to just over 12 percent. In 1947, on the eve of Taft-Hartley, fully 35 percent of the labor force was unionized, the high point in U.S. history, and this level was maintained until the mid-1950s. Moreover, the share of union membership represented by government employees, who are bound by law to be less militant, has increased dramatically.

The story of the institutionalization of the labor movement in the United States is a long and complicated one and one that continues to develop. At the same time, in broad outline, it is remarkably similar to that of the agricultural workers behind the Populists. There were many efforts to organize both groups that differed in terms of their inclusiveness and their engagement with mainstream American politics, with ongoing organizing battles among competitors. In both cases, over a long period of time, the more moderate, perhaps pragmatic, tendency was able to win out over more universalistic political tendencies. Instead of focusing on the basic structure of American politics, the successful organizers focused on securing a place for their constituents within the existing political and economic structure. Unlike the farmers, organized labor was able to help elect presidents who had some sympathy with their concerns, but in office, even Roosevelt and Truman brokered compromises for labor to balance other concerns. The establishment of direct routes of access and institutional rules of participation surely helped reduce discriminatory practices and violence against organizers, and the development of routinized relationships between large unions and employers led, at least for a long while, to stable, predictable, increased wages and continued production. Over time, however, institutionalization provided routes for opponents, as well as activists, to weigh in on the politics of the issues, limiting the sorts of claims that social movement organizers could make. Over time, the number of people represented by both farmers' organizations and organized labor has decreased, and their political power has eroded.

REVISITING INSTITUTIONALIZATION

The notion of bringing conflict into the mainstream political process is easily traced back to James Madison's constitutional design. Although we certainly don't want to sugarcoat difficult organizing and political battles that sometimes included violence, gaining access to mainstream political institutions in the United States remains *relatively* easy. At the same time, routine representation within mainstream politics comes with a cost but also often brings benefits. It's not always clear that when representatives of a social movement buy into the system, they are selling out their constituents. Rather, it's a question of maximizing the impact a movement can have and cutting the best deal that it can.

We can think of institutionalization as taking place along three dimensions that don't necessarily move in sync. First, *claims* or concerns can be institutionalized, recognized as legitimate, and routinely dealt with in mainstream politics. Second, constituencies can become recognized players in mainstream American politics, getting a seat at the negotiating table when decisions are made about particular sets of issues. In the politics of public education, for example, both teachers' unions and representatives of African Americans are routinely consulted by policymakers. Third, tactics and processes can become institutionalized such that a range of groups imitates successful tactics, and all players in the political conflict know what to expect from use of those tactics. Again, they become routinized, repeatable, essentially normal politics.

This analytical frame helps organize the cases we reviewed earlier in this chapter. We saw that *some* of the claims or demands of both the Populist movement and the labor movement won recognition, although they may be redefined in the process. In the case of labor, government provided a formal institutional habitat for labor concerns and regulated—and to some degree routinized—the organizing and bargaining process, affording security about some of labor's issues for some constituents for the better part of the last hundred years. In the case of nuclear power, a range of concerns about the politics and economics of nuclear power plant construction was accepted and accommodated by federal agencies, whereas others were excluded and redefined primarily as safety. Since the advent of the nuclear age, movements against nuclear weapons have generally succeeded in getting rhetorical recognition of their concerns about the dangers of nuclear fallout or nuclear war as well as the establishment of an arms control process that remains, generally, even in the absence of pressure from social movements. The existence of the Equal Employment Opportunity Commission, for example, reflects a response to a social movement and an acceptance of at least one version of the concerns that motivated a movement. Indeed, if we look at a roster of federal government offices, we can note scores of bureaus and office founded exactly in response to social movements.

Similarly, American government offers the opportunity for incorporating constituencies, generally recognized by their representatives. This process takes place at absolutely every part of the political process. At the grassroots level, in local electoral politics ethnic minorities are courted as they establish themselves, sometimes even before they mobilize. In exchange for the votes of new communities, politicians and political parties offer a mix of symbolic and substantive enticements, ranging from rhetoric to positions on policy to plain patronage. At the federal level, constituencies are incorporated and institutionalized through the appointment process and through the establishment of dedicated agencies, for example, the establishment of the Department of Education in response to labor mobilization by teachers and the establishment of the Environmental Protection Agency in response to the environmental movement. We know, for example, that any president from either party will try to offer a slate of cabinet officers that represents some of the range of American demography as well as politics. There will be not only women and ethnic and regional diversity, but also some amount of occupational and interest diversity. This is also institutionalization.

Finally, there is what we might describe as the institutionalization and routinization of social movement tactics, as well as government responses. We have seen in reviewing the development of tactics that many forms of protest have histories that date to the founding of the United States—and prior. When any group uses a tactic in a way that seems successful, other challengers, including political opponents, will pick up on it, adopting it for their own. In seeking to manage this process, and to limit the amount of disruption that protesters cause, both federal and state governments, particularly police departments, have developed a ready capacity to manage demonstrations and protests, effectively ensuring the right of the people peaceably to assemble, as promised in the First Amendment to the Constitution, while limiting the amount of influence such protests can have. In the next chapter, we will see that the tactic of protest itself has become firmly institutionalized in American politics.

CHAPTER 8

WHEN EVERYONE PROTESTS

The Democratic national convention in Chicago in 1968 was a watershed for both protest and party politics.[1] Demonstrators outside the convention site camped in Lincoln Park, using Vice President Hubert Humphrey's nomination as occasion to protest against the war in Vietnam and for increased attention to civil rights and social justice. Humphrey had publicly defended President Johnson's policies in Vietnam even while suggesting that he might do things differently as president. Despite the salience of the war, the convention nominated Humphrey—even though he had not entered a single primary. National media projected a range of protest activities, including nonviolent marches, street theater, and overt conflict with police. The tumult outside the convention center amplified the conflicts within as police clashed with party activists and journalists (Farber 1988).

That convention provided an obvious target for activists. At once, political leaders responsible for both the war and federal action on behalf of civil rights were meeting inside the convention hall, arguing about not only the party's nominee for president, but also the platform on which he would run. The convention was a site for *direct access* to decision makers. More than that, national media attention to the convention offered activists the prospects of projecting their concerns to a far broader audience, potentially influencing policy by expanding the scope of the political conflict and mobilizing new actors in other efforts. When the federal government chose to prosecute eight political organizers (Rennie Davis, David Dellinger, John Froines, Tom Hayden, Abbie Hoffman, Jerry Rubin, Bobby Seale, and Lee Weiner) for inciting a crowd to riot, the political conflict around the convention extended over a period of years. The protests at the convention reflected a coalition effort as a variety of groups came to Chicago each bringing its own concerns and tactics. Pacifists Davis and Dellinger, for example, came from the National Mobilization against the War and focused on the war issue. Hayden represented the schism-riddled Students for a Democratic Society (SDS), and Bobby Seale, who appeared for only a relatively brief speech, was a leader of the Black Panther Party. Meanwhile, Hoffman and Rubin, who had founded the Youth International Party (Yippies), were fronting a countercultural challenge to far more than the Democratic Party and employed creative street theater, including nominating their own candidate for president, "Pigasus," a pig. The ensuing trial of the defendants was at least as theatrical as the protests at the convention and extended the political conflict over a period of years.

---

[1] I am grateful to Annie Peshkam for research assistance on political conventions.

But although the Chicago protests were a departure in scope from previous convention protests, the recognition of the party convention as a political opportunity was already well established in American politics. Political conventions in the United States always seem to provide such a dual benefit to activists: direct access to political elites and media attention for political issues. As such, they provide a regularly recurring opening for activists (see Hilgartner and Bosk 1988). Because the conventions are regularly scheduled and relatively infrequent (every four years) occasions, they provide a window through which to see change and continuity in American protest politics.

We will see that increased numbers of constituencies are protesting at political conventions, reflecting the spread of social movement approaches throughout American politics. In this chapter we will focus first on how protest at political conventions has changed. We will then focus on the broader implications of the increasing use of political protest in American politics. Protest has now become so widespread that it is common to see both sides of a political conflict using social movement forms and tactics, which we will consider in looking at movement-countermovement dynamics. We will conclude with a discussion of the ubiquity of protest in America.

PROTEST AT CONVENTIONS

In looking at protest at political conventions, we can see a kind of institutionalization and routinization of protest politics in America. We can see the mobilization of a more diverse collection of people organizing on behalf of a wider variety of causes, as well as the development of resilient systems of social control that make protest both more manageable and likely less disruptive (McCarthy and McPhail 1998)—and probably less effective.

Both the Democratic and Republican parties have staged national four-day conventions during every presidential election year for more than a century. As a result, the conventions afford a clear window through which to observe potential changes in the nature of protest politics. To assess such changes in protest politics over the past several decades, we can look at political conventions held from 1948 to 2000.

Looking at *The New York Times'* coverage of protest around a political convention (the four days of the convention at the center of a two-week period, five days before and five after), we can see which protests generated attention at each of twenty-eight conventions that took place during this period.[2] In this way, we can see not only changes over time in protest politics, but also differences between the two major parties.

Figure 8.1 shows the number of protests that take place at political conventions, demonstrating that protest is a recurrent feature of conventions, historically slightly more prevalent at Democratic conventions than at Republican. The year 1968 is actually a

---

[2] Scholars have criticized the use of *The New York Times* as being too limited in assessing protest politics, but the paper does provide a consistent, readily available source of historical data (e.g., Earl, Martin, McCarthy, and Soule 2004; Rucht, Koopmans, and Neidhardt 1999). Although we would not presume that all events were covered, we do assume that the distortions would be relatively constant, thus allowing a meaningful look at changes over time.

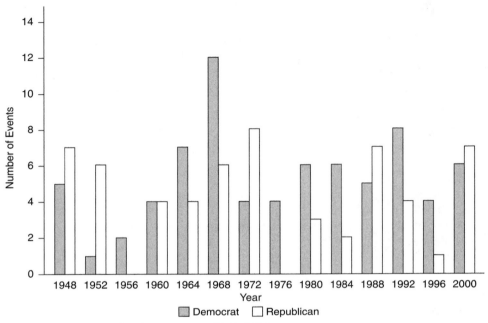

Figure 1. Protest at political conventions, 1948–2000.

watershed for the Democratic Party; however, both party conventions witnessed substantial numbers of protests since that time.

But what are the protesters protesting about? Figure 8.2 notes the presence of twenty issues at various times. A few points are worth noting. First, labor is virtually always present as an issue, even as the labor movement has declined over the past half-century (Goldfield 1987). Whereas unions sometimes skip Republican conventions, they almost never skip Democratic conventions. Civil rights is also a recurrent issue, again more prevalent at Democratic than at Republican conventions. The large number of new issues that appears in 2000 is generally present during the conventions of both parties. Importantly, even if the grievance is not directed at one party or another, the presence of a convention affords an opportunity for activists to make their claims heard.

Figure 8.3 shows the number of events and the number of issues together, combining the conventions of both parties. Here we see that the number of protests has increased far less dramatically than has the number of issues. Contrasting the years 1968 and 2000 is instructive. Many protests staged in the former year were directed at the war and civil rights. The message projected in the mass media then would include the issues as well as the tactics. In contrast, in the year 2000, a somewhat smaller number of events carried a much larger number of issues, including animal rights, environmental protection, the death penalty, and peace. Any activist group will have more difficulty in getting its message out amid the clutter of issues. And any activist group is much less likely to be alone.

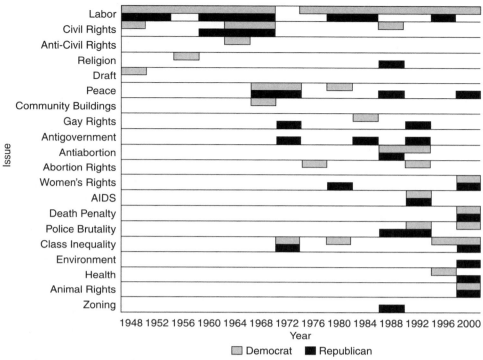

Figure 2. Issues protested during political conventions, 1948–2000.

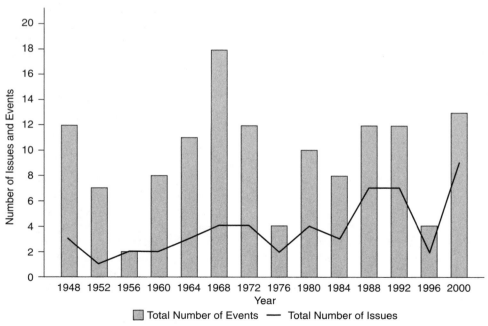

Figure 3. Number of protests and number of issues at political conventions, 1948–2000.

BOTH SIDES NOW

For forty-five days, beginning in July 1991, thousands of protesters marched in the streets of Wichita, Kansas, converging on a clinic run by Dr. George Tiller, one of the few clinics in the area that performed late-term abortions. Antiabortion forces had bombed Tiller's Women's Health Care Services clinic six years before, but Tiller was committed, and the clinic stayed open. The Summer of Mercy, organized by Operation Rescue, represented the success of a strategic shift for the antiabortion movement. Rather than depend upon the efforts of a few extremely committed individuals, those willing to use bombs, for example, Operation Rescue adopted the tactics of the civil rights movement, calling for mass action in targeting a local evil to raise broader concerns.

An estimated thirty thousand people participated in the summer's events, which included prayers, demonstrations, and blockades of Tiller's clinic. According to an abortion rights Web site (www.nnaf.org.pledge), all three clinics performing abortions in Wichita closed their doors for a week, and the "rescuers" persisted when the clinics reopened. Armed with an injunction from a federal judge against the demonstrators blocking access to the clinics, federal marshals began making arrests when the clinics reopened. All told, some twenty-seven hundred people were arrested for the blockades over those six weeks, and the event, in many ways, marked the height of the antiabortion movement's visibility. The massive, sustained, and targeted protests brought the antiabortion movement national visibility—again—while simultaneously imposing high costs on the city of Wichita, which had to pay for more police and for detaining and trying the arrested. And if the protests caused some of the clinic workers to seek other job opportunities, that would be easy to understand.

Dr. Tiller, however, was undaunted and continued his practice. Even two years later, when an antiabortion activist shot him in both arms, Tiller was still committed to providing late-term abortions to women, returning to work the next day. And ten years later, when Rescue America, the successor to Operation Rescue, sought to revive its prominence, Tiller was still continuing his work. For Rescue America, however, the struggle to con-tinue was somewhat more difficult. Reverend Flip Benham announced the start of an anniversary campaign that he promised would be even more effective than the Summer of Mercy. "You mark these words: they will not be there next year," Benham said. "That is a prophetic witness." Tiller disagreed, posting a sign in the entrance to the clinic's parking lot that read: "Women need abortions and I'm going to do them. George Tiller" (Hegeman 2001).

But the tenth anniversary of the Summer of Mercy was considerably smaller and less disruptive than the event it commemorated. Antiabortion activists from around the country gathered again in Wichita but prayed, protested, engaged in civil disobedience, and fasted in spurts over one week, rather than over more than six weeks. The largest rallies drew an estimated five-hundred participants, and fewer than ten people were arrested. The city of Wichita, its citizens, and Dr. Tiller were generally able to conduct their business as usual (Glasser 2001). Local abortion rights groups claimed this state of affairs as a victory, noting that access to safe and legal abortions remained whereas the antiabortion movement had largely faltered. Indeed, abortion rights supporters used the anniversary as an opportunity to do their own mobilizing and organizing. Local activist groups, tapping into national networks of support, stood vigil outside the clinic whenever the antiabortion pro-testers were present, with the two sides occasionally clashing. They raised money, escorted women seeking abortions, monitored the actions of the other side, and publicized their ef-forts, proclaiming Tiller's clinic an "Outpost of Reproductive Freedom" (National Network of Abortion Funds [NNAF] Web site: www.nnaf.org).

Prophecies aside, Dr. Tiller continued performing abortions in Wichita, including late-term abortions. Indeed, he has made it a practice to work for free on the anniversary of *Roe v. Wade* (Hegeman 2002) as antiabortion protesters demonstrate outside his clinic. More than the availability of abortions in Wichita, however, the story of politics around Tiller's clinic demonstrates the changing nature of social movements in the United States by underscoring the ongoing interactions of movements and countermovements and by demonstrating the firm institutionalization of protest tactics as part of the normal political repertoire.

The abortion battles in Witchita underscore the extended development of social move-ments and their opponents, and the interaction in which activists on more than one side of an issue use social movement approaches.

Ongoing Movement Interaction: The Makah Whale Hunt

Like most American Indian tribes, the Makah have struggled to maintain their identity and their well-being in the United States. The treaty negotiated with the Governor of Washing-ton Territory in 1855 explicitly protected the Makah's right to continue harvesting whales. By the 1920s, however, with stocks of gray whales decimated by commercial hunting, the Makah abandoned whaling. In the late 1990s, pointing to dramatically increased gray whale populations, the Makah sought to resume whaling in Neah Bay, in the upper Northwest cor-ner of Washington State.[3]

The federal government recognized the tribe's treaty rights, but urged the Makah to ob-tain permission from the International Whaling Commission (IWC). Even as the Makah made their case before the IWC, they were met by opponents of whaling, including members of the U.S. Congress, who testified against the resumption of whaling in 1997. The United States, however, supported the hunt and negotiated an exchange of whaling quotas with Russia, assigning the U.S. allotment of whales to the Makah.

With the help of a large federal grant, the Makah established their own whaling commission in 1998, which worked to establish a humane way to hunt whales. The plan was to hunt in a thirty-two-foot canoe, accompanied by modern high-speed boats, harpoon the whale, then immediately shoot it with a fifty-caliber gun. Once the whale was dead, a man would dive into the water and sew its mouth shut to prevent it from sinking; all the hunting vessels would then tow the whale to shore where it could be ritually butchered and distributed to the tribe, which includes just over twelve hundred registered members.

---

[3] This account draws from information provided on websites of the parties in this dispute. See http://www.cnie.org/NAE/cases/makah/index.html, http://www.makah.com/whaling.htm, http://www.seashepherd.org/news/media_050922_3.html.

Most of the Makah support the hunt, and the tribe's leadership see whaling as a critical component of culture. "More than anything else," announces the tribe's website (http://www.makah.com/whaling.htm), "whaling represents the spiritual and technological preparedness of the Makah people and the wealth of culture." The Makah argued that their whaling, in addition to being legally protected, was an essential component of their tribal identity.

The revival of the Makah whale hunt generated great opposition, including more than 250 animal rights and conservation groups (but not Greenpeace or the Sierra Club). Opposition also came from whale-watching interests in Washington state, others who oppose tribal exercise of old treaty rights, and still others who object to the financial cost to the American government (often estimated in excess of $1.5 million). Led by the Sea Shepherd Conservation Society, whaling opponents have deployed a wide range of arguments against Makah whaling, including: emphasizing that the Makah are clearly not dependent on whale meat; that the Makah are being manipulated by the Japanese to expand the internationally-accepted rationales for whaling; that Makah tribal elders, representing the real Makah identity, oppose the hunt. (Whaling opponents within the tribe claim to have faced reprisals, including dismissal from tribal jobs.)

When the Makah first tried to reinstate the whale hunt, in the fall of 1998, the hunt boat was surrounded by a flotilla of protest boats, which committed to staying between the Makah and any whales. For two months, environmental groups essentially occupied Neah Bay. Fighting back, the Makah Tribal Council passed an ordinance preventing any of the boats from docking at their marina. On land, opponents of whaling staged protest marches and demonstrations, sometimes ending in arrests. Each side has charged the other with gratuitous insults and harassment. The occupation ended only when the whale migration had passed and the prospects of actually catching a whale had disappeared.

The following year, however, the Makah resumed their hunt, this time protected by U.S. Coast Guard ships, which enforced a five hundred-foot buffer zone around the hunt canoe and seized several of the protest boats. The hunters killed one whale, which they brought back to shore, butchered, and distributed among the tribe. To date, this is the full yield of the Makah hunt. Whaling opponents, defeated at Neah Bay, went to federal courts to stop the hunt. They argued that the federal government was hasty in authorizing the hunt, neglecting studies and environmental impact statements required by the Marine Mammal Protection Act of 1972. This conflict continues in the courts and each side has worked to enlist outside support in the United States and abroad, including allies within various bureaucratic agencies, elected officials, and international support.

The story of the Makah quest for the whale hunt directs our attention to the ongoing interactions among opposing movements. Activists on more than one side of an issue must deal not only with each other, but also the outsiders drawn into the conflict. Activists on one side will shop for allies and venues friendly to their claims, and their opponents are virtually forced to follow them. Also, opposing movements will frequently challenge not only the claims and arguments of their opponents, but also their right to make them. In the United States, where more than one side of a conflict is likely to be able to find allies in government, social movement conflicts extend over long periods of time, and do not generally end easily or neatly.

MOVEMENT-COUNTERMOVEMENT DYNAMICS

It's appealingly simple to think about protest movements as the province of those who can't win in any other way and who are working in opposition to a reasonably unified government representing some kind of policy consensus of those interested and relevant to the issue. In reality, however, life and politics are more complicated, particularly in the United States, where the separation of powers and federalism ensure that a broad range of groups is likely to find both allies and opponents in government.

Think, for example, of the civil rights movement, which in its heyday organized against state and local governments in the American South that enforced segregation. By the mid-1950s, aided by the Supreme Court decision *Brown v. Board of Education,* civil rights activists sometimes enjoyed the support of the federal government in their efforts to desegregate public schools and then other public facilities and then to register people to vote. At the same time, acting in opposition to the movement were not only the local and state governments, but also organized groups of white southerners who not only disagreed with the civil rights movement's claims, but also distrusted the willingness or capacity of their governments to resist change effectively. Citizens' councils throughout the South, sometimes covertly, organized opposition to the civil rights movement. Such opposition included all the trappings of a social movement: letters and lobbying directed at elected officials, intensive work in electoral campaigns, and demonstrations and visible opposition to civil rights demonstrations, augmented by often-vigorous harassment of civil rights activists, including surveillance, physical intimidation, violence, and, occasionally, murder. The white resistance movement as a whole operated with more autonomy and flexibility than did often-allied local and state governments. Both movements, civil rights and white resistance, found allies in government, and both directed some portion of their efforts at government and some portion at each other.

In fact, the development of countermovements that engage social protest over the long haul has become the rule, rather than the exception, of American politics. A countermovement is interested in the same issues as the social movement it responds to but wants everything to turn out differently. The white resistance movement wanted to maintain legally supported segregation and, more generally, to stifle a movement that wanted change. "Wise use" activists on environmental issues want to limit government oversight of the use of private property and to reverse and limit the influence of environmental activists. Proponents of a constitutional amendment to strictly define marriage want to counter the claims of lesbian and gay activists. And protesters who routinely show up to challenge antiwar demonstrators want to counter the public influence of an antiwar movement. The existence of opposition that sometimes uses the forms and tactics of social movements has become a permanent feature of American political life. And the notion of a limited response to a movement during its peak mobilization has been replaced by the long-term institutionalization of social movement groups that pursue their goals through a variety of means. Instead of an occasional movement-countermovement response, we've seen the development of long-term oppositional movements operating in pairs (Meyer and Staggenborg 1996).

Let's return to the example of the abortion debate in the United States to see how these politics play out over an extended period of time. The movement for access to birth control, which later turned to the pursuit of legal access to abortion, dates back to the suffrage movement. In the 1960s, what came to be called the "abortion movement" pressed for legalized abortion, which was becoming more available throughout the world. Abortion access was variously tied up with the women's movement, efforts to control population growth, and professional efforts at legal reform. One component of the movement pressed for reform, while another, housed in local feminist networks, provided services, including referrals for illegal abortions, to pregnant women.

In 1966, as the abortion movement was growing, an opposition also emerged, initially funded by the Roman Catholic Church through the efforts of the National Council of Bishops' Committee on Family Life. Because abortion was generally illegal, its efforts were limited, and its political mobilization was almost invisible until called to action by state legislatures considering reform of abortion laws (Blanchard 1994; Staggenborg 1991). By the early 1970s, four states provided ready access to abortion, and a campaign for other statewide campaigns was growing—along with the number of women crossing state lines to obtain abortions.

At the same time, not quite independent of the larger movement, two lawyers in Texas sought a plaintiff for making a legal, rights-based claim on abortion rights. Veterans of women's groups and well acquainted with the successes of the civil rights movement, Linda Coffey and Sarah Weddington used a pregnant woman unable to get a legal abortion in Texas as a plaintiff. Although the plaintiff had given birth and had put her little girl up for adoption by the time the case got to the Supreme Court, the Court saw a constitutional issue and took the case. It handed down its *Roe v. Wade* decision in January of 1973. With a 6–3 majority, the Court ruled that women have a fundamental right to make decisions about pregnancy and abortion during the first trimester, that states have an interest in protecting an unborn child during the third trimester, and that in between there has to be a balancing of rights. Immediately this decision struck down laws on abortion in forty-six of fifty states, and abortion rights activists hoped that they had won a victory that put an end to their struggle. Initially the antiabortion side was offended but quiet, and the decision generated surprisingly little attention—at least in retrospect.

Opponents of abortion organized in response to the decision at a time when the basic rules of electoral politics were changing. As political parties grew weaker, the direct primary process for choosing candidates for the presidency became well established, and as the costs of campaigning grew, antiabortion leaders found ways to enter the political process that made them increasingly powerful. In the 1976 campaign for the presidency, both Democrat Jimmy Carter and aspiring Republican candidate Ronald Reagan sought to cultivate evangelical Christians to support their efforts. Carter won the Democratic nomination and ultimately the presidency while avoiding a strong position on abortion, but the movement had found a tactic and an opening in politics.

Lobbying Congress, antiabortion activists pressed for an end to government funding, through Medicaid, of abortions for poor women. The Hyde Amendment, adopted by Congress in 1976, didn't reverse the Supreme Court's decision, but it prohibited the federal government from paying for abortion. Abortion remained reasonably accessible for women who could afford it. Meanwhile, Ronald Reagan, positioning himself for another run at the presidency, used the abortion issue to raise money and mobilize support from grassroots activists, who were developing their expertise working in campaigns for Congress in the 1978 elections. Reagan won the Republican Party's nomination in 1980, emphasizing his strong opposition to abortion and defeating his closest rival, George H. W. Bush, who until that time had supported abortion rights. Reagan asked Bush to join the Republican ticket as candidate for vice president, and Bush reconsidered his position on abortion.

The antiabortion movement was fairly quiet in the early years of the Reagan administration, no doubt anticipating that Reagan would deliver on his commitment, somehow
finding a way to make abortion illegal. By the mid-1980s, however, the movement saw little
progress at the federal level, and activists experimented with different ways of making their
positions on abortion impossible for politicians to avoid. The first visible efforts included
violence at abortion clinics, which mobilized abortion rights supporters and alienated many
abortion opponents. Activists innovated; emphasizing a different term, "pro-life," activists
diversified their tactics. The early 1980s brought bombings of abortion clinics, large demonstrations, and lobbying at the state level to restrict access to abortion.

Responding to the successful mobilization of their opponents, abortion rights activists,
adopting the term "pro-choice," found a home within the Democratic Party. (Notably, Jesse
Jackson, anticipating a run for the Democratic presidential nomination, reconsidered his
antiabortion position in 1983, adopting instead a "pro-choice" stance.) By the mid-1980s,
both sides were fully mobilized. Antiabortion activists sought to limit access to abortion bit
by bit, reducing funding, promoting restrictions such as parental notification for minors,
working in electoral campaigns, and looking forward to a reversal of *Roe*. Abortion rights
activists worked within the Democratic Party, essentially establishing a pro-choice position
as a litmus test for presidential hopefuls and trying to counter every proposed restriction at
every level.

The two sides developed a certain odd symmetry. Both sides were comprised of broad
coalitions, including both single-issue and multi-issue groups. Both sides developed local
networks engaged in street action, conventional politics, and campaigns of all kinds, loosely
coordinated by national groups. Each side developed an increasingly exclusive relationship
with one of the major political parties, making it increasingly difficult for abortion rights
supporters in the Republican Party and for abortion opponents in the Democratic Party.
Both sides litigated, lobbied, raised money, called demonstrations and press conferences,
engaged in public education, and constantly warned partisans that the next piece of legislation, election, or demonstration represented a grave threat to the future of their cause.
Each side sought new ways to approach the broader issues of reproductive rights but was
constantly on the defensive in response to the other side's initiatives. In essence, the two
sides created a kind of structural mirror image. If one side sought to testify in judicial
confirmation hearings, for example, the other side pressed its allies in Congress to have the
same opportunity. Lobbying by one side at the state level had to be countered by lobbying
by the other side at the state level. Perhaps most dramatically, effective action in the streets,
such as the Rescue America effort in Wichita, had to be countered by defensive action in
the streets—augmented by proactive efforts to sue antiabortion leaders for the costs associated with policing such demonstrations and direct actions. Antiabortion "sidewalk counseling," usually comprised of accusatory screams accompanied by horrific visual aids depicting destroyed fetuses, was countered by "escorts" provided by abortion rights activists.
And so on.

When one side had a strong ally in the presidency, it pressed the president to make favorable statements and appointments, particularly to the judiciary, and to initiate helpful
legislation. In 1994, for example, at the urging of President Clinton, Congress passed the
Freedom of Access to Clinic Entrances Act (FACE), which made it much more difficult for
antiabortion activists to shut down clinics. When President George W. Bush won a second
term as president in 2004, everyone concerned with the issue expected the president to

make judicial appointments reflecting his longstanding opposition to abortion and dependence on the pro-life movement for support.

In short, we have two well-developed, integrated, politicized, and institutionalized movements, each prepared to respond to every initiative of its opponent. Each has found allies in institutional politics. While working to eliminate (or preserve) the larger legacy of *Roe*, activists on both sides focus on issues that seem more immediately actionable: imposing— or preventing—limits on certain medical practices; ensuring that physicians can—or can't—learn how to perform abortions; and forcing candidates for all sorts of political offices in the United States to take clear positions on abortion. Each side holds annual demonstrations to commemorate *Roe v. Wade* and grows stronger, larger, and more volatile in response to the victories of its opponent. The issue—and the movements around it—is not likely to disappear, no matter what else happens. More than that, each side has attached other issues and values to the issue of access to abortion, and this development makes resolution more difficult. For opponents of abortion rights, for example, the abortion issue has come to be the leading edge of many other grievances, including prayer in the schools, rights of gays and lesbians, and one broad set of moral values. On the other side, abortion rights proponents view their position as something that reflects a broader set of concerns about individual rights and autonomy, freedom of (and from) religion, and, most generally, the rights of women. The accretion of values to the policy dispute makes it harder and harder for mainstream institutional politics to resolve the dispute and, as a result, makes it more likely that this political battle will continue to engage movements on both sides.

ROOTS AND STRATEGIC INTERACTION

Importantly, countermovement responses do not spring into life from nothing. Rather, they are rooted in other organizations and other social movements. To take the example of the abortion struggle, we know that the abortion rights movement had its roots in the second wave of the women's movement of the 1960s and 1970s as well as among legal reformers and population control advocates. Its opponent, the antiabortion movement, was rooted in the support of the Roman Catholic Church, ultimately augmented by traditionalist strains of other religious orders. Both sides built upon foundations of groups and individuals who shared certain values and saw abortion as the most critical, urgent, or promising issue at a particular moment. Both movements grew from these foundations to win new converts and spawn new organizations on their own.

Such ongoing interaction of opposing movements has become well established in American politics for a number of reasons and is well reflected in the abortion debate. First, because of the separation of powers and federalism, each side can find allies in institutional politics, and each can try to affect legislation it finds favorable at some level of government somewhere. Second, and a direct result of the first factor, a victory, even a small victory, for one side is a provocation and a threat to its opponent. Recognizing a large and long-term political struggle, neither side can afford to let small defeats pass unchallenged. Third, and again this is a result of the first two factors, no level of government has been able to resolve decisively the issue of abortion.

Although abortion provides a ready example, it is by no means the only one. Indeed, as the level of organized interests promoting their claims in institutional politics has grown, it has become harder and harder for government and a diverse society to resolve decisively any issue. When most activists can find some kind of ally somewhere in government, virtually all activists can also find organized opponents in government. Fewer and fewer groups are comfortable relying exclusively on conventional politics. When one side begins to make inroads using social movement tactics, its opponents are increasingly likely to do the same thing.

We can see the press for countermovement development through all levels of the political process. When an activist coalition organizes a demonstration against a war, for example, its opponents recognize an opportunity for both expression and publicity by turning up as counterdemonstrators. (The conventions of reporting also encourage this kind of movement-countermovement development. When journalists cover a demonstration, for example, the need for balance requires them to look for opponents as well as demonstrators.) Not only is it a chance to temper the message of their opponents, but also counterdemonstrators can get out their own message at the same time. Above the level of the street demonstration, successful organizations—and potentially effective movements—inspire not only imitators, but also opponents. The social movement group that lobbies a state legislature virtually invites a countereffort by its opponents, engaging in the same venue with roughly parallel tactics, just as the organization that files a lawsuit virtually ensures that its opponents will also engage the struggle.

Struggles over Gay and Lesbian Rights

In the ongoing strategic interaction, groups will have to respond to the (potentially) effective efforts of their opponents, but they will also seek strategic advantages by innovating in terms of tactics, venues, and rhetoric. In contemporary American politics, we are witnessing a good example of such innovation and response in the unfolding conflict about gay and lesbian rights. Of course, the gay and lesbian movement has ebbed and flowed over at least the past thirty-five years, but more recently, as it has won some successes and broader social support, it has provoked a serious political opposition.

Gay and lesbian activists had their greatest early successes in making effective claims for acceptance in local communities. In cities with relatively large and visible gay populations, such as San Francisco, Boston, and New York, gay pride parades became important events that mainstream politicians would ritualistically attend, just as they would attend Columbus Day parades. More than anything else, this easy accommodation reflected activists' success in establishing themselves as legitimate and potentially powerful actors in local politics. By the 1980s, city governments and local police departments established formal liaisons with the gay communities, and openly gay people could work in local politics and sometimes win elective office.

Such inroads, however, didn't necessarily add up to significant influence in national politics. Again, Madison's institutional design explains a great deal: whereas a member of San Francisco's Board of Supervisors could ignore the concerns of organized gay and lesbian groups only at his or her peril, national politicians embraced the concerns of a geographically concentrated minority only at their own political risk. Moreover, the successful mobilization of the gay community at the local level provoked an opposition rooted in conservative religious traditions. As with opposition to abortion, conservative politicians and political organizers found that they could use the threat of gay and lesbian activism as a means to mobilize their faithful.

In 1986, in a case that arose from Georgia (*Bowers v. Hardwick*), the Supreme Court ruled that state laws that discriminate against gay people by outlawing sodomy do not violate the U.S. Constitution. The majority decision was narrow, 5–4, and was a severe disappointment to gay and lesbian organizers around the country, who had watched the case moving to the Supreme Court with optimism. Organizations took the defeat as an occasion for mobilizing more aggressively in new venues. Most directly, they sought to overturn sodomy laws at the state level; working through state legislatures, they succeeded in repealing sodomy laws in twelve of the twenty-five states with such laws on the books by 2003.[4]

They also turned to other issues. By the early 1990s, activists had challenged the military's policy prohibiting gays from serving in the armed forces, arguing that second-class status based on sexual orientation was akin to the discrimination African Americans had faced in the military nearly fifty years earlier. Military leaders rejected this analogy but accepted an odd compromise policy that prohibited the military from inquiring about sexual orientation and that officially allowed gays to serve so long as they didn't tell anyone they were gay or engage in gay sex. This "don't ask, don't tell" policy, predictably, didn't satisfy gay activists, but it did provoke the opposition. Both sides shifted the fight to other issues, most notably, marriage.[5]

The gay and lesbian movement's focus on marriage emerged from material as well as symbolic concerns (Soule 2004). Because many social and economic benefits, health insurance, for example, are dispensed through the family unit, the costs of being barred from marriage are substantial. Stories about gay people being barred from hospital rooms of their critically ill lifetime partners or lacking any standing to see their children in the event of a partner's death gave impetus to organizing. Beyond that, the institution of marriage, well established around the world, affords gay couples a legal and social legitimacy.

It is this legitimacy, at least as much as the material benefits, that irritated the opposition. Seeing a threat to their values, conservative activists pressed elected officials to prevent gays from securing new rights. Seeking an issue for the 1996 election, conservatives in Congress presented a "Defense of Marriage Act" (DOMA), which guaranteed states the right to define marriage as a mixed-sex institution and not to recognize different sorts of marriages performed elsewhere.[6] President Clinton signed the act in September of 1996, antagonizing some of his allies but denying his opponents the issue for the presidential election.

Some activists, and some politicians, looked for alternatives and found "civil unions," an institution established in Denmark in the late 1980s. Supporters argued that such unions would provide the legal protections of marriage but avoid the backlash of symbolic

---

[4] I am grateful to Steve Boutcher for his insights on these cases.

[5] The military's new difficulties in recruiting volunteers, in the wake of the long deployment in Iraq, seem likely to promote a reconsideration of this policy.

[6] The U.S. Constitution provides that "Full faith and credit shall be given in each State to the public acts, records, and judicial proceedings in every other State" (Article IV, Section 1). The constitutionality of a congressional act that would have explicitly violated this guarantee was hotly debated and ultimately served to put more attention on the Supreme Court, which has yet to rule on DOMA.

acceptance. But many gay activists were less sanguine, noting that civil unions authorized at the state level would not provide federal protections and that enforcement in other states might be problematic. Still, Vermont was the first state to craft a civil union provision, and other states began efforts to follow. Incremental state-level adoption of civil union policies might have pushed the broader cultural and political debate about gay rights elsewhere, but the Supreme Court, a state court, and a presidential election intervened.

In June of 2003, the Supreme Court explicitly reversed its own *Bowers* decision in a case from Texas. By a 6–3 majority, in *Lawrence v. Texas*, the Court ruled that private sexual conduct between adults represents a liberty right, which states cannot intrude upon. The majority opinion even cited the wave of sodomy law repeals as evidence for public recognition of this liberty right. In December of the same year, the Supreme Judicial Court of Massachusetts ruled that a state law providing for civil unions between gay people violated the guarantees of equal treatment established by the Massachusetts Constitution. Citing its own opinion months before, the state court held that the state constitution "affirms the dignity and equality of all individuals" and "forbids the creation of second-class citizens" (*Goodridge v. Public Health,* Id. at 312). The Massachusetts court delayed immediate implementation of its decision but set a short deadline for legislative action.

Seeking to prevent gay marriages in Massachusetts, the state legislative leaders hastily called a constitutional convention with the express intent of avoiding this day of reckoning by amending the state Constitution to eliminate any such protections against discrimination. The Supreme Judicial Court's decision, however, prevented any easy compromise that afforded gays the benefits of marriage without marriage, and advocates on both sides of the issue aggressively mobilized their supporters.

Opponents of gay marriage pointed to natural law. As example, Representative Marie Parente opined, "Nature left her blueprint behind and she left it in DNA, a man and a woman. . . . I didn't create that combination, Mother Nature did" (Associated Press 2004). At the same time, supporters of gay marriage repeatedly drew analogies to the civil rights movement. Senator Dianne Wilkerson recalled growing up as a black woman in the South. "I know the pain of being less than equal and I cannot and will not impose that status on anyone else. . . I was but one generation removed from an existence in slavery. I could not in good conscience ever vote to send anyone to that place from which my family fled" (Associated Press 2004). Given the high rhetorical stakes and the limited ground for compromise, the state legislature was, unsurprisingly, unable to craft an amendment commanding majority support, and gay marriages legally commenced in Massachusetts on May 17, 2004. Elsewhere in the United States, however, politicians and activists began their responses to the Court's decision months earlier.

Using the language of rights, a few local officials began to act. Gavin Newsom, recently elected mayor in San Francisco, ordered the city to issue marriage licenses to same-sex couples. The Constitution of the United States, he argued, provides for this fundamental right—even in opposition to a recently passed state referendum prohibiting gay marriage and a federal law "defending" marriage. In effect, he claimed, he was not breaking the law but rather following the Constitution's higher law. The mayor of New Paltz, New York, adopted a similar analysis and began performing marriages himself.

In response, an embattled president, George W. Bush sought to use the issue to mobilize his own support, calling for a constitutional amendment to define marriage as a mixed-sex institution. Given the difficult and time-consuming process of actually amending the

Constitution, it is likely that he was more concerned with his upcoming reelection campaign than with legislative or constitutional progress on the issue. At the same time, referenda defining marriage as a mixed-sex institution were on the ballot in eleven states—along with George Bush and John Kerry. Gay rights played an odd role in the campaign; both presidential candidates proclaimed an opposition to gay marriage altogether, and both called for tolerance. Whereas Senator Kerry argued that states should continue to set policy on marriage, President Bush claimed that a national definition, enshrined in the Constitution, should stop states from allowing gay marriage. Both men allowed for the possibility of some kind of civil union. The most visible organized group of gay Republicans, the Log Cabin Society, refused to endorse the Republican candidate for president, and John Kerry won the largest share of openly gay voters—at least according to exit polls—but self-identified gays and lesbians comprise a very small part of the electorate.

Bush won reelection, and referenda strictly defining marriage passed in every place they appeared on the ballot by at least 10 percentage points—often by much more. These outcomes, however, don't end either the political debate or the mobilization of groups on both sides of the issue. Whereas gay and lesbian rights groups viewed the election results as a call for reevaluating strategies and finding new means for pursuing their interests (Liptak 2004), leaders of socially conservative groups proclaimed that their critical role in Bush's reelection had earned their cause substantial political capital with the second Bush administration and expected the president to deliver on their concerns about a constitutional amendment (Kirkpatrick 2004).

Importantly, neither side gave any hint about giving up at what each described as a critical time. The core groups involved in the battle on both sides have a clear interest in inflating the threats and opportunities of the moment in order to maintain their membership, their fundraising, their space on the agenda, and their access to allies in government. Unless one side can win so decisively that it eliminates all prospects for influence for the other, the movement-countermovement dynamic continues, with each side constantly prospecting for supporters and seeking new strategic approaches. The losers of the moment, of course, are those most likely to innovate, inviting responses from their opponents.

Movement-Countermovement Dynamics: A Warning

The increasing inability of the American government to resolve domestic political issues decisively invites political mobilization and countermobilization, filling all of the institutional channels for participation but spilling over into social movement efforts as well. Finding more than one side of a political conflict represented by social movement organizations and actions is becoming the rule, rather than the exception, in contemporary American politics. At the same time, it's a mistake to assume that movements on either side of an issue are equivalent, not only in terms of the merits of the claim, but also in terms of resources, allies, and influence. Although journalists ritualistically portray demonstrators and counterdemonstrators as equivalent—two sides of a political conflict—this portrayal may distort reality. As we saw in the second round of demonstrations in Wichita, one side, the abortion rights activists, far outnumbered their opponents, those protesting against abortion. Antiwar demonstrators are virtually always met by a much smaller number of supporters of a war—although the two sides are often portrayed as symmetrical.

Opposing movements vary not only in size, but also in other resources, including money, allies in government, legal support, relations with police, and media image. We can watch these relationships and resources change over time, and movement strategies change with them. Civil disobedience, for example, became a popular tactic among antiabortion activists because, like antiwar activists, they challenged a policy supported by the government, whereas their movement opponents mostly counted on the government to enforce the law and protect them—but this can change over time. The important thing here is to recognize that movement tactics are now employed by all sorts of claimants in the political debate and not by only one side, sympathetic or not. Thus, it is not one movement against state policy but rather (at least!) two movements, each having allies in government, each using a variety of means to make claims on political matters.

SOCIAL MOVEMENT SOCIETY

The growth of movement-countermovement pairs and the persistence of longstanding political conflicts, often expressed through movement politics, reflect a larger phenomenon in American politics, the institutionalization of protest as a political tactic. Whereas once protest was the province of those without other means to make political claims effectively, it is now an add-on or component of the political strategy of an increasingly broad range of groups; of course, when more people protest for more causes, its meaning and efficacy are likely to change. The routinization, diffusion, and firm institutionalization of the social movement as a means of political participation have created what we might call a "social movement society" (Meyer and Tarrow 1998).

Three historical trends underscore the development of a movement society: social protest has moved from being a sporadic feature of American politics to being one that is perpetual; protest is used with greater frequency, is used by more diverse constituencies, and is used to represent a wider range of claims than ever before; and protests are coordinated by professional social movement organizations that derive their legitimacy, at least in part, from participation in movements. As protest becomes routine, less disruptive, and more accepted, we have to wonder whether movements become less important, particularly to those who formerly depended upon them.

These trends, accelerating since the end of World War II, reflect numerous changes in American politics and society. As government has taken up more activities and issues, an increasing number of defined constituencies have mobilized to shape government activity. These newly organized interests represent the strong emergence of formerly excluded categories of people (e.g., women, ethnic minorities), as well as new trade and occupational groups, and a wide range of groups built around constituencies unified by belief in a position on a set of issues, such as human rights, abortion, or nuclear power. With a broader range of groups making claims on government, and with weakening political parties, government is increasingly unable to resolve disputes decisively and to choose among various claims, producing a kind of stalemate that frustrates everyone involved (Ginsberg and Shefter 2002). Increased wealth, coupled with increased information about protest and organizational formation, has encouraged more groups to take to the streets—after a fashion. Furthermore, as travel has become more accessible and as information has become more readily available through television, radio, the Internet, and even cell phones, it's far easier to organize than in the past. At the same time, the increased familiarity with the basic forms of protest by all concerned, including media, activists, and authorities, has resulted in a more routine—and safer—management of most sorts of protests (McCarthy and McPhail 1998).

Let's take some of these issues in turn. To begin, over the past thirty years the percentage of Americans who report having engaged in a protest activity has increased substantially; more than one-quarter of Americans say that they have engaged in some kind of protest (Dalton 2002). Note, however, that the reported activities heavily lean toward the least confrontational and least disruptive sorts of protest activities, including petitioning (more than two-thirds of those who protested). Even as we recognize that the surveys ask only if the individual has *ever* engaged in a protest, they still tell us that an increasing share of the population has partaken of social movement politics at some point. Still, more than 16 percent of Americans claim to have attended a demonstration—roughly twice the percentage that has ever contributed money to an electoral campaign. This means, at least, increased awareness and acceptance of what used to be seen as an unusual form of participation. This point is underscored when we look a little more deeply and note that protest activities are more common among those people who are more educated and more affluent—hardly what we would usually see as the desperate and disenfranchised.

Supporting this development is the explosion of interest organizations, which began in the early 1970s. As identified by Jeffrey Berry (1997), the number of political action committees based in Washington, DC, increased from 608 in 1974 to more than 3,992 in 1994; other political organizations also increased in number over the same period of time. Although not all of these groups use protest, a large number do. Moreover, the wealth of organizations in Washington allows the committed organizer and activist to make a career working at politics on the left or the right, engaging in public education and lobbying, working on issues, and even organizing protests (Minkoff 1994; Walker 1991).

As a result of these changes, as well as the commonly assumed efficacy of protest—at least sometimes—the use of social movement forms and tactics has spread across the political spectrum, across the country, and across social and demographic categories. Even if younger people on the left are still more likely to use protest, it is nonetheless a tactic now commonly embraced by conservative movements and by groups and movements filled with different sorts of people.

This spread of social movements and protest tactics has been caused at least partly by the rise of professional activists, although the popular image of the protester remains that of the average citizen, suddenly pushed into protest by the emergence of a salient issue. Having engaged in protest action, she then returns to her normal life, carrying a memory, but perhaps little else from the experience. There is little reason to believe that this was ever the case, and it certainly isn't now. Although the mass movements that capture the imagination are invigorated by all sorts of people not normally engaged in contentious politics, they are organized through campaigns that are built around the ongoing efforts of organizers for whom social movements are a vocation. Increasingly, however, core activists today support themselves through social change efforts as organizing became a career option and the mass movements of the past gave way to episodic campaigns animated by small cores of permanent organizers surrounded by much larger numbers of people whose activism is just as episodic.

The firm establishment of professional organizers means that there is some cumulative learning, at least about the tactics of mobilizing. Professional activists have frequently conducted outreach campaigns to other organizations, printed leaflets, set up telephone or e-mail communication trees, worked at getting their messages into the mass media, established permanent contacts within the media, raised money, applied for police permits, and posted bail. In short, with the details of social movements now the province of professional knowledge, it is easier for organizers to put a crowd into the streets and to have a reasonable estimation of what will happen as a result. Of course, professionalization comes with costs— organizers who work at it over decades are likely to pick tactics that they can continue to use for decades, and they may develop more stakes in maintaining an organization than in inciting disruptive mobilization on the issues of the moment. At the same time, it also means that a cadre of experienced organizers is always prospecting for opportunities to work on a set of issues (Staggenborg 1988) and prepared to mobilize when they find viable opportunities.

All told, the increased use of social movement forms and tactics reflects and encourages the process of institutionalization that we discussed in the last chapter. It means that activists can engage in movement politics with less risk and that the government can manage protest with less difficulty. It also means that most movements have professionals representing their concerns in some fashion, even between episodes of broad public awareness or political mobilization.

These changes, taken together, may reflect an exaggeration of a longstanding bias in the American political system. Since America's founding, there has been a general opening of political institutions to new constituencies. Those excluded from the centers of power have used the routines and tactics on the margins to open the political system to their interests. Nearly two hundred years ago, Andrew Jackson's followers established the mass political party as a means of making claims effectively for those excluded from the pristine elite politics of the previous age. Ultimately political parties were overwhelmed by all sorts of political interests and claimants, and ultimately both major parties have been dominated by well-established interests. In a similar way, during the twentieth century excluded actors used interest groups and social movement forms to gain access to mainstream political institutions. The social movement form is no longer the exclusive province of those without other means to represent themselves.

In thinking about what this means for American politics more broadly, it's hard not to see cumulative political disadvantages for those already disadvantaged. At once, as professionals are increasingly responsible for mobilizing social movements, constituencies lacking in well-established and well-funded organizations will have a harder time negotiating the technologies and politics of contemporary movements. In effect, the same biases of the interest group universe become replicated rather than counterbalanced in the world of social movements (Schlozman 1984; Berry 1999).

Perhaps even more problematic is the clutter created in mass politics by the proliferation of protest. The clutter takes place not only on the Washington Mall, where organizers have to coordinate their preferred dates with other social movement organizers, but also in the mass media and politics, where the tactics of social protest no longer rip through the imagination with the possibilities of disruption and something new. In the next chapter, we will see that the influence of social movements often amounts to preserving a policy stalemate.

THE POLICY
CONNECTION

How Movements Matter

At the height of the Great Depression, in the spring of 1932, unemployed veterans of the First World War (then called the "Great War"), desperate for work, called for the federal government to pay them their service bonus, amounting to no more than $1,000—and often much less—immediately rather than waiting until 1945, when the bonus was originally scheduled to be paid. Across the country, groups of veterans started separate marches to Washington, D.C., where the federal government might consider such a demand, conducting parades along the way.[1] As reports of the marches spread, new marches started, and other veterans (sometimes surreptitiously) rode freight trains, organized car caravans, or hitchhiked. Ultimately more than twenty thousand veterans would converge on the Capitol.

In February of 1932, a Democratic congressman from Texas had introduced a bill calling for the accelerated payment of the bonus, but the bill faced opposition from both the right (too expensive!) and the left (why not money for all people in need, rather than just veterans?). The Bonus Marchers hoped that their presence would force Congress to vote on the bill and that then they would be able to defeat its opponents at the polls in November. At once, the idea behind the Bonus March was both radical (government spending provoked by direct action) and profoundly conservative (money directed to veterans who had proved their patriotism, delivered through the most conventional political means). The eventual outcomes of this bold idea illustrate much about protest politics in America and draw our attention directly to the relationships among protest, institutional politics, and public policy.

By the end of May 1932, the first three hundred marchers from Oregon had reached the outskirts of Washington, with thousands more following on their heels. President Herbert Hoover and District of Columbia Police Superintendent Pelham Glassford welcomed the veterans, guardedly, warning them about associating with Socialists and Communists. Glassford, himself a veteran of the war, met frequently with the "Bonus Expeditionary Forces," numbering more than five thousand by early June, and arranged for a safe campground in Anacostia, across the Potomac River from the District of Columbia. He also helped the marchers set up their camps and makeshift kitchens and raised money from local merchants to find food for the marchers. The Bonus Marchers asked him to serve as their "secretary-treasurer," and he agreed, even while still preparing to protect the Capitol from

---

[1] This account follows Lucy Barber's (2002). Barber's wonderful book traces the establishment of the march on Washington as a staple political tactic in the United States.

the veterans, including securing tear gas for the district's police force. At the same time, the newly appointed chief of staff of the U.S. Army, Douglas MacArthur, much less sympathetic than Glassford, developed his own militarized plans to control the marchers and the streets of Washington.

On June 7, the Bonus Army conducted its first large parade, displaying in an orderly fashion decorated war heroes, disabled veterans, and veterans (including African Americans) from diverse backgrounds and regions of the country. They emphasized their service, their patriotism, and their discipline, winning some support from Congress and the press in the process. Implicitly, they also emphasized their desperation, because men with jobs could not spend months traveling to the Capitol and camp out on lawns to support a demand for a relatively small cash payment. Their parades were complemented by organized visits to the offices of members of Congress, a kind of grassroots lobbying. Although some members of Congress expressed sympathy for the marchers, others proclaimed that they would never vote for such a payment when under the implicit pressure of men encamped at the nation's capital.

On June 17, the Bonus Army gathered outside the Capitol while the Senate considered the Bonus Bill inside. When the Bonus Bill was soundly defeated (62–18), the veterans were forced to reconsider their strategy. Although they marched in an orderly fashion back to their camp across the river, they refused to leave the city; indeed, more Bonus Marchers continued to arrive, with close to twenty thousand veterans encamped throughout Washington, most in Camp Anacostia. In response to legislative defeat, the veterans refocused on extending their message to reach a new audience, the broader public, rather than just Congress, and expanded their demands to include relief for all needy people. They also welcomed some families into their camps, stressing the presence of women and children within their ranks. Some of their leaders traveled to other cities on the East Coast to raise money to feed the marchers.

The tensions of the long encampment affected everyone as the marchers grew frustrated and the police impatient. A faction of Communist veterans tried to press others to escalate their rhetoric and to include the White House in their targets for protest, and District of Columbia police conducted preemptive arrests on those near the White House. By the end of July, as Congress prepared to adjourn its legislative session, authorities grew more determined to clear the veterans out of the city. Local and national officials issued eviction orders to the encamped veterans, and General MacArthur and the army began enforcing those orders on July 28, overrunning the camps, using tear gas, and burning the shacks the protesters were living in. Most of the veterans fled the encampments in the face of the army's superior force, but some men fought back by throwing rocks, effectively encouraging MacArthur's strategy of relatively aggressive force. Seeking to justify the use of bayonets and tear gas, MacArthur, publicly supported by President Hoover (who kept his own misgivings private), suggested that a strong Communist presence had hijacked the Bonus March effort and that many of the men present weren't even veterans. Both charges proved false, but the veterans were routed from the Capitol, and pictures and movies of the burning shacks filled newsreels across the country.

In November 1932, Franklin Delano Roosevelt defeated Hoover's bid for reelection in a landslide. When Bonus Marchers reappeared in early 1933, President Roosevelt arranged for lodging, food, and bathrooms at an army post in Virginia and provided ready transport for veterans who wished to demonstrate in the capital. Roosevelt received a delegation of

Bonus veterans at the White House, and his wife, Eleanor, followed by newsreel cameras, visited their encampment. Although Roosevelt initially opposed paying the bonus, he offered the veterans priority for employment in the newly established Civilian Conservation Corps; by 1936, in the context of a rapidly expanding set of relief programs and the beginnings of a social safety net, he agreed to pay the bonus as well (Amenta 1998).

The story of the Bonus March cuts through many of the issues involving protest movements and American politics and focuses our attention particularly on the interaction of movements with the larger policy process. Although the Bonus Marchers didn't get what they wanted in 1932, over time they saw their influence through a range of other policies. Of course, the Bonus Marchers were not alone in opposing President Hoover's reelection, or in calling for more expanded social programs from the federal government. The Bonus Marchers were part of a much larger political process, and the extent and limits of what they achieved put many of the issues we've discussed in high relief.

To begin, the Bonus Marchers continued what had already become a well-established tradition of personally carrying their claims to Washington. It began, according to Lucy Barber (2002), in 1894 with Coxey's Army, an offshoot of Populist dissatisfaction with American politics that marched to call for public spending to create jobs, employing what activists called a "petition with boots." The tactic and the space were emulated in 1913 by the suffragettes, who paraded throughout the city and called for the extension of the franchise. The Mall has become a common place for people with grievances. In our time, we see the same space used, and then imitated, by all sorts of contemporary movements, ranging from the Million Man March, which called for African American men to gain control of their communities, to the Million Mom March, which called for governments at all levels to work for handgun control. There is no shortage of grievances. McCarthy, McPhail, and Smith (1996), reviewing both mass media accounts and police permits, describe a contemporary Washington that is visited by hundreds of demonstrations, most small, each year.

Groups go to Washington for a number of reasons, not the least of these being that it is where government works, where decisions are made, policies made, and money allocated. Demonstrating near the buildings that house American government, activists send a direct message to legislators, to the Supreme Court, and to the president. More than that, by demonstrating in Washington, they try to use the nation's press to speak to their allies across the country and to inspire other sorts of action, including the most routine conventional politics as laid out in the Constitution. The demonstration is an expression of a cause, an expression of a constituency, and an analysis about what is to be done.

All of this is predicated on an assumption that protest might matter, that through a variety of means the direct efforts of those assembling in front of national building might affect what government officials do inside those buildings, that protest can affect policy. And *sometimes* it does—even if protesters rarely get all they want when they ask for it. In this chapter, we will focus on the policy connection for social movements, laying out how we can tell that protest matters and how it might affect the shape of policy over the short and long terms.

Returning to the Bonus March, a few things should be clear. First, the veterans had allies in government, and the boundaries between their supporters and themselves sometimes blurred, as demonstrated by secretary-treasurer Glassford, who resigned from the Bonus Army after Congress defeated the Bonus Bill. Second, the veterans had reasonably diverse interests and analyses of the problems they faced and potential solutions; the demand for early payment of the bonus unified a broad spectrum of veterans and supporters, and when that failed, they expanded their agenda to bring in more support. Third, the move to Washington and the adaptation of encampment and demonstration tactics affected government, a broader public audience, and the veterans themselves. Fourth, people in government also had diverse interests and ideas for dealing with not only the problems of the Depression, but also the more immediate problem of thousands of veterans camping out in Washington. And fifth, the responses to the Bonus Marchers played out over an extended period of time and had many causes and consequences beyond the march itself. Indeed, we will see when we look at other social movements and the policy process that the Bonus March episode is relatively brief and contained in comparison with other movements. We will then examine how stories about social movement influence, develop, and affect politics and protest over a long period.

TRACING SOCIAL MOVEMENT INFLUENCE[2]

The Bonus Marchers got exactly what they initially demanded within four years of their protest, as Franklin Roosevelt initiated a massive transformation of federal government social welfare policies (Amenta 1998). Indeed, full payment of the bonus was a very small piece of that transformation. The legacies of most movement effects, however, play out over a longer period of time and are more difficult to trace. Take, for example, the movement against American involvement in the Vietnam War.

There were already all kinds of good reasons to oppose U.S. participation in the Vietnam War in 1965, when Lyndon Johnson announced that he would increase the American military presence in Vietnam by nearly fifty thousand troops. Providing these troops meant expanding the military draft, and the expanded draft turned a distant issue,[3] the war in faraway Vietnam, into a proximate one and stoked the fledgling antiwar movement. The draft provided both a focus for the antiwar movement and a sense of urgency on college campuses to do something to stop the war.

The salience of the draft invigorated what had formerly been small pacifist and leftist organizations mobilizing and coordinating the initial opposition to the war, flooding local chapters and national events with larger numbers of new activists than any of the organizations was prepared to handle (Gitlin 1980; Miller 1987). The expanded draft created much greater potential audiences for the committed peace lobby. It helped groups such as Students for a Democratic Society (SDS), which expressed a broad commitment to comprehensive democratic change in the United States, to spread quickly across American college campuses (Heineman 1993). Draft resistance, often by the ritualized (and criminal) act of burning a draft card, was a tactic for expressing opposition to the war, physically accessible to the millions of young men who had to carry draft cards.

The rapid growth of the antiwar movement also created difficulties for those who would organize it. New recruits to organizations working against the war didn't necessarily share commitments to pacifism or "participatory democracy." The newly swollen antiwar

---

[2] These issues are taken up in more detail in Meyer, Jenness, and Ingram (2005).

[3] Dieter Rucht (2000) coined the term *distant issue* to refer to political issues that don't directly affect those who mobilize for them.

organizations also provided a larger venue, as well as the prospects of higher payoffs, for everyone involved in the movement, encouraging internecine fights about ideology and tactics. Many organizations didn't survive.

More significant for this chapter, the larger, more volatile, more public, and more diverse antiwar movement made life even more difficult for government seeking, minimally, domestic peace. In his memoirs, Richard Nixon (1978: 396–404) claims that the antiwar protesters constrained his options in Vietnam, preempting his using nuclear weapons in Vietnam—or even his making a credible threat to use nuclear weapons. Of course, at the time President Nixon repeatedly proclaimed that the antiwar movement would not affect his policies. Politicians are understandably reluctant to admit that social movements affected their conduct. Such an admission could only undermine the politicians' credibility.

Still, politicians respond to movements, even if they don't acknowledge doing so. Richard Nixon certainly did. One obvious response to the antiwar movement was extending the franchise to eighteen-year-olds, who were already eligible for the draft. Another response was instituting a draft lottery before ultimately ending the draft. Of course, it wasn't only the political problems at home that encouraged the end of the draft. Conscripts created discipline problems in the field and were more likely to attack their own officers with guns and grenades than were volunteers (DeBenedetti and Chatfield 1990: 308).

The end of the draft in 1972, following ratification of the twenty-sixth Amendment the previous year, altered the political terrain dramatically for the antiwar movement. As electoral possibilities for organizing opened, organizers simultaneously lost some portion of the zealous new converts, terrified for their own lives even as they opposed the war. James Fallows (1981: 136) observes, "the history of Vietnam demonstrated the difference between abstract and self-interested actions. Resistance to the war went up in proportion as the effects of the war (primarily, the draft) touched the children of influential families." Although the antiwar movement may well have won, as U.S. involvement in Vietnam ultimately ended, the pacifists lost their connections with movement politics, and broader claims about invigorated and genuine democracy, as expressed by SDS, mostly disappeared from American political life or were reformulated in much more moderate terms as procedural reforms.

The example of the draft, like the earlier one of disgruntled veterans at home, points up a range of connections among protest, policy, and democracy: activists respond to government policy, and government responds, partly through policy, to the disruption that activists create, which changes the circumstances under which activists can mobilize their efforts. For this reason, understanding the effect of social movements on policy requires us to consider the effects of policy on social movements as well; preventing or softening an unwanted policy initiative, for example, without pushing policy sharply in a favored direction, can be quite a substantial effect for a movement, although surely not one that activists become excited about or mobilize around. In order to understand the relationship between policy and protest in America, we'll use the preceding examples to lay out a list of mutual effects.

POLICY/PROTEST: A FIRST LOOK

Both the Bonus March and the antiwar movement thirty years later underscore the ways in which government policies create constituencies. In the first case, the promise of a bonus to World War I veterans offered a focal point for out-of-work veterans in a desperate economic climate in which many Americans were out of work. When the Bonus Bill failed, the marchers were essentially forced to turn their attentions to building a broader constituency and seeking more ambitious remedies. In some contrast, the draft in the 1960s gave one group of Americans, young men, special reason to join with those who already opposed the war. Conscription became a provisional target for the antiwar movement ("Stop the Draft, End the War"), and the draft provided a series of sites or targets at which to launch protests (draft boards), as well as a set of tactics (burning draft cards, defacing files, providing draft counseling). Both opposition to the draft in general and concern about one's individual fate pushed young men—and those who cared about them—into the full range of American political institutions, including the Selective Service bureaucracy, local draft boards, the courts, and electoral campaigns.

The effects of the coalitions of groups and movements of the 1930s and 1960s are also wide ranging—and different. The expansion of the social welfare state, following the Bonus Marchers and many others, increased the numbers of Americans directly affected by the federal government. Over time, it led to an increased rate of government services and taxation and the national dominance of the Democratic Party for nearly fifty years. The expansion of social welfare programs helped to erode the power of local political party machines, which dispensed smaller-scale services and jobs in exchange for partisan loyalty; partly as a result, partisan identification began a decades-long decline, which has contributed to a dramatic change in American electoral politics. The movements following the Second World War were about bringing new groups into the sunshine of the larger social welfare state: African Americans, other ethnic minorities, women, and young people. The Bonus March and its contemporaries produced more mobilization and a larger, more ambitious national government.

The effects of opposition to the draft and its contemporaries pushed in a very different direction. In conjunction with the broader movement against the Vietnam War, the antidraft movement has affected all sorts of policies since. Although President Jimmy Carter restored draft *registration* of young men in 1980, the United States has relied on a volunteer military force since Vietnam, at least partly because of the antiwar movement. More generally, the political fallout of the antiwar movement constrained U.S. foreign policy for nearly thirty years. The so-called Vietnam Syndrome led to a reluctance to commit ground troops abroad unless the United States deployed overwhelming force and could reasonably expect to win and exit within a reasonably short time period. First articulated by Defense Secretary Caspar Weinberger (1990), it was embraced by his assistant, future Secretary of State Colin Powell, and defined policy for nearly twenty years—until finally repudiated directly by President George W. Bush's initiation of war in Iraq.

Ending the draft also changed personnel practices within the military, which now had to manage employees who had the option of quitting. Absent a draft, policymakers and administrators paid more attention to the quality of life for military personnel, devoting far more attention to recruiting, as well as to issues of compensation, housing, child care, and career advancement for service people. Service in the military, formerly a nearly universal experience for young American men, is now an experience confined to a relatively small portion of Americans. Whereas the legacy of the New Deal was a more inclusive and ambitious government, the longer-term effects of the 1960s movements were diminished faith and ambition for the national government and more individuated policy responses to social problems.

Laying out these two stories of effects of movements that enjoyed some influence underscores the larger set of questions about how and why social movements sometimes achieve influence. The question is even more difficult than it initially seems, so we'll now try to unpack it.

SOCIAL MOVEMENTS AND POLICY CHANGE

In the 1960s, at the height of a range of social movements, scholars sought to determine whether protest, as an addition to more routine politics, helps activists get what they want. The initial answers, focusing on movements on behalf of the poor (Lipsky 1970; Piven and Cloward 1971, 1977) were positive. For people poorly positioned in the political system, protest and disruption proved to be a way to get their concerns taken to a broader audience and, sometimes, to have them addressed. Frances Fox Piven and Richard Cloward looked particularly at social welfare spending, finding that government often increased spending on social welfare in response to political unrest; essentially, spending was a way to buy quiet during difficult political times. Absent political turmoil, however, that spending could be withdrawn.

Sociologist William Gamson, writing at about the same time, looked at a broader range of social movements. He randomly selected fifty-three groups that had challenged government to act on a broad variety of issues between 1800 and 1945, then followed the historical record forward fifteen years from the height of a challenge. If some of what a group had wanted became policy (new advantages) or if it won formal recognition as a legitimate political player (acceptance), Gamson coded it as a winner, then set out to discover the characteristics of groups that won or lost. This pioneering analysis, however, raised more questions than it answered. For example, how can you tell which group affected policy change when more than one group was involved and they were all doing different things? How did groups translate their efforts into policy change? Why did policy responses seem to come in flurries and at defined times, rather than gradually in direct responses to movements?

Although these critical works in the 1970s opened up an important area for research, few of the critical questions identified were pursued systematically in the following decades. Scholars of social movements addressed the context and outcomes of political mobilization, but public policy was treated as a relatively minor part of the structure of political opportunities that might spur social movements. From the social movement side, policy is often treated as an outcome of mobilization, and changes in policy are traced back to find the influence of movements.

In fact, the policy process is long and complicated, with many steps between an idea for reform and the adoption and implementation of a new policy. This is particularly true in the United States where Madison and the founders designed a system that they intended to slow the process of political change. Even in the simplest model of policy reform, recounted in grade school as "how a bill becomes a law," introduction of a policy proposal in one House in Congress is followed by committee hearings, revisions, consideration in the other House of Congress, followed by more revisions, negotiations between leaders of both Houses of Congress, and then presidential approval. It's not surprising that social movement activism can weigh in more heavily in the earlier stages in the policy process, when much of the activity takes place in public and many officials have the opportunity to act, than in later stages of the process when rules are more rigid, the number of significant actors smaller, and much of the action takes place behind closed doors (King et al. 2005; Soule and King 2006). In order to understand the relationship between social movements and public policy, we need to recognize a longer and more complicated policy process, and to realize that even when social movements affect change, they rarely get all they want.

MOVEMENTS AND POLICY: FIRST PREMISES

From what had been established in scholarship on public policy and on social movements, we can sketch out a set of potential relationships between policies and movements. Importantly, we need to emphasize that movements respond to, as much as create, changes in public policy and that just because activists don't get what they ask for, it doesn't mean that they don't exercise influence.

The policy process is complicated and doesn't operate as any simple textbook about American government would suggest. A wide range of actors, including elected officials, civil servants, outside interest groups, academic experts, and committed amateurs, is episodically involved in making and implementing policy, often dropping in and out of influence. Disputes among all of these people involve not only *how* to accomplish a particular goal (housing poor people? protecting the environment? stopping drunk driving?), but also *whether* some goal is an appropriate one for government altogether, and disputes about one frequently masquerade as arguments about the other. Oddly, policy change is normally incremental, with marginal adjustments in spending or rules, even as great conflict surrounds important policy issues. In fact, vigorous disputes themselves serve to stabilize the content of public policies, with stability reflecting stalemates among interested people, rather than anyone's satisfaction. In effect, policies are maintained by networks of groups and individuals, operating inside and outside of government, linked by their mutual interest—and recognition of each other—as legitimate actors concerned with a particular set of policies.[4] Legislators, bureaucrats, and activists in established interest groups all have defined stakes in particular areas, and their conflicts play out, most of the time, in an ongoing tug-of-war that allows only incremental reforms, and scores of networks are built around the vast range of policy areas. Change efforts launched from outside these networks are, generally, easily ignored. But sometimes an outside event, an accident or threat, or the determined efforts of activists can open up that network to a different mix of actors or a different balance of power among them and allow the possibility of substantial reform.

Public policies reflect—and shape—the way we view both social problems and the people involved in them (Ingram and Smith 1993; Schneider and Ingram 1997). By identifying some people, veterans, for example, as worthy and deserving, government legitimates political and social action on their behalf; it also helps those actors to mobilize for themselves, as we saw in the case of the Bonus March. Of course, the reverse is also true: by identifying certain people as authors of their own misfortunes, government not only

---

[4] Baumgartner and Jones (1993) call this group a "policy monopoly." Burstein (1991) refers to basically the same network as a "policy domain," a term adopted by Jenness and Grattet (2001) and Sawyers and Meyer (1999).

justifies official inaction (or punitive or paternalistic action), but also creates social, political, and psychological obstacles for their own mobilization. For example, many people convicted of crimes lose the right to vote in many states, even after serving their prison sentences. These people become politically irrelevant to all policymakers. A policy change on this matter could fundamentally alter American politics, however, because even very limited participation by this group would have affected several Senate races and at least one presidential contest (Uggen and Manza 2002).

From our reading on social movements, we understand that social movements include diverse interests and activities, stretching between the inside and outside of government. That coalition is likely to be broader and more diverse when an issue is salient on the public agenda, although not necessarily when the prospects for change are greatest.

Government action can provoke or preempt protest, depending upon the positioning of a particular constituency. Groups that can achieve their goals without protest politics will do so; groups that have little prospect for influence regardless of their tactics are unlikely to mobilize. Thus, government action to bring some constituencies into the polity and to respond to their claims can spur protest, whereas the same pattern can dampen the prospects for protest for other constituencies. Because social movement organizations work not only to achieve policy reforms, but also to support themselves (McCarthy and Zald 1977; Wilson 1995), organizers constantly prospect for issues and tactics, looking for visibility, influence, and support.

When public attention to an issue is growing, and resources are relatively readily available, groups are more likely to cooperate, and groups without a primary interest in an issue are likely to develop one. This situation creates a pattern of rise and decline in which scores of groups, politicians, and citizens sporadically get involved with an issue, engage in an effort to promote or resist change, and then retreat and regroup, looking to other issues or private concerns.

Activists can also find or build safe spaces within mainstream institutions, including political institutions. Mary Katzenstein (1998) traced feminist activists working in difficult environments: the Roman Catholic Church and the American military. She found that activists survived, made some progress, and sustained themselves for better days by building such safe spaces, or *habitats*. Such habitats can also serve as places within government to promote particular policies over the long haul, as we saw in the case of new institutions (e.g., Clemens 1997; Hansen 1991). One effect of the civil rights movement, for example, was the establishment of the Equal Employment Opportunity Commission, which served as an habitat not only for African Americans, but also, subsequently for other ethnic minorities and for women (Burstein 1985; Minkoff 1995). The establishment of the Arms Control and Disarmament Agency in 1963, partly as a response to the peace movement (Meyer 1993b), and the Environmental Protection Agency in 1970, partly as a response to the growing environmental movement (Switzer 2001), has also sometimes provided habitats for individuals concerned with moderation in the arms race and in environmental despoliation.

We know that in the United States, government is especially prone to allowing access to challengers and to setting up new institutions within government. This doesn't mean, however, that government is especially responsive to social movements in terms of policy reform. Knowing what we do about the American context, we can lay out a set of potential effects and relationships between policies and social movements, as well as explain the routes through which movements can affect policy.

POSSIBLE EFFECTS

Policy, that is, what government does or doesn't do, can work in numerous ways to influence the development of social movements.

Policy can directly affect the openness and receptiveness of mainstream politics by making voting easier or harder, for example, or by mandating citizen participation in hearings. Policies affect the attractiveness of a protest movement as a political strategy. Importantly, openings and rules affect different groups differently. In this way, public policy creates constituencies and the terrain on which strategies are made.

Government action can also encourage certain strategies of political organization, offering tax breaks, for example, to groups that incorporate and agree to stay out of electoral politics (McCarthy, Britt, and Wolfson 1991). Changes in the laws regulating funding national elections in the 1970s, for example, encouraged groups to form somewhat independent political action committees to contribute to campaigns and to develop direct-mail fundraising. Using surveillance, repression, or harsh criminal penalties, government can also foreclose some tactics. Federal and state enforcement of civil and criminal penalties on antiabortion demonstrators who blocked clinics mostly shut down peaceful clinic protests during the early 1990s. In effect, public policies about participation channel advocates to adapt particular tactics, organizational forms, and even claims.

Policy also creates causes or grievances, as we saw in the case of the draft, which became much more salient for young men when the United States accelerated its participation in the Vietnam War. Changes in policy, or changes in conditions that seem to mandate changes in policy, provide the concerns that drive people into mobilization (Meyer 2002). We can see how a shocking event, such as a nuclear reactor accident, a violent terrorist attack, or an economic slowdown, can affect not only the salience of an issue, but also the extent of public trust in government and the attractiveness of a social movement strategy for influence.

Just as the policy process often invites protest, it also responds to social movements. Movements, in conjunction with institutional political action, can produce increased expenditures or regulations in an established policy area, such as welfare spending or environmental regulation. Movements can also create new categories of policies, instituting payments or other benefits to a newly recognized political constituency, such as senior citizens in the 1930s (e.g., Amenta 1998; Amenta, Dunleavy, and Bernstein 1994) or physically disabled people in the 1970s (Fleischer and Zames 2001). Movements can also provoke or inspire regulation of a previously unregulated area, such as the environment (e.g., Switzer 2001) or the food industry, a result of the Progressive movement.

Mobilization can affect policies that define just who is relevant to the process of making decisions. When crime victims and their families organized to define themselves as an aggrieved group in the 1970s, for example, policymakers responded by changing the law to allow "victim impact statements" at criminal trials and sentencing hearings (Weed 1995). This development affected not only the sentences of individual criminals, but also the organized representation of victims in subsequent discussions about policy reform. Similarly, groups concerned with civil rights or environmental quality have established permanent roles for themselves in monitoring the implementation of the policies they care about, and the quality of monitoring ends up affecting substantially the effects of the policy (Andrews 2001).

Seeing policy outputs as the outcomes of social movements is important, but the effects are also indirect, as movements raise issues, allow (or force) politicians to address their issues, and even promote value change in the absence of policy reform (Rochon 1998). Although the Equal Rights Amendment for women failed in the early 1980s, there is no doubt that the movement that supported it fundamentally changed the way most Americans viewed not only abstractions, such as equal rights, but also specific policies, such as school spending on girls' and boys' sports (Costain 1993).

HOW MOVEMENTS MATTER

By recognizing the add-on role that movements play in the normal policy process, we can see *how* social movements sometimes matter, identifying the means through which successful movement activists exercise influence.

Most of the time, policy—government action or inaction—is supported by stalemate, rather than satisfaction, with the key players in a policy area committed to working inside mainstream politics to achieve incremental reforms that push policy in their preferred direction. Whereas advocates of progressive taxation, for example, work to include some elements of progressivity, their opponents work to flatten the tax code in steps. Most of their debates and discussions don't generate much public attention, and normal political participation (elections, interest group lobbying, for example) ends up supporting advocates on both sides of the issue. Essentially, as in a tug-of-war, they exert great force to fight a long-term war of position.

Activists committed to some alternative vision of policy work, largely below government's radar, to reach the public and the government, unsuccessfully most of the time. Changes in policy, changes in the political climate, or an outside event can create an opportunity for those activists to reach a broader audience for a reconfiguration of the boundaries of the actors involved in making policy in the area. Social mobilization becomes easier when an issue seems more urgent, the prospects of favorable change more likely, or the threats of unfavorable change more likely. Sometimes the chance or need to protest becomes apparent when an insider, frustrated about losing, goes public and seeks the support of a social movement to augment his or her influence. This is what has happened when opponents of government policy on nuclear weapons have engaged a broader public.

In either case, the key change is the composition of just who is relevant on the policy matter. Either by including new actors or excluding established ones, changes in the composition of the policy network alter the prospects for social movement action. During the peak period of mobilization, connections between the margins and the mainstream define social movement politics. The positions and criticisms of those on the margins no longer appear irrelevant and can reach a larger audience; government policies, unusually visible and salient to a broad public, appear to be changeable.

An active social movement alters the calculations that those inside mainstream politics—and in office—make about their actions. When a mobilized effort demonstrates strength and commitment, it can make the current policy course untenable or make long-simmering ideas appear suddenly viable. At the same time, mainstream political figures suddenly have to address the same broader audience engaged by the movement, and they must explain and justify their policies more frequently and in more detail. As we saw with the Bonus March, President Hoover had to explain why, in a time of widespread unemployment, he didn't favor helping veterans with a relatively small cash payment. Similarly, during the period of antiapartheid protests in Washington, D.C., President Reagan was forced to explain his policies toward South Africa far more frequently than were any of his predecessors, all of whom had managed essentially the same policy. Richard Nixon, facing the antiwar movement, had to explain again and again just what his plan for peace was, and each subsequent version was a little different. More outside attention to the content of policy and the policymaking process can make more substantial reforms possible.

MEANS OF INFLUENCE

Social movements can then influence policy by altering the composition of the relevant policy network in at least four ways: *replacement, conversion, creation,* and *reconfiguration.*

Replacement is the mechanism of influence most obviously fundamental to conventional democratic politics: throwing a rascal out and putting an ally in office instead. In the United States, this happens most often through elections (although we've seen social movements try to use impeachment as well). The direct influence of movements in electoral campaigns is generally on the margins, but margins can matter. The Bonus Marchers were not the only ones responsible for replacing Hoover with Roosevelt, but the critical change of occupancy in the Oval Office dramatically affected not only the reception they got in Washington, but also the policies on unemployment and welfare coming from the federal government.

The threat of that marginal influence is one factor that can lead to *conversion.* Exposing a recalcitrant legislator or administrator to the power of a movement's ideas—or, alternatively, the power of the ideas' promoters—means altering the composition of a policy network without changing the identity of the players. It's not really all that important to determine whether conversions, such as George H. W. Bush's decision to oppose abortion rights in 1980 or Jesse Jackson's decision to adopt a pro-choice position in 1983, come from opportunistic calculus or reflective soul-searching. Each man recognized that he had to change his position in order to be a viable candidate for his party's presidential nomination—but, of course, this doesn't mean the change wasn't sincere. Indeed, someone who has callously calculated a policy change for partisan advantage may be more likely to display the zeal of the newly converted and perhaps to operate more effectively and strategically in institutional politics.

Creating a new policy area, institutional setting, or network is a third way to alter, often radically, the composition of the relevant policy network. In this regard, the creation of new agencies or habitats, such as the Arms Control and Disarmament Agency, the Environmental Protection Agency, or the Department of Agriculture, means the permanent institutional presence of concerns that would previously be represented idiosyncratically, dependent upon the shifting preferences, constituencies, and skills of elected officials. Social movements can encourage policymakers to create these habitats, and once established, these habitats develop lives, constituencies, and concerns of their own. We see this dramatically with the creation of cabinet-level agencies directed to education, under Jimmy Carter, and veterans' affairs, under George H. W. Bush. President Lyndon Johnson established the cabinet-level Department of Housing and Urban Development as a cornerstone of his Great Society programs. The department was a response to the civil rights movement and to urban riots in the earlier part of the decade and provided an institutional setting for ongoing social welfare and urban development programs.

Finally, social movements can *reconfigure* existing policy monopolies by establishing new actors within them. Weed's (1995) tale of the victim's rights movement shows how the newly institutionalized presence of actors who were formerly spectators in the courtroom changes what happens not only in the courtroom, but also in the legislatures. Similarly, Nancy Matthews's (1994) analysis of the feminist antirape movement shows how political mobilization by feminists against rape altered the content and implementation of policy and established new institutions: rape crisis centers (also see Gornick and Meyer 1998). Essentially, activists in both cases expanded the scope of a political conflict to alter the bias in the arena.

But changes in policy alter the conditions under which activists mobilize. As policymakers respond to social movements, the environment in which the movements make claims—the "structure of political opportunities"—changes, making some kinds of tactics seem unnecessary or inappropriate and some kinds of claims impractical. Government response to a movement includes not only making narrowly defined policy outputs, but also taking on some of the language of a movement, officially recognizing movement groups or individuals, and finding places for movement actors in government. The feminist campaign against rape as the most threatening and egregious element of patriarchy turned into a public safety effort. Activists who initially campaigned to eliminate the oppression of women established a working relationship with local governments to "manage" the problem of rape (Matthews 1994). Civil rights activists who demonstrated in front of the Lincoln Memorial for an end to segregation and for increased access to jobs negotiated a voter registration strategy with a Democratic president, John Kennedy, who had narrowly won office just a few years earlier.

The institutionalization of movement concerns can mean changes in policies, if not in what activists ask for; it also makes it harder for activists to mobilize active support in the same way. Generally, organizers see their most visible policy demand, be it banning DDT, passing a voting rights act or an equal rights amendment, or freezing the nuclear arms race, as the leading edge in a broad movement to remake the world. Institutionalization of concerns means, to varying degrees, settling for something less than that. Thus, appointees to the Arms Control and Disarmament Agency learn to speak of only the first objective in the agency's name, and opponents of pollution learn to negotiate acceptable levels of contaminants. And feminists learn to rely on legislators who make it easier to convict and punish rapists, even if ignoring larger oppressions in society.

Social movement coalitions respond to these changes, often by redefining themselves, their claims, and their allies. Policy reforms split movement coalitions and fracture and demobilize movements. Because participating groups enter social movements with a range of goals, it isn't surprising that they view acceptable outcomes differently. Activists must constantly redefine the demand of the moment, and that redefinition affects their alliances and their opponents.

To summarize: changes in policy, particularly in the composition of policy networks, mean the terrain on which social movements mobilize is constantly shifting. Opportunities for inclusion always threaten to undermine the urgency of a social movement's claims or the apparent necessity of its tactics. Our government does not have to satisfy even the largest part of a social movement coalition to make its continued mobilization much more difficult.

For elected officials, understanding this reality means the constant search for balancing points on policy to stabilize their political environment: giving enough to quell disturbances, but not so much as to generate disruption from the other side. For activists, understanding this reality means making hard calculations about the costs, as well as the benefits, of concessions on matters of policy and political inclusion. It also means there is always work to be done.

CLAIMING CREDIT

Even when social movements affect policy, activists often don't get the credit for their efforts. This fact matters; getting the credit for making something good happen is an essential element of politics, only partly related to the process of actually making something good happen in the past, but critically important to political effectiveness in the future.

The civil rights movement of the 1950s and 1960s, for example, is central in virtually all discussions of race in contemporary politics. When President Ronald Reagan, a political opponent of Martin Luther King Jr., signed into law a bill establishing a national holiday commemorating King's birth—even as Reagan proclaimed his misgivings about doing so—we saw the consolidation of a story of movement influence in mainstream politics. The civil rights movement is consistently portrayed as a successful and heroic struggle for equality for African Americans, in consonance with values expressed by the Declaration of Independence. Today virtually all of the southern states organize and promote "civil rights tourism," as does the National Park Service.[5] The struggles of the 1950s and 1960s have become every bit as accepted as a part of the great American story as the American Revolution, even accepted, promoted, and distorted by those who opposed the movement.

The civil rights movement represents a key example of a movement successful in claiming credit, but many more movements exemplify the failure to do so. Indeed, often the people who lead contemporary social movements downplay their own impact. Christian Smith (1996), for example, investigated Central America Solidarity activists to appraise their influence. In the 1980s, the movement, employing the full range of tactics from civil disobedience to testimony before Congress, actively opposed the Reagan administration's efforts to overthrow the Sandinista government in Nicaragua. For the most part, the activists were mercilessly self-critical, quick to acknowledge falling short of their goals and scattering blame in all directions, but particularly at themselves.

Of course, the civil rights movement changed the face of America, affecting laws, public opinion, culture, and politics. At the same time, we know that it did not achieve all that its partisans demanded, as demonstrated by ongoing inequalities in education, employment, and elsewhere in American life. There is much the movement didn't win; but opponents, bystanders, and participants all recognize some accomplishments, even if they view the work still to be done differently.

---

[5] On civil rights tourism, see a Debbie Elliott report, "Civil Rights and Tourism," on National Public Radio's *All Things Considered*, broadcast July 4, 2000. Elliott reports that the southern states, once ashamed of their role in civil rights history, have discovered that it's a good source of tourism and money. The states now promote black heritage sites. The National Park Service offers an inventory of historic sites and suggests that one has to consider a longer view of American history, including slavery, to understand the civil rights movement and to consider the civil rights movement to understand any politics since. For example, see http://www.cr.nps.gov/delta/home.htm

And there are real accomplishments that veterans of the Central America Solidarity movement *could* claim. Although the Sandinista government fell in Nicaragua, it did so in an election, not in a military invasion from the North. Smith (1996) makes a compelling case that multinational peace politics and American policy were affected by the citizen movements of the 1980s. Although the outcomes were not exactly what activists asked for, promoting procedural democracy and peace is hardly trivial. Because activists didn't claim credit for their efforts, however, the field was clear for the Reagan administration to tell a largely uncontested tale in which it ousted the Sandinistas—over the objections of a misguided and diffuse American left.

It's not only actual influence that affects the popular story of a movement's influence. Although scholars work to assess the relative weights of numerous factors and actors on some policy change, the popular story is far more important to what happens next. The stories that people hear about the past influence how they view future possibilities and, most significantly, their prospective role in making it.

HOW STORIES MATTER

The old axiom that history belongs to the winners should be rephrased: *those who win in the writing of history shape the future*. A dominant story about the influence of a citizens' movement on politics and policy legitimizes protest as a tactic and social movements in general, providing encouragement for future movement efforts. Indeed, as Kim Voss (1998) notes, even a story about a movement defeat can help sustain future activism—if it offers an explanation of why and strategies for improvement. In contrast, a dominant story that emphasizes the power of institutional actors to do what they want, for good or evil, robs incipient movements and activists of the sense of efficacy that makes mobilization possible.

Organizers can use stories of movements of the past to spur or support new efforts. Narratives of past influence can maintain the enthusiasm of the faithful, mobilize new activists by providing a plan for contemporary actions, and make sense of current political challenges (Polletta 1998). That the civil rights movement is broadly accepted as a cause of significant improvements in the lives of millions has been a source of inspiration for other social movements—on the right as well as the left—providing a sense that movement efforts in the service of a moral cause against great odds are worthwhile. In contrast, when movement efforts are viewed by those who initiated them as costly and ultimately futile, recruiting activists in the future may be difficult.

In looking at the stories of influence told by social movement activists and their competitors, we can identify the implicit negotiations in constructing accepted narratives of influence. Perhaps the most successful case, that of the civil rights movement for African Americans, demonstrates both the extent and limits of success claimed. Although the movement is widely given credit for winning basic civil rights, its popular image emphasizes charismatic leadership, rather than political organizing, most notably in the eventual inclusion of Martin Luther King Jr. in the pantheon of national heroes. The frequently told story of Rosa Parks's civil disobedience on a bus in Montgomery in December 1955 is taken out of the organizational and political context of the day. Parks is remembered as a tired old lady, with rarely a mention of her connections to long-standing organizations such as the NAACP and the Highlander Folk School's leadership programs.

In short, although the movement's influence is acknowledged, the movement itself is often portrayed as something inevitable or mystical, almost apart from politics, and not something that people today could organize. Even in a story of influence, the neglect of context and organization in favor of spontaneity or magic, what Taylor (1989) terms a myth of "immaculate conception," undermines the prospects of subsequent mobilization, giving little clear direction to today's organizers. We need to think about why some movements are more successful at claiming credit than are others.

American Politics: You Can't Ever Get All You Want

Most activists are always going to be able to find disappointments in the outcomes of their efforts. First, because movements are comprised of coalitions, in which people and groups unify around common demands, many activists are going to see their most cherished goals left out of the movement campaign, much less any ultimate policy reform. Second, the nature of the American political system prizes compromise, even as politicians and organizers are rewarded for using polemics outside of *government*. Whereas mobilization is generally based on promising more than you can deliver, legislation is based on making sure you deliver whatever you can. Third, because the ultimate translation of protest into policy is undertaken by mainstream political figures, including elected officials and bureaucrats, social movement activists will always have to compete with more established figures to get their story out. And those established figures will have an incentive to oversell the programs they enact.

In American politics, polemical rhetoric dominates. Politicians talk about "saving Social Security", fighting a "war" against drugs after losing another one against poverty, or adopting "zero tolerance" for crime or environmental pollution. *There is a mismatch between political rhetoric that emphasizes absolutes and a political process that prizes compromise and incrementalism.* Thus, the dynamics of contemporary American politics virtually mandate that *most people are going to be disappointed most of the time.*

Paradoxically, disappointment is most likely for the movements that achieve the most. Effecting social and political change is a result of the process of institutionalization, that is, getting people into positions of power and, even more importantly, getting your ideas into mainstream culture and politics. Social movements carry new ideas to a broader audience, and when they succeed in getting their ideas into the mainstream, they lose control of how those ideas are presented (Rochon 1998). American social movements are poorly positioned to reject institutional figures who claim to speak for them. An opponent of government regulation of pollution can claim to be an environmentalist, and the more successful a movement has been, the more attractive its labels are—and the easier they are to poach. People with no previous connection to a movement such as the women's movement, for example, can claim to be feminists—or environmentalists or animal rights supporters or peace activists. In doing so, they make explicit claims not only about their own identity, but also about the politics and identity of the larger movements.

Although most social movements leave a trail of actions and statements that can provide the raw materials of a claim for credit, only rarely can activists translate those raw materials into a compelling and broadly resonant claim of influence. Let's think about why.

WHY SOME MOVEMENT STORIES STICK

First, although the processes through which broad social and political change are inordinately complex, *simple stories* usually triumph in the political arena. The mass media and popular history alike are drawn to stories of conflict with a limited number of key players and unambiguous heroes and villains (Stone 1997). Social movements are rarely well positioned to offer such simple tales. The legislator who wants to claim credit for passing some kind of legislation can often edit out of the story the movement that inspired—or allowed—him to do it. Activists who want to claim credit for the same legislation can't edit out the legislator. Institutional politics is closer to the ultimate political outcome, even if not so important, and elected officials generally have greater resources for getting their version of the story out.

Second, *groups* within a social movement have diverse *goals,* and a story of influence has to have an achievement that can impress a broad public as being significant. Although activists work mightily to secure a space for a demonstration (della Porta 1999), for example, that achieving and bearing witness hardly seem substantial enough to rate broad public recognition. Because all victories in American politics are partial, translated through mainstream politics, activists often focus on what they did not win. There is what we might call the problem of the *moving finish line.* Having won a battle to end legal segregation of schools, for example, civil rights activists turn to ending the actual segregation of schools and improving the quality of education. A victory commences a new political battle (Gornick and Meyer 1998). The more ambitious goals are not only harder to win, but also more difficult to claim credit for achieving; there are always many other competitors.

Third, like Coleridge's "Ancient Mariner," someone must be around to tell the story. *Organizational survival* is key to claiming credit. Although organizations that do not focus on sustaining themselves may have substantial influence (Piven and Cloward 1977), they are poorly positioned to take credit for that influence. Activists, professional organizers, and groups move on to other issues and other organizations, often shifting the emphasis of their political concerns. The movement against nuclear power, for example, was antagonistic to developing formal and permanent leadership structures (Dwyer 1983), and individual activists drifted in and out of participation. When the movement faded and activists and organizations moved to other issues, there was no one committed to claiming the victory of stopping the development of new power plants. Further, because the more moderate groups within a coalition are those most likely to survive, the prevalent stories of social movements tend to focus on institutional politics.

Fourth, organizers are keenly aware of the *risks of victories.* Movements recognized as successful can provoke their opponents (Meyer and Staggenborg 1996) while simultaneously risking complacency among their supporters. Organizers understand that risk and threat rather than support from government often generate mobilization of activism and financial contributions. In abortion politics, for example, Supreme Court decisions are routinely followed by press conferences in which groups on both sides of the issue claim defeat. Organizers want to heighten urgency, keep the faithful engaged, and solicit financial contributions. Claiming victory risks lessening urgency and ceding what is always a limited agenda space (Hilgartner and Bosk 1988) to other causes and claimants; there is always more important work to be done.

Fifth, *members who enter government, either by being appointed or by winning elective office, present a special challenge for movements.* Frequent elections at all levels of government and a relatively open political system are constant temptations for activists seeking to do good—and/or to promote themselves. Although movements that make inroads into government produce individuals with both stake and status to make claims about movement influence, those people can overshadow the movement.

Policies cannot speak for themselves. When a movement is about the treatment of identifiable and distinct groups of people, for example, African Americans, women, gays and lesbians, individual careers can readily be seen as social movement successes. Appointment or election to government positions, or anointment by the mass media, enables them to claim credit for partial victories, even if those so advantaged are not hard-core movement activists or represent a more moderate wing of the movement.

Paradoxically, individuals who win elective office, even veterans of radical organizations, such as John Lewis from SNCC, or Tom Hayden from Students for a Democratic Society (SDS), by virtue of their hard-won careers in mainstream politics can't help but emphasize the importance of institutional politics. Winning access to such positions becomes both a movement triumph and the signal for a shift toward institutionally oriented politics (Polletta 1998). When activists gain access to political institutions and the capacity to get a movement story out, it is a story fixed in the past, emphasizing conventional politics for the future.

In contrast, individuals who win access through policy-focused movements have a more difficult time claiming credit for their movement; indeed, exercising influence within policymaking circles frequently entails disavowing movement connections. The peace activist who takes an appointment in the Arms Control and Disarmament Agency and the environmentalist who works for the Environmental Protection Agency, as example, disavow activist identification as part of the bargain. Even if they did not, activists in the street would quickly disavow them for excessive moderation. For some movements, winning access to political institutions essentially means slipping an identity, something that people identified by characteristics beyond beliefs cannot easily do.

Movements based on providing targeted advantages to an identifiable constituency are thus better positioned to claim credit than are those that build support on the basis of beliefs. Whereas skin color, gender, ethnicity, and even sexual orientation are relatively "sticky" identities, movements based on beliefs are far more "slippery." But identities can become more slippery over time. Whereas women in mainstream politics can now sometimes ignore the impact of the feminist movement (Sawyers and Meyer 1999), African Americans who try to shed that identity have it thrust back upon them by mainstream politics.

SOCIAL MOVEMENTS AND PUBLIC POLICY

We've seen how social movements are the product of public policy and how they sometimes can change public policy. We've also seen that the actual impact of a movement is often quite separate from the popular understanding of its impact. Campaigns that seek inclusion of a disadvantaged minority are better positioned to make claims of influence than are those that seek collective benefits. Organizations that survive and flourish are far better positioned to get their version of the story out and make it stick than are those that fade away. Both of these factors affect the capacity of sponsors to project a narrative of political influence effectively and aren't inherently surprising: well-established organizations and well-placed individuals have better access to both resources for cultivating and projecting preferred narratives and to the mass media that will amplify them.

But placing people in power isn't enough. Activists who enter politics often claim allegiance with the movements of the past, even emphasizing their own careers as the product of those movements. At the same time, the very visibility of such people in positions of power makes it harder to make claims about either ongoing collective disadvantages or the necessity of protest politics as a strategy.

For groups that mobilize on the basis of beliefs, the prospects of claiming credit are even worse. People identified with an environmental or peace movement, for example, when in power are likely to qualify that identification. The demands of the legislative process require a willingness to compromise and qualify that bodes badly for social movement politics, which do best with sharp absolutes. Would-be allies outside government will disparage the self-proclaimed environmentalist in Congress who supports an acceptable standard of toxic discharge or the declared peace activist who votes for a military budget that includes money for nuclear weapons. Additionally, groups that must mobilize on the basis of beliefs encounter serious risks in claiming victories and may be loathe to do so. Such groups cultivate support by emphasizing the threats and urgency of the moment. The inherent problem for activists is the challenge of *claiming victories gracelessly while continuing to mobilize*. There is always work to be done.

PROTEST AND
AMERICAN POLITICS

What's Next?

The inauguration of a president is a ritual of American politics, a time when Americans acknowledge the choice of a leader and their identity as Americans and make plans and promises for the future. Since George Washington left office, presidential elections have been contested, often bitterly, and activists have often questioned the integrity of the electoral process. Nonetheless, the inauguration event, typically including a processional, a swearing-in, a speech, and numerous balls and parties, is an expression of some sort of unity and orderliness in government. The president rides or walks down Pennsylvania Avenue and takes his place in front of the Capitol building, the seat of Congress. Surrounded by congressional leaders of both parties, families and friends, the president takes the responsibility for governing the nation, even those who opposed him, and leaders of both political parties acknowledge this assumption of power.

The new American president, prompted by a justice of the Supreme Court, takes a constitutionally prescribed "Oath or Affirmation" to "faithfully execute the Office of the President of the United States, and will to the best of my Ability, preserve, protect and defend the Constitution of the United States." He then speaks to the nation, announcing priorities for the future. Amid all the politics, the ceremony puts the Constitution and other symbols of America, the Capitol dome, the justice's robe, for example, at center stage. But politics doesn't disappear, nor does protest. The second inauguration of President George W. Bush provides a window for looking at protest politics and their relation to conventional politics in America.

In November 2004, George W. Bush won reelection by more than three million votes, 62,041,268 (50.73 percent) to 59,028,548 (48.27 percent). Bush won more votes than any presidential candidate in American history; his opponent, John F. Kerry, with more than 59 million votes, won the second-highest vote total ever—substantially more than anyone previously elected president. Both men were buoyed by the highest voter turnout in forty years, approaching 60 percent of eligible voters, a growing population, and a deeply conflictual election with intense emotions and rhetoric on both sides. Although a majority of voters supported Bush over Kerry, public opinion polls showed that a majority of Americans also opposed Bush's management of the key issues of the day: the war in Iraq and the economy (Nagorney and Elder 2005).

But elections are crucial not only for choosing leaders, but also for managing and channeling conflict in American politics. The election over, Americans across the political spectrum moved on to establish their political strategies until, at least, the next election.

Deciding on a leader doesn't resolve or end differences of opinion on war, the economy, taxes, or hundreds of other issues, but it does establish the composition of government and thus the lay of the land for politics and policy. President Bush's reelection came with an enhanced Republican majority in both the Senate and the House of Representatives. In democracy, however, and particularly in America, the losers don't go away but instead plan to win the next time and try to influence policy in the meantime. Kerry, a U.S. senator from Massachusetts, had good seats at the inaugural and watched his opponent proclaim a mandate for policies that Kerry had campaigned against. Although Senator Kerry had pledged to continue to fight President Bush's policies in government, he ritualistically applauded all the nonpartisan elements of the ceremony, leaving aside the strategies of tomorrow's politics for the moment.

Many of Kerry's supporters, however, were considerably less sanguine about President Bush's second term. Across Washington, D.C., the losers protested in a wide variety of ways, riding bicycles, holding signs, wearing costumes, chanting, and organizing for the next four years. The diversity of events, issues, and constituencies provides a dramatic testament not only to the breadth of opposition to the newly elected president, but also to the firm establishment of protest as a normal part of American politics, intricately connected to more conventional politics.

For the counterinaugural, the day opened with bike rides organized by Critical Mass, a decentralized group concerned with promoting bicycle transportation across the United States. For most, the bike rides were also a way to make a positive statement about environmental protection. Although most riders obeyed traffic laws, some blocked traffic and tried to enter blocked-off streets. Another group, self-described "Billionaires for Bush," conducted a kind of street theater as they claimed to "auction off" Social Security to protect their own wealth. Opponents of the war marched carrying dozens of cardboard coffins to draw attention to the American servicemen and women who had died in Iraq, then numbering more than eleven hundred (www.counter-inaugural.org). Code Pink, a feminist social justice group, staged an antiwar beauty pageant, with "contestants" sporting black sashes marked "RESIST." Less dramatically, the president's opponents organized demonstrations, fundraising events, and parties for the inaugural night in Washington and in other cities across the country (Mendoza 2005; Montgomery and Vargas 2005).

On this cold day, several women stripped and paraded naked to protest wearing fur; another woman dressed as Jesus Christ to challenge the morality of President Bush's policies. One man posed on a platform, his head covered by a black hood, imitating a photo of a tortured prison camp inmate in Iraq. Along with these theatrical poses, a wide variety of demonstrators engaged in an equally wide variety of actions: activists marched, waved signs (e.g., "You Didn't Get a Mandate from Me"; "War Begins with W"; "Worst President Ever"; "Four More Years: God HELP America"), chanted, banged drums, turned away from the street when the president's limousine passed, made speeches, issued press releases, and burned a flag. Other antiwar activists staged a "die-in." They dramatically collapsed on the street and waited for police to arrest them for blocking traffic, but police left them alone. Disappointed and cold, the activists got up themselves. Police did arrest other activists at other locales; clad in riot gear late at night, police arrested sixty-five activists they described as anarchists for marching without a permit. There were other "scuffles" with demonstrators at a few points along Pennsylvania Avenue; some demonstrators crossed metal security barricades and reportedly threw water bottles and trash while police used batons, water cannons, and pepper spray (Armas and Quaid 2005; Fernandez and Rich 2005; Shogren 2005; Stout and O'Neil 2005).

Indeed, because this was the first inaugural since the September 11, 2001, terrorist attacks, the police and security presence was unprecedented. More than seven thousand members of the armed forces were deployed in security roles, augmenting a force of more than six thousand local, state, and federal police. The security forces stationed sharpshooters on building tops, stationed police on horses everywhere, blocked off large portions of the city, and set up numerous security screening stations (Newman 2005). The extent and cost of the security arrangements became a political issue in themselves. Some demonstrators complained that "excessive" concern with security was used to stifle their voices and reduce their numbers. The mayor of Washington, Anthony A. Williams, complained, "In general, we've struck a balance too far in favor of security and not enough in favor of openness." It wasn't just the principles at stake for Mayor Williams. He complained that the event would cost the always cash-strapped city more than $17 million, while the federal government would pay only $6 million for the arrangements it required from the city (Janofsky 2005a).

The issues represented did not stop with the inaugural itself and were every bit as diverse—and familiar—as the tactics. Although the war in Iraq and inequities in the economy received the most attention from both the mass media and the protesters, activists in the streets were concerned with many other issues as well, including abortion, civil liberties, Cuba, electoral reform, environmental protection, fraud, homophobia, housing, Iran, jobs, marriage, meat, North Korea, the Patriot Act, racism, sexism, Social Security, torture, Venezuela, and war crimes. This alphabetized list, drawn from newspaper reports on the protests, is surely *not* complete. In contemporary American politics, protest is a tool embraced by virtually every interest with a grievance. The national inauguration was a prime-time opportunity for anyone with a gripe to gather with others who shared, minimally, the same target for their frustrations and to jostle with them for a space in the mass media.

Part of the motivation was surely to make it clear to political friends and foes alike that the election had done more to engage and enrage the opposition than to vanquish it. The counterinaugural events were all about demonstrating that these activists and their concerns would not go away. As one activist, Jared Maslin, nineteen, who had come from his home in New Hampshire, said, "It's important to show that when Bush's second inauguration goes into the record books, there was healthy dissent" (Associated Press 2005). For some, this was enough. They viewed the successful staging of broad-based protest as a victory in itself. For Brian Becker, national coordinator of Act Now to Stop War and End Racism (ANSWER), this was the case. "We think this is a significant achievement for the antiwar movement," he reported. "We have bleachers, a stage, a sound system, and we're right along the parade route. We feel we have succeeded" (Janofsky 2005b).

Some of President Bush's supporters, who also teemed into Washington for the inaugural, were considerably less enthusiastic. Viewing at least some of the broad collection of protesters as unpatriotic—or at least sore losers—some of those who joined the crowds *celebrating* the second inaugural tried to shout down the demonstrators, chanting "USA, USA, USA"; others threw snowballs. But this reaction wasn't shared by all those present. Laura Flaherty, a high school teacher from Columbus, Ohio, who had supported Bush's re-election, brought forty of her social studies students to the inauguration and viewed the totality of the event, inauguration, and counterinauguration as a lesson about America. Asked about the demonstrators, she said, "I think this is what makes the country great. They have as much right to be here as we do" (Shogren 2005).

Ms. Flaherty recognized that democracy continues even between elections and that those who don't—or can't—get what they want through participation in elections can search out other ways to make their voices heard. But it's more than this.

STAKE AND STANDING

From what we know about protest in American politics, it's likely that the vast majority of the inaugural demonstrators was also actively engaged in the election campaign that preceded it. Having lost at the polls, they took to the streets. Much earlier in the campaign, Democratic candidate Kerry had hinted that he had spoken with "foreign leaders" and had learned that they were much more supportive of his putative presidency than that of his opponent, President Bush. Kerry quickly backed away from this statement; if it were true, he certainly had to know that no foreign leader would publicly acknowledge such a preference. Perhaps even more significantly, Kerry's campaign managers surely realized that the endorsement of foreign leaders could only be a handicap for his presidential prospects.

Months later, on the eve of the election, enterprising pollsters, no doubt facing increasingly fatigued subjects in the critical battleground states, took their surveys abroad, reporting that the challenger, John Kerry, would win in a landslide of historic proportions if non-Americans could have voted. Of course, they couldn't.

At the same time, it is abundantly clear that people all over the world had a *stake* in the election's outcome. Israelis and Palestinians, French and British, Colombian and Chinese people are all affected by the policies of the American president. The positions of the United States on issues of war and peace, the environment, and global trade dramatically affect the interests of people far outside its borders. Here *stake* means an interest in the outcome of the election. These people, however, lack *standing* to participate in American elections. Even as they have an interest in the outcome, they have no institutional means of affecting that outcome. To the extent that they have any means of affecting the outcome, it is by doing something to persuade those with standing, that is, a recognized right and means to participate in the election, to consider their interests. Global citizens' means of affecting influence here are extremely limited: they might write letters or songs to American voters, lobby their own leaders to resist certain policies—or protest against them and offer threats or inducements to voters. All of these efforts are likely to have minimal impact directly on an American election and, indeed, are as likely to be counterproductive. It's hard to imagine many American voters responding positively to a foreign endorsement of a political candidate. And excluding non-Americans from fundamental decisions about American politics is easy to justify.

The conflict, both real and potential, between *stake* and *standing* is not limited to those without citizenship. Now we routinely deny the franchise to some Americans who have obvious interests in what the American president does. In most states, convicted felons are prohibited from voting. Citizens under the age of eighteen are also prohibited from voting, as we hope their interests are effectively represented by adults who care about them. In the first case, by the lights of American law, felons have forfeited their right to vote by demonstrating lack of concern about the rule of law and the well-being of society. In the second case, we assume that children have yet to develop sufficient judgment or independence to be entitled to influence the outcome of elections. Without much controversy, we separate stake in the outcome from standing to influence it.

But, as we know, there is a long history of other groups being denied the right to vote; as we also know, the right to vote, that is, the formal extension of some element of standing, is only one small piece of what it takes to affect the content of American politics. But, by noting the distinction between stake and standing, we can begin to see the essential role that social movements play in American politics; simply, social movements are one vehicle for transforming stake in a decision into effective standing.

American women organized for suffrage for nearly eighty years before winning a constitutional amendment providing the right to vote. In essence, this amendment afforded individual women standing to participate in the basic routines of politics. The ratification of the Nineteenth amendment in 1920 did not afford the organized groups that had promoted suffrage any recognition or access to make claims on behalf of women; indeed, they faded after the adoption of the amendment, and women's impact on politics via election is hard to discern. Organized groups really didn't emerge strongly until the so-called second wave of the women's movement in the early 1960s, and elected officials responded not only by creating liaison positions in government and targeting women as a constituency, but also by altering public policy toward women and families.

The story was somewhat different for African Americans, who also organized around meaningful suffrage. The guarantees of the thirteenth, fourteenth, and fifteenth Amendments meant little to black people in the South until the pressure of the civil rights movement led to a series of legislated electoral reforms and guarantees. At least partly because critical organizations were well established before the Voting Rights Act, many of the groups—or "factions," in Madison's terms—that pushed for civil rights were able to maintain standing as representatives of African American interests. Likely even more important, the relative homogeneity of African American interests and the geographic concentration of blacks in certain areas in certain states made it easier for both activists and audiences to believe that their collective interests could be represented by organized groups both during and between elections. Thus, the civil rights movement succeeded in establishing both individual rights for African Americans and organizational standing for groups that represented them.

The antiwar movement during the Vietnam era made much of the fact that young men could be drafted and forced to put their lives at risk in support of a policy that they could not hope to influence through the most rudimentary democratic means—voting. Clearly here, too, there was a sharp distinction between stake and standing, and the resultant twenty-sixth Amendment, ratified in 1971, which grants eighteen-year-olds the vote, afforded young people the right to represent themselves as individuals but not collective representation of any kind. Of course, the influence that eighteen-to-twenty-one-year-olds could effect, particularly when participation has historically been low and their interests have been divided, has been limited.

In all three of these cases of an expanded franchise, political mobilization of a disadvantaged constituency has translated into formal recognition of standing to make claims on government, although in two of the three cases, that standing was granted to individuals, not organized groups—at least initially. Collective standing is contingent upon some kind of recognition of broad collective interest. It is most likely to occur when the constituency at hand is one with a recognizable identity, defined at least partly by interests, and some kind of concentrated geographic identity—in cities or rural areas or some states.

Now what are we to make of the numerous social movements that have mobilized on behalf of other kinds of identities, defined, say, by occupation (e.g., workers or farmers) or, even more commonly, by beliefs (e.g., antiabortion or antifur)? Membership in such a group is clearly volitional, that is, people *choose* to identify with a group and its claim, and you can't necessarily pick partisans out of a crowd by the way they look or how they dress. In such cases, individuals recognize an interest that isn't necessarily obvious to others, and the process of turning their stake into standing through social movement action is even more pronounced. Their efforts underscore the necessity of some kind of collective identity and collective representation beyond just the collection of all individuals. The very existence of the tractorcade drive-in to Washington, D.C., underscores the belief of the participating farmers, and presumably many others who weren't driving their tractors to Washington, that they have a set of interests that isn't being served through conventional politics. They seek political recognition of a collective interest that can't be achieved through individual efforts alone.

This is similarly true of numerous political mobilizations based on beliefs: that nuclear weapons are dangerous; that the environment is insufficiently protected; that gun owners are under fire; that people accused of crimes are mistreated; that a war is a bad idea; that fundamental religious values are being undermined; and so and so on through thousands of issues. Mobilization, when successful, brings a constituency of belief attention from mainstream politics and brings people who can credibly speak for that constituency a place in mainstream politics.

The history of American politics, as we've seen here, is of diverse groups mobilizing to win routine access to the political system for their representatives and, in effect, the capacity *not* to stage social movements in order to have their interests taken into account. In other words, *most people mobilize, go to demonstrations, write letters, knock on doors, or commit civil disobedience so that they don't have to do so in order to be heard.* We have seen that the political mobilization of all sorts of constituencies, from farmers to veterans to organized labor to women to environmentalists, including virtually all ethnic minorities at one time or another, has often achieved meaningful and routinized representation of new interests in American politics.

But such concessions and recognitions are hardly permanent. The access that organized representatives of once-mobilized constituencies enjoy ebbs and flows depending upon larger currents in politics, including the balance of power among other groups; the availability of elected officials as allies; the salience of older and newer issues; and the mobilization of older and newer actors. Whereas social movements have become a constant part of American political life, the mobilization and balance of power among social movement activists are constantly in flux. Advantages gained at one moment can disappear later, and groups that once mobilized to protect their interests often need to do so again or else risk losing access and influence. As a result, the need for social movement action, that is, finding additional channels of influence beyond conventional politics, doesn't disappear when a group wins routine access.

Social movements then become almost a routine part of the political landscape, and we have to recognize that the surprise and disruptive threat offered by, say, the Bonus Marchers rarely attend contemporary movement events, which have become safer and more predictable but no less important. We can return to the colorful protests of President Bush's second inaugural to assess how social movements can affect politics and policy.

It's critical to start by remembering that the protests in Washington probably weren't the only thing that the demonstrators have done—or will do. We have to see the Critical Mass bicyclists, the Code Pink feminist demonstrators, or the Billionaires for Bush as one expression within lifetimes of more or less engaged political activism. When the demonstrators returned home, they turned not only to voting, but also maybe to organizing community politics, serving on a Parent Teacher Association, calling elected officials, and writing op-ed pieces for newspapers. The episode in Washington provided contacts for people who share similar concerns and some sense of a larger politics that can animate smaller, less visible, and often local efforts.

Of course, the point of protest isn't to influence the protesters or counterprotesters,[1] but rather to challenge authorities, embolden allies, and educate bystanders. It's unlikely, of course, that even the most clever and thoughtful action at the inaugural will change the minds of people who came to celebrate President Bush's inaugural, much less directly affect the president's stance on the war in Iraq or Social Security. The protests will, however, force a wrinkle into the record of the inaugural, affording journalists the chance to write not only about Bush's opponents, but also about their concerns. Projected to a broader audience through television, newspapers, or the Internet, they can undermine the apparent political unanimity and explicitly encourage at least some citizens to act on their beliefs or even to reexamine them. In conjunction with other political actions, the protests suggest an energy and commitment that potentially allied politicians can draw from—or exploit—in choreographing their own responses to President Bush's second-term agenda. Again, in conjunction with other political actions, the protests can offer a little bit of cover to Bush allies who may wish to temper their support of some of his policies. If the activists are successful, the president and his allies will have to spend more time explaining and justifying their policies. Additional exposure and scrutiny might inspire more action, and this action may lead to moderation in policies or sufficient worry about political fallout to stall or stifle the next initiative.

What You Can Do

It's frustrating to write about—as it must be to read about—all of the qualifiers that are inescapable when assessing the actual effects of either individual protests or longer-lived social movements. The fact is that it is never just a single action or one tactic that changes politics and policy, and it is impossible to know in advance just what the outcome of any one action will be. Social movements interact with all of the other actors, events, and interests that comprise politics, inside and outside of government. Uncertainty, however, suggests possibilities.

First, the most important thing to recognize is that in a country like America, where the historical record is filled with instances of individuals bucking all the odds to try to work on behalf of their beliefs, we all bear some responsibility for the policies our government pursues. This is an awesome responsibility, one that the activists who have animated social movements in American history have taken very seriously. Learning that you live

---

[1] I'm grateful to Hannah Miller for discussions on this point.

with a system that is designed to absorb and deflate pressure and realizing that there are determined activists engaged in promoting policies you detest lead to the recognition that doing nothing is tantamount to accepting responsibility for those policies. Recognizing that you can do something, the question is then to figure out what.

Second, whatever your point of view is, you are not alone. Probably not far away from you is a group that shares your concern; people write from your perspective, and specialized magazines represent your point of view in some way. Although popular history emphasizes extraordinary individuals, social change comes from groups of like-minded people working together. Reading a little bit deeper into history, you can see that those extraordinary individuals are embedded in dense networks of people who care about the same things. Finding your allies allows you to know more and to figure out where and how you can be most effective.

Third, although always impossible to know for certain, the prospects for change are much better than you think. Every substantial change in American history was preceded by large numbers of powerful people explaining that it wasn't possible. Most people are easily convinced of the futility of their efforts. Those brave enough to believe otherwise make history.

REFERENCES

Abraham, Yvonne. 2004. "Progressive Organization: Influence of MoveOn Undeniable." *The Boston Globe,* February 16.

Amenta, Edwin. 1998. *Bold Relief: Institutional Politics and the Origins of Modern American Social Policy.* Princeton, NJ: Princeton University Press.

Amenta, Edwin, Kathleen Dunleavy, and Mary Bernstein. 1994. "Stolen Thunder? Huey Long's 'Share Our Wealth,' Political Mediation, and the Second New Deal." *American Sociological Review* 59:678–702.

Andrews, Kenneth T. 2001. "Social Movements and Policy Implementation: The Mississippi Civil Rights Movement and the War on Poverty, 1965–1971." *American Sociological Review* 66(1):21–48.

Aristophanes. 1990. *Lysistrata.* Trans. Alan H. Sommerstein. Warminster, England: Aris and Phillips.

Armas, Genaro C., and Libby Quaid. 2005. "Protesters Opposing the Inauguration of President Bush and the War in Iraq Gather Near the US Capitol Today." Associated Press, January 20.

Associated Press. 2004. "Mass. Debate on Gay Marriage Continues." February 12.

———. 2005. "Protesters Target Bush's Inauguration." January 20.

Banaszak, Lee Ann. 1996. *Why Movements Succeed or Fail: Opportunity, Culture, and the Struggle for Woman Suffrage.* Princeton, NJ: Princeton University Press.

Barakso, Maryann, 2004. Governing NOW. Ithaca: Cornell University Press.

Barber, Lucy G. 2002. *Marching on Washington: The Forging of an American Political Tradition.* Berkeley: University of California Press.

Baumgartner, Frank R., and Bryan D. Jones. 1993. *Agendas and Instability in American Politics.* Chicago: University of Chicago Press.

Bedau, Hugo Adam. 1969. "Introduction." In *Civil Disobedience: Theory and Practice,* ed., Hugo Adam Bedau, 15–24. Indianapolis, IN: Pegasus.

Bell, Terrel. 1988. *The Thirteenth Man.* New York: Free Press.

Benford, Robert D. 1993a. "Frame Disputes within the Nuclear Disarmament Movement." *Social Forces* 71:677–701.

———. 1993b. "'You Could Be the Hundredth Monkey': Collective Action Frames and Vocabularies of Motive within the Nuclear Disarmament Movement." *Sociological Quarterly* 34:195–216.

Bernstein, Iver. 1990. *The New York City Draft Riots: Their Significance for American Society and Politics in the Age of the Civil War.* New York: Oxford University Press.

Berry, Jeffrey. 1997. *The Interest Group Society.* 3rd ed. New York: Longman.

———. 1999. *The New Liberalism: The Rising Power of Citizen Groups.* Washington, DC: Brookings Institution Press.

Bigelow, Albert. 1959. *The Voyage of the Golden Rule: An Experiment with Truth.* Garden City, NY: Doubleday.

Blanchard, Dallas A. 1994. *The Anti-Abortion Movement and the Rise of the Religious Right.* Boston: Twayne.

Blee, Kathleen M. 2002. *Inside Organized Racism: Women in the Hate Movement.* Berkeley: University of California Press.

Boles, Janet K. 1991. "Form Follows Function: The Evolution of Feminist Strategies." *Annals of the American Academy of Political and Social Sciences* 515 (May):38–49.

Boorstin, Daniel J. 1973. *The Image: A Guide to Pseudo-Events in America.* New York: Atheneum.

Breines, Wini. 1982. *Community and Organization in the New Left: The Great Refusal.* Philadelphia: Temple University Press.

Brown, Richard D. 1987. "Shays's Rebellion and the Ratification of the Federal Constitution in Massachusetts." In *Beyond Confederation: Origins of the Constitution and American National Identity,* ed. Richard Beeman, Stephen Botein, and Edward C. Carter II, 113–127. Chapel Hill: University of North Carolina Press.

Brownmiller, Susan. 1975. *Against Our Will: Men, Women, and Rape.* New York: Simon & Schuster.

Burstein, Paul. 1985. *Discrimination, Jobs, and Politics.* Chicago: University of Chicago Press.

———. 1991. "Policy Domains: Organization, Culture and Policy Outcomes." *Annual Review of Sociology* 17:327–350.

——— 1999. "Social Movements and Public Policy." In *How Social Movements Matter,* ed. Marco Giugni, Doug McAdam, and Charles Tilly, 3–21. Minneapolis: University of Minnesota Press.

Bustillo, Miguel, and Kenneth R. Weiss. 2004. "Election Becomes a Fight over Sierra Club's Future." *Los Angeles Times,* January 18.

Cannon, Lou. 1991. *President Reagan: The Role of a Lifetime.* New York: Touchstone.

Carson, Rachel. 1962. *Silent Spring.* New York: Fawcett Crest.

Carter, April. 1973. *Nonviolent Action and Liberal Democracy.* London: Longman.

Clemens, Elisabeth. 1993. "Women's Groups and the Transformation of U.S. Politics, 1892–1920." *American Journal of Sociology* 98:755–798.

———. 1997. *The People's Lobby.* Chicago: University of Chicago Press.

Cook, Adrian. 1974. *The Armies of the Streets: The New York City Draft Riots of 1863.* Lexington: University Press of Kentucky.

Costain, Ann N. 1993. *Inviting Women's Rebellion.* Baltimore: Johns Hopkins University Press.

Craig, Barbara Hinkson, and David M. O'Brien. 1993. *Abortion and American Politics.* Chatham, NJ: Chatham House.

Dahl, Robert A. 1956. *A Preface to Democratic Theory.* Chicago: University of Chicago Press.

Dalton, Russell J. 2002. *Citizen Politics.* 3rd ed. Chatham, NJ: Chatham House.

DeBenedetti, Charles, and Charles Chatfield. 1990. *An American Ordeal: The Antiwar Movement of the Vietnam Era.* Syracuse, NY: Syracuse University Press.

della Porta, Donatella. 1999. "Protest, Protesters, and Protest Policing: Public Discourse in Italy and Germany from the 1960s to the 1980s." In *How Movements Matter: Theoretical and Comparative Studies on the Consequences of Social Movements,* ed. Marco Giugni, Doug McAdam, and Charles Tilly, 66–96. Minneapolis: University of Minnesota Press.

DeNovella, Elizabeth. 2003. "Interview: Janeane Garofalo." *The Progressive,* May.

Divine, Robert A. 1978. *Blowing on the Wind: The Nuclear Test Ban Debate, 1954–1960.* New York: Oxford University Press.

Downs, Anthony. 1957. *An Economic Theory of Democracy.* New York: Harper & Brothers.

Dudziak, Mary L. 2000. *Cold War Civil Rights: Race and the Image of American Democracy.* Princeton, NJ: Princeton University Press.

Dwyer, Lynn E. 1983. "Structure and Strategy in the Antinuclear Movement." In *Social Movements of the Sixties and Seventies,* ed. Jo Freeman, 148–161. New York: Longman.

Earl, Jennifer, Andrew Martin, John D. McCarthy, and Sarah A. Soule. 2004. "The Use of Newspaper Data in the Study of Collective Action." *Annual Review of Sociology* 30:65–80.

Eisinger, Peter K. 1973. "Conditions of Protest Behavior in American Cities." *American Political Science Review* 67:11–28.

Epstein, Barbara. 1991. *Political Protest and Cultural Revolution.* Berkeley: University of California Press.

Fallows, James. 1981. *National Defense.* New York: Random House.

Farber, David. 1988. *Chicago '68.* Chicago: University of Chicago Press.

Fernandez, Manny, and Eric Rich. 2005. "Unwelcome and Unfazed, Demonstrators Push Messages: Administration Foes Are Seemingly Everywhere; Dozens Are Arrested, Others Disappointed They're Not." *The Washington Post,* January 21.

Finnegan, William. 2000. "After Seattle: Anarchists Get Organized." *The New Yorker,* April 17, 40–51.

Flacks, Richard. 1988. *Making History.* New York: Columbia University Press.

Fleisher, Doris Zames, and Frieda Zames. 2001. *The Disability Rights Movement: From Charity to Confrontation.* Philadelphia: Temple University Press.

Fortas, Abe. 1968. *Concerning Dissent and Civil Disobedience.* New York: World Publishing.

Friedan, Betty. 1963. *The Feminine Mystique.* New York: Norton.

Gamson, Josh. 1989. "Silence, Death, and the Invisible Enemy: AIDS Activism and Social Movement 'Newness.'" *Social Problems* 36:351–367.

Gamson, William A. 1990 [1975]. *The Strategy of Social Protest.* 2nd ed. Homewood, IL: Dorsey.

———. 1992. "The Social Psychology of Collective." In *Frontiers of Social Movement Theory,* ed. Carol M. Mueller and Aldon D. Morris, 53–76. New Haven, CT: Yale University Press.

Gamson, William A., and David S. Meyer. 1996. "Framing Political Opportunity." In *Comparative Perspectives on Social Movements,* ed. Doug McAdam, John D. McCarthy, and Mayer N. Zald, 275–290. New York: Cambridge University Press.

Garrow, David. 1978. *Protest at Selma: Martin Luther King, Jr. and the Voting Rights Act of 1965.* New Haven, CT: Yale University Press.

Gerhards, Jürgen, and Dieter Rucht. 1992. "Meso-Mobilization: Organizing and Framing in Two Protest Campaigns in West Germany." *American Journal of Sociology* 98:555–596.

Ginsberg, Benjamin, and Martin Shefter. 2002. *Politics by Other Means.* 3rd ed. New York: Norton.

Ginsburg, Faye D. 1989. *Contested Lives: The Abortion Debate in an American Community.* Berkeley: University of California Press.

Gitlin, Todd. 1980. *The Whole World Is Watching: Mass Media in the Making and Unmaking of the New Left.* Berkeley: University of California Press.

———. 1993. *The Sixties: Years of Hope, Days of Rage.* Rev. ed. New York: Bantam.

Glasser, Jeff. 2001. "Like a Bad Sequel, the Protest Flopped." *U.S. News & World Report,* July 30.

Goldfield, Michael. 1987. *The Decline of Organized Labor in the United States.* Chicago: University of Chicago Press.

———. 1997. *The Color of Politics: Race and the Mainsprings of American Politics.* New York: New Press.

Goodwyn, Lawrence. 1978. *The Populist Moment.* New York: Oxford University Press.

Gornick, Janet C., and David S. Meyer. 1998. "Changing Political Opportunity: The Anti-Rape Movement and Public Policy." *Journal of Policy History* 10(4):367–398.

Gould, Debbie. 2002. "Life during Wartime: Emotions and the Development of ACT-UP." *Mobilization* 7(2):177–200.

Greenhouse, Steven. 2005. "Two Large Unions Say They Are Leaving the AFL-CIO." *The New York Times,* July 25.

Greider, William. 1987. *Secrets of the Temple: How the Federal Reserve Runs the Country.* New York: Simon & Schuster.

Griswold, Wesley S. 1972. *The Night the Revolution Began: The Boston Tea Party, 1773.* Brattleboro, VT: S. Greene Press.

Hansen, John Mark. 1991. *Gaining Access: Congress and the Farm Lobby, 1919–1981.* Chicago: University of Chicago Press.

Harrington, Michael. 1962. *The Other America: Poverty in the United States.* New York: Macmillan.

Harris, Leslie M. 2003. *In the Shadow of Slavery: African Americans in New York City, 1626–1863.* Chicago: University of Chicago Press.

Hathaway, Will, and David S. Meyer. 1997. "Competition and Cooperation in Social Movement Coalitions: Lobbying for Peace in the 1980s." In *Coalitions and Political Movements: The Lessons of the Nuclear Freeze,* ed. Thomas R. Rochon and David Meyer, 61–79. Boulder, Co: Lynne-Rienner.

Hegeman, Roxana. 2001. "Summer of Mercy Protesters Hope Wichita Again Bolsters Nation's Anti-Abortion Movement." *The Lawrence Journal-World,* July 23.

———. 2002. "Protests Counter Clinic's Free Abortions." *The Lawrence Journal-World,* January 20.

Heineman, Kenneth J. 1993. *Campus Wars: The Peace Movement at American State Universities in the Vietnam Era.* New York: New York University Press.

Hersey, John. 1989. *Hiroshima.* New York: Vintage.

Hilgartner, Stephen, and Charles Bosk. 1988. "The Rise and Fall of Social Problems: A Public Arenas Model." *American Journal of Sociology* 94:53–78.

Hill, Julia Butterfly. 2000. *The Legacy of Luna: The Story of a Tree, a Woman and the Struggle to Save the Redwoods.* San Francisco: Harper.

Hirschman, Albert O. 1982. *Shifting Involvements: Private Interest and Public Action.* Princeton, NJ: Princeton University Press.

Hoffer, Eric. 1951. *The True Believer: Thoughts on the Nature of Mass Movements.* New York: New American Library.

Imig, Douglas R. 1996. *Poverty and Power: The Political Representation of Poor Americans.* Lincoln: University of Nebraska.

Ingram, Helen, and Steven Rathgeb Smith, eds. 1993. *Public Policy for Democracy.* Washington, DC: Brookings Institution Press.

Ithaca Journal. 1992. July 22, 21.

Jankofsky, Michael. 2005a. "Washington Mayor Describes Inaugural Precautions as Excessive." *The New York Times,* January 20.

———. 2005b. "Demonstrators Revel in Opposition on Big Day for President." *The New York Times,* January 21.

Jasper, James. 1990. *Nuclear Politics.* Princeton, NJ: Princeton University Press.

Jasper, James M., and Dorothy Nelkin. 1992. *The Animal Rights Crusade: The Growth of a Moral Protest.* New York: Free Press.

Jenkins, J. Craig, and Craig M. Eckert. 1986. "Channeling Black Insurgency: Elite Patronage and Professional Social Movement Organizations in the Development of the Black Movement." *American Sociological Review* 51:812–829.

Jenness, Valerie, and Ryken Grattet. 2001. *Building the Hate Crime Policy Domain: From Social Movement Concept to Law Enforcement Practice.* New York: Russell Sage.

Jezer, Marty. 1977. "Learning from the Past to Meet the Future." *WIN,* June, 17–23.

Joppke, Christian. 1993. *Mobilizing against Nuclear Energy.* Berkeley: University of California Press.

Katz, Michael B. 1989. *The Undeserving Poor: From the War on Poverty to the War on Welfare.* New York: Pantheon.

Katzenstein, Mary. 1998. *Faithful and Fearless: Moving Feminist Protest inside the Church and the Military.* Princeton, NJ: Princeton University Press.

Katznelson, Ira. 1981. *City Trenches: Urban Politics and the Patterning of Class in the United States.* New York: Pantheon Books.

Kehler, Randy. 1992. "What I Would Have Told the Judge." *Peacework,* February, 3.

Keniston, Kenneth. 1968. *Young Radicals.* New York: Harcourt, Brace and World.

Kimmeldorf, Howard, and Judith Stepan-Norris. 1992. "Historical Studies of Labor Movements in the United States." *Annual Review of Sociology* 18:495–517.

King, Brayden G., Marie Cornwall, and Eric C. Dahlin. 2005. "Winning Woman Suffrage One Step at a Time: Social Movements and the Logic of the Legislative Process." *Social Forces* 83:1211–1234.

King, Martin Luther, Jr. 1969. "Letter from Birmingham Jail." In *Civil Disobedience: Theory and Practice,* ed. Hugo Adam Bedau, 73–90. Indianapolis, IN: Pegasus.

Kingdon, John W. 1984. *Agendas, Alternatives, and Public Policies.* Boston: Little, Brown.

Kirkpatrick, David D. 2004. "Some Bush Supporters Say They Anticipate a 'Revolution.'" *The New York Times,* November 4.

Kitschelt, Herbert P. 1986. "Political Opportunity Structures and Political Protest: Anti-Nuclear Movements in Four Democracies." *British Journal of Political Science* 16:57–85.

Klatch, Rebecca. 1999. *A Generation Divided: The New Left, the New Right and the 1960s.* Los Angeles: University of California Press.

Kluger, Richard. 1975. *Simple Justice.* New York: Vintage.

Kornhauser, William. 1959. *The Politics of Mass Society.* Glencoe, IL: Free Press.

Kozol, Jonathan. 1967. *Death at an Early Age: The Destruction of the Hearts and Minds of Negro Children in the Boston Public Schools.* Boston: Houghton Mifflin.

Krasniewicz, Louise. 1992. *Nuclear Summer: The Clash of Communities at the Seneca Women's Peace Encampment.* Ithaca, NY: Cornell University Press.

Krikorian, Greg, and Jia-Rui Chong. 2004. "Caltech Grad Student Held in Arson Fires of 125 SUVs." *Los Angeles Times,* March 10.

Kurtz, Howard. 2003. "No Kidding: On Iraq, Janeane Garofalo Fights to Be Taken Seriously." *The Washington Post,* January 27.

Labaree, Benjamin W. 1964. *The Boston Tea Party.* New York: Oxford University Press.

Layton, Azza Salaama. 2000. *International Politics and Civil Rights Policies in the United States.* Cambridge, England: Cambridge University Press.

Levin, Stephanie A. 1992. "Grassroots Voices: Local Action and National Military Policy." *Buffalo Law Review* 40 (Spring):321–371.

Lipktak, Adam. 2004. "Caution in Court for Gay Rights Groups." *The New York Times,* November 12.

Lipset, Seymour Martin, and Earl Raab. 1973. *The Politics of Unreason: Right Wing Extremism in America.* New York: Harper & Row.

Lipsky, Michael. 1968. "Protest as a Political Resource." *American Political Science Review* 62 (December):1144–1158.

———. 1970. *Protest in City Politics.* Chicago: Rand McNally.

Maier, Pauline. 1972. *From Resistance to Revolution: Colonial Radicals and the Development of American Opposition to Britain, 1765–1776.* New York: Knopf.

Manegold, Catherine. 1992. "Abortion Foes See Tactics Backfire in New York." *The New York Times,* July 17, 27.

Mansbridge, Jane. 1986. *Why We Lost the Era.* Chicago: University of Chicago Press.

Marina, William. 2004. "Only 1/3rd of Americans Supported the American Revolution?" History News Network, June 28, 2004. http://hnn.us/articles/5641.html (accessed August 16, 2005).

Matthews, Nancy. 1994. *Confronting Rape: The Feminist Anti-Rape Movement and the State.* New York: Routledge.

Matthews, Richard K. 1995. *If Men Were Angels: James Madison and the Heartless Empire.* Lawrence: University Press of Kansas.

McAdam, Doug. 1982. *Political Process and the Origins of Black Insurgency.* Chicago: University of Chicago Press.

———. 1983. "Tactical Innovation and the Pace of Insurgency." *American Sociological Review* 48:735–754.

———. 1988. *Freedom Summer.* New York: Oxford University Press.

McCammon, Holly J. 2001. "Stirring Up Suffrage Sentiment: The Emergence of the State Woman Suffrage Movements, 1866–1914." *Social Forces* 80:449–480.

McCammon, Holly J., and Karen E. Campbell. 2002. "Allies on the Road to Victory: Coalition Formation between the Suffragists and the Woman's Christian Temperance Union." *Mobilization: An International Journal* 7:231–251.

McCammon, Holly, Karen Campbell, Ellen Granberg, and Christine Mowery. 2001. "How Movements Win: Gendered Opportunity Structures and U.S. Women's Suffrage Movements, 1866 to 1919." *American Sociological Review* 66(1):47–70.

McCarthy, John D., David W. Britt, and Mark Wolfson. 1991. "The Institutional Channeling of Social Movements by the State in the United States." *Research in Social Movements, Conflict, and Change* 13:45–76.

McCarthy, John D., and Clark McPhail. 1998. "The Institutionalization of Protest in the United States." In *The Social Movement Society: Contentious Politics for a New Century,* ed. David S. Meyer and Sidney Tarrow, 83–110. Lanham, MD: Rowman & Littlefield.

McCarthy, John D., Clark McPhail, and Jackie Smith. 1996. "Images of Protest: Dimensions of Selection Bias in Media Coverage of Washington Demonstrations, 1982 and 1991." *American Sociological Review* 61(3):478–499.

McCarthy, John D., and Mayer N. Zald. 1977. "Resource Mobilization and Social Movements: A Partial Theory." *American Journal of Sociology* 82:1212–1241.

McFarland, Andrew. 1984. *Common Cause: Lobbying in the Public Interest.* Chatham, NJ: Chatham House.

Mendoza, Martha. 2005. "Hundreds Mark Inauguration with Protests." Associated Press, January 20.

Mettler, Suzanne. 1998. *Dividing Citizens: Gender and Federalism in the New Deal.* Ithaca, NY: Cornell University Press.

Meyer, David S. 1990. *A Winter of Discontent: The Nuclear Freeze and American Politics.* New York: Praeger.

———. 1993a. "Institutionalizing Dissent: The United States Structure of Political Opportunity and the End of the Nuclear Freeze Movement." *Sociological Forum* 8 (June): 157–179.

———. 1993b. "Political Process and Protest Movement Cycles." *Political Research Quarterly* 46 (September):451–479.

———. 1993c. "Peace Protest and Policy: Explaining the Rise and Decline of Antinuclear Movements in Postwar America." *Policy Studies Journal* 21:35–51.

———. 1995. "Framing National Security: Elite Public Discourse on Nuclear Weapons during the Cold War." *Political Communication* 12:173–192.

———. 2002. "Opportunities and Identities: Bridge-Building in the Study of Social Movements." In *Social Movements: Identity, Culture, and the State,* ed. David S. Meyer, Nancy Whittier, and Belinda Robnett, 3–21. New York: Oxford University Press.

———. 2004. "Protest and Political Opportunities." *Annual Review of Sociology* 30:125–145.

Meyer, David S., and Catherine Corrigall-Brown. 2005. "Coalitions and Political Context: US Movements against Wars in Iraq." *Mobilization* 10:327–346.

Meyer, David S., and Joshua Gamson. 1995. "The Challenge of Cultural Elites: Celebrities and Social Movements." *Sociological Inquiry* 65:181–206.

Meyer, David S., and Douglas R. Imig. 1993. "Political Opportunity and the Rise and Decline of Interest Group Sectors." *Social Science Journal* 30:253–270.

Meyer, David S., Valerie Jenness, and Helen Ingram, eds. 2005. *Routing the Opposition: Social Movements, Public Policy, and Democracy.* Minneapolis: University of Minnesota Press.

Meyer, David S., and Suzanne Staggenborg. 1996. "Movements, Countermovements, and the Structure of Political Opportunity." *American Journal of Sociology* 101:1628–1660.

Meyer, David S., and Sidney Tarrow, eds. 1998. *The Social Movement Society: Contentious Politics for a New Century.* Lanham, MD: Rowman & Littlefield.

Meyer, David S., and Nancy Whittier. 1994. "Social Movement Spillover." *Social Problems* 41 (May)2:277–298.

Michels, Roberto. 1962 [1915]. *Political Parties.* New York: Collier.

Miller, James. 1987. *Democracy Is in the Streets: From Port Huron to the Siege of Chicago.* New York: Simon & Schuster.

Miller, William. 1982. *Dorothy Day: A Biography.* San Francisco: Harper & Row.

Minkoff, Debra C. 1994. "From Service Provision to Institutional Advocacy: The Shifting Legitimacy of Organizational Forms." *Social Forces* 72:943–969.

———. 1995. *Organizing for Equality: The Evolution of Women's and Racial-Ethnic Organizations in America, 1955–1985*. New Brunswick, NJ: Rutgers University Press.

———. 1999. "Bending with the Wind: Strategic Change and Adaptation by Women's and Racial Minority Organizations." *American Journal of Sociology* 104:1666–1703.

Montgomery, David, and Jose Antonio Vargas. 2005. "Counter-Inaugural Ballgoers Don't See Red." *The Washington Post,* January 21.

Morris, Aldon D. 1984. *The Origins of the Civil Rights Movement: Black Communities Organizing for Change*. New York: Free Press.

Mueller, Carol M., and Aldon D. Morris, eds. 1992. *Frontiers of Social Movement Theory*. New Haven, CT: Yale University Press.

Muste, A. J. 1969. "Of Holy Disobedience." In *Civil Disobedience: Theory and Practice,* ed. Hugo Adam Bedau, 133–145. Indianapolis, IN: Pegasus.

Nader, Ralph. 1965. *Unsafe at Any Speed: The Designed-In Dangers of the American Automobile*. New York: Grossman.

Nagorney, Adam, and Janet Elder. 2005. "Public Voicing Doubts on Iraq and the Economy, Poll Finds." *The New York Times,* January 20.

Neier, Aryeh. 1979. *Defending My Enemy: American Nazis, the Skokie Case, and the Risks of Freedom*. New York: E. P. Dutton.

Nepstad, Sharon Erikson. 2004. "Persistent Resistance, Commitment and Community in the Plowshares Movement." *Social Problems* 51:43–60.

Newman, Maria. 2005. "Heightened Security Turns Washington into a Quiet Scene." *The New York Times,* January 20.

Nixon, Richard M. 1978. *RN: The Memoirs of Richard Nixon*. New York: Grosset & Dunlap.

Oliver, Pam. 1984. "'If You Don't Do It, Nobody Else Will': Active and Token Contributions to Local Collective Action." *American Sociological Review* 49:601–610.

Olson, Mancur. 1967. *Theory of Collective Action*. Cambridge, MA: Harvard University Press.

Peacework. 1992. "Home 'Sold,' Kehler, Corner Vow Resistance." March, 3.

Perry, Michael J. 1988. *Morality, Politics and Law*. New York: Oxford University Press.

Piven, Frances Fox, and Richard A. Cloward. 1971. *Regulating the Poor*. New York: Vintage.

———. 1977. *Poor People's Movements*. New York: Vintage.

Polletta, Francesca. 1998. "'It Was Like a Fever. . .': Narrative and Identity in Social Protest." *Social Problems* 45:137–159.

Purnell, Brian J. 2001. "Drive Awhile for Freedom: Brooklyn CORE and the 1964 World's Fair 'Stall-In.'" Presented at the Gotham Center's History Festival, October 6. New York.

Rakove, Jack N. 1979. *The Beginnings of National Politics*. New York: Alfred A. Knopf.

Reger, Jo. 2002. "More Than One Feminism: Organizational Structure, Ideology and the Construction of Collective Identity." In *Social Movements: Identity, Culture, and the State,* ed. David S. Meyer, Nancy Whittier, and Belinda Robnett, 171–184. New York: Oxford University Press.

Reynolds, David S. 2005. *John Brown, Abolitionist: The Man who Killed Slavery, Sparked the Civil War, and Seeded Civil Rights*. New York: Knopf.

Rimmerman, Craig. 2002. *From Identity to Politics: The Lesbian and Gay Movements in the United States*. Philadelphia: Temple University Press.

Robnett, Belinda. 2002. "External Political Change, Collective Identities, and Participation in Social Movement Organizations." In *Social Movements: Identity, Culture, and the State,* ed. David S. Meyer, Nancy Whittier, and Belinda Robnett, 266–285. New York: Oxford University Press.

Rochon, Thomas R. 1998. *Culture Moves: Ideas, Activism, and Changing Values.* Princeton, NJ: Princeton University Press.

Rochon, Thomas R., and David S. Meyer, eds. 1997. *Coalitions and Political Movements: The Lessons of the Nuclear Freeze.* Boulder, CO: Lynne-Rienner.

Rohlinger, Deana A. 2002. "Framing the Abortion Debate: Organizational Resources, Media Strategies, and Movement-Countermovement Dynamics." *The Sociological Quarterly* 43:479–507.

Rohlinger, Deana A. 2004. "Getting into Mass Media: A Comparative Analysis of Social Movement Organizations and Mass Media Outlets in the Abortion Debate. PhD diss., University of California, Irvine.

Rohlinger, Deana A. and David A. Snow. 2003. "Social Psychological Perspectives on Crowds and Social Movements," pp. 503–527. *Handbook of Social Psychology: Sociological Perspectives,* John DeLamater, editor. New York: Kluwer-Plenum.

Rojecki, Andrew. 1999. *Silencing the Opposition: Antinuclear Movements and the Media in the Cold War.* Urbana and Chicago: University of Illinois Press.

Rosenstone, Stephen J., and John Mark Hansen. 1993. *Mobilization, Participation, and Democracy in America.* New York: Macmillan.

Rothenberg, Lawrence. 1992. *Linking Citizens to Government: Interest Group Politics at Common Cause.* New York: Cambridge University Press.

Rucht, Dieter. 2000. "Distant Issue Movements in Germany: Empirical Description and Theoretical Reflections." In *Globalizations and Social Movements: Culture, Power, and the Transnational Public Sphere,* ed. John A. Guidry, Michael D. Kennedy, and Mayer N. Zald, 76–105. Ann Arbor: University of Michigan Press.

Rucht, Dieter, Ruud Koopmans, and Friedhelm Neidhart, eds. 1999. *Acts of Dissent: New Developments in the Study of Protest.* Sigma: Berlin.

Rupp, Leila J., and Verta Taylor. 1987. *Survival in the Doldrums: The American Women's Rights Movement, 1945 to the 1960s.* New York: Oxford University Press.

Ryan, Charlotte. 1991. *Prime Time Activism.* Boston: South End Press.

Salisbury, Robert H. 1970. *Interest Group Politics in America.* New York: Harper & Row.

Samuels, David. 2000. "Notes from the Underground: Among the Radicals of the Pacific Northwest." *Harpers,* May, 35–47.

Sawyers, Traci M., and David S. Meyer. 1999. "Missed Opportunities: Social Movement Abeyance and Public Policy." *Social Problems* 46(2):187–206.

Schattschneider, E. E. 1960. *The Semi-Sovereign People.* New York: Holt, Rinehart & Winston.

Schneider, Anne Larason, and Helen Ingram. 1997. *Policy Design for Democracy.* Lawrence: University Press of Kansas.

Scholzman, Kay Lehman. 1984. "What Accent the Heavenly Chorus: Political Equality and the American Pressure System." *Journal of Politics* 46:1006–1032.

Schlozman, Kay Lehman, and John T. Tierney. 1986. *Organized Interests and American Politics.* New York: Harper & Row.

Selznick, Philip. 1953. *TVA and the Grassroots.* Berkeley: University of California Press.

Shilts, Randy. 1988. *And the Band Played On.* New York: Penguin Books.

Shogren, Elizabeth. 2005. "Protesters Come from across the Country to March, Chant and Turn Their Backs on the Inaugural Festivities for a President They Oppose." *The New York Times,* January 21.

Shridharani, Krishnalal J. 1962. *War without Violence.* Bombay: Bharatiya Vidyha Bhavan.

Sikkink, Kathryn. 1986. "Codes of Conduct for Transnational Corporations. The Case of the WHO/UNICEF Code." *International Organization* 40:815–840.

Sinclair, Upton. 1906. *The Jungle.* New York: New American Library.

Singer, Peter. 2001 [1975]. *Animal Liberation.* New York: Ecco.

Sitkoff, Harvard. 1981. *The Struggle for Black Equality, 1954–1980.* New York: Hill and Wang.

Smith, Christian. 1996. *Resisting Reagan: The U.S. Central America Peace Movement.* Chicago: University of Chicago Press.

Smith, Jackie, and Hank Johnston, eds. 2002. *Globalization and Resistance: Transnational Dimensions of Social Movements.* Lanham, MD: Rowman & Littlefield.

Snow, David A. 2005. "Social Movements as Challenges to Authority: Resistance to an Emerging Hegemony." In *Authority in Contention (Research in Social Movements, Conflicts and Change),* ed. Daniel J. Myers and Daniel M. Cress. Greenwich, CT: JAI Press.

Snow, David A., and Robert D. Benford. 1992. "Master Frames and Cycles of Protest." In *Frontiers of Social Movement Theory,* ed. Carol M. Mueller and Aldon D. Morris, 133–155. New Haven, CT: Yale University Press.

Sophocles. 1987. *Antigone.* Trans. Andrew Brown. Warminster, England: Aris and Phillips.

Soule, Sarah A. 2004. "Going to the Chapel? Same-Sex Marriage Bans in the United States, 1973–2000." *Social Problems* 51:453–477.

Soule, Sarah A., and Brayden G. King. (in press). "The Stages of the Policy Process and the Equal Rights Amendment, 1972–1982." *American Journal of Sociology.*

Staggenborg, Suzanne. 1986. "Coalition Work in the Pro-Choice Movement." *Social Problems* 33:374–389.

———. 1988. "The Consequences of Professionalization and Formalization in the Pro-Choice Movement." *American Sociological Review* 53:585–605.

———. 1991. *The Pro-Choice Movement.* New York: Oxford University Press.

Steinem, Gloria. 1990. "Sex, Lies & Advertising." *Ms. Magazine,* (July–August).

Stepan-Norris, Judith, and Maurice Zeitlin. 2003. *Left Out: Reds and America's Industrial Unions.* Cambridge, England: Cambridge University Press.

Stone, Deborah. 1997. *Policy Paradox: The Art of Political Decision Making.* New York: Norton.

Stout, David, and John O'Neil. 2005. "Bush, Beginning a New Term, Stresses Liberty Abroad." *The New York Times,* January 20.

Stowe, Harriet Beecher. 1852. *Uncle Tom's Cabin.* London: J. Cassell.

Switzer, Jacqueline Vaughn. 2001. *Environmental Politics: Domestic and Global Dimensions.* 3rd ed. Boston and New York: Bedford/St. Martin's.

Szatmary, David P. 1980. *Shays' Rebellion.* Amherst: University of Massachusetts Press.

Szymanski, Ann-Marie E. *Pathways to Prohibition: Radicals, Moderates, and Social Movement Outcomes.* Durham: Duke University Press.

Tarrow, Sidney. 1998. *Power in Movement.* 2nd ed. New York: Cambridge University Press.

References

Tarrow, Sidney. 2005. *The New Transnational Activism.* New York: Cambridge University Press.

Taylor, Verta A. 1989. "Social Movement Continuity: The Women's Movement in Abeyance." *American Sociological Review* 54:761–775.

Taylor, Verta A., and Nancy Whittier. 1992. "Collective Identity in Social Movement Communities: Lesbian Feminist Mobilization." In *Frontiers of Social Movement Theory,* ed. Carol M. Mueller and Aldon D. Morris, 104–129. New Haven, CT: Yale University Press.

Thomas, Janet. 2000. *The Battle in Seattle: The Story Behind and Beyond the WTO Demonstrations.* Golden, CO: Fulcrum.

Thoreau, Henry David. 1969. "Civil Disobedience." In *Civil Disobedience: Theory and Practice,* ed. Hugo Adam Bedau, 27–48. Indianapolis, IN: Pegasus.

———. 1975. *Selected Works,* ed. Walter Harding. Boston: Houghton Mifflin.

Tilly, Charles. 1978. *From Mobilization to Revolution.* Reading, MA: Addison-Wesley.

———. 1992. "How to Detect, Describe, and Explain Repertoires of Contention." New School for Social Research Working Paper 150.

———. 1993. "Contentious Repertoires in Great Britain, 1758–1834." *Social Science History* 17:253–280.

———. 1994. "Social Movements as Historically Specific Clusters of Political Performances." *Berkeley Journal of Sociology* 38:1–30.

Tilly, Charles, and Sidney Tarrow. 2006. *Contentious Politics.* Boulder, CO: Paradigm.

Tocqueville, Alexis de. 2000 [1835]. *Democracy in America.* Trans. and ed. Harvey C. Mansfield and Delba Winthrop. Chicago: University of Chicago Press.

Uggen, Christopher, and Jeff Manza. 2002. "Democratic Contraction? Political Consequences of Felon Disenfranchisement in the United States." *American Sociological Review* 67:777–803.

Useem, Bert. 1980. "Solidarity Model, Breakdown Model, and the Boston Anti-Busing Movement." *American Sociological Review* 45:357–369.

Van Dyke, Nella. 2003. "Crossing Movement Boundaries: Factors That Facilitate Coalition Protest by American College Students, 1930–1990." *Social Problems* 49:497–520.

Voss, Kim. 1993. *The Making of American Exceptionalism: The Knights of Labor and Class Formation in the Nineteenth Century.* Ithaca, NY: Cornell University Press.

———. 1998. "Claim Making and the Framing of Defeats: The Interpretation of Losses by American British Labor Activists, 1886–1895." In *Challenging Authority: The Historical Study of Contentious Politics,* ed. Michael P. Hanagan, Leslie Page Moch, and Wayne Te Brake, 136–148. Minneapolis: University of Minnesota Press.

Voss, Kim, and Rachel Sherman. 2001. "Breaking the Iron Law of Oligarchy: Union Revitalization in the American Labor Movement." *American Journal of Sociology* 106:203–249.

Waldman, Steven. 1996. *The Bill: How Legislation Really Becomes Law: A Case Study of the National Service Bill.* Rev. ed. New York: Penguin Books.

Walker, Jack L. 1991. *Mobilizing Interest Groups in America.* Ann Arbor: University of Michigan Press.

Wallace, Michael, Larry J. Griffin, and Beth A. Rubin. 1989. "The Positional Power of American Labor, 1963–1977." *American Sociological Review* 54:197–214.

Wallace, Michael, Beth A. Rubin, and Brian T. Smith. 1988. "American Labor Law: Its Impact on Working-Class Militancy, 1901–1980." *Social Science History* 12:1–29.

Walzer, Michael. 1970. *Obligations: Essays on Disobedience, War, and Citizenship.* Cambridge, MA: Harvard University Press.

Weed, Frank J. 1995. *Certainty of Justice: Reform in the Crime Victim Movement.* New York: Aldine de Gruyter.

Weinberger, Caspar W. 1990. *Fighting for Peace: Seven Critical Years in the Pentagon.* New York: Warner Books.

Whalen, Jack, and Richard Flacks. 1989. *Beyond the Barricades: The Sixties Generation Grows Up.* Philadelphia: Temple University Press.

Whittier, Nancy. 1995. *Feminist Generations: The Persistence of the Radical Women's Movement.* Philadelphia: Temple University Press.

Wilcox, Fred A. 1991. *Uncommon Martyrs: The Berrigans, the Catholic Left, and the Plowshares Movement.* Reading, MA: Addison-Wesley.

Wilde, Melissa. Forthcoming. *Catholicism Contested: A Sociological Study of Vatican II.* Princeton, NJ: Princeton University Press.

Wills, Gary. 2003. *Negro President: Jefferson and the Slave Power.* Boston: Houghton Mifflin.

Wilson, James Q. 1995. *Political Organizations.* 2nd ed. Princeton, NJ: Princeton University Press.

Wittner, Lawrence S. 1984. *Rebels against War: The American Peace Movement, 1933–1983.* Philadelphia: Temple University Press.

———. 1993. *One World or None: A History of the World Disarmament Movement through 1953.* Vol. I of *The Struggle against the Bomb.* Palo Alto, CA: Stanford University Press.

———. 1997. *Resisting the Bomb: A History of the World Disarmament Movement, 1954–1970.* Vol. II of *The Struggle against the Bomb.* Palo Alto, CA: Stanford University Press.

———. 2003. *Toward Nuclear Abolition: A History of the World Disarmament Movement, 1971 to the Present.* Vol. III of *The Struggle against the Bomb.* Palo Alto, CA: Stanford University Press.

Wofford, Harris, Jr. 1969. "Non-Violence and the Law: The Law Needs Help." In *Civil Disobedience: Theory and Practice,* ed. Hugo Adam Bedau, 59–71. Indianapolis, IN: Pegasus.

Wolff, Robert Paul, Barrington Moore Jr., and Herbert Marcuse. 1969. *A Critique of Pure Tolerance.* London: Cape.

Wood, Gordon S. 1993. *The Creation of the American Republic, 1776–1787.* New York: Norton.

Zald, Mayer, and Patricia Denton. 1963. "From Evangelism to General Service: The Transformation of the YMCA." *Administrative Science Quarterly* 8(2):214–234.

Zald, Mayer N., and John D. McCarthy. 1987. *Social Movements in an Organizational Society.* New Brunswick, NJ: Transaction.

Zashin, Elliot M. 1972. *Civil Disobedience and Democracy.* New York: Free Press.

Zinn, Howard. 1964. *SNCC: The New Abolitionists.* Boston: Beacon.

———. 1968. *Disobedience and Democracy: Nine Fallacies on Law and Order.* New York: Random House.

INDEX

Index